BREAKING NEWS

BREAKING NEWS

A Stunning and Memorable Account
of Reporting from Some of the Most
Dangerous Places in the World

Martin Fletcher

Thomas Dunne Books
St. Martin's Press ≈ New York

THOMAS DUNNE BOOKS.
An imprint of St. Martin's Press.

www.thomasdunnebooks.com
www.stmartins.com

Frontispiece photograph: courtesy of NBC News

Library of Congress Cataloging-in-Publication Data

Fletcher, Martin, 1947–
    Breaking news : a stunning and memorable account of reporting from some of the most dangerous places in the world / Martin Fletcher.—1st ed.
        p. cm.
    ISBN-13: 978-0-312-37118-0
    ISBN-10: 0-312-37118-7
    1. Fletcher, Martin, 1947– 2. Television journalists—Great Britain—Biography. I. Title.
    PN5123.F44A3 2008
    070.4'332092—dc22
    [B]   2007042762

First Edition: March 2008

10 9 8 7 6 5 4 3 2 1

To my father:
A son, a tree, a book.

Contents

Acknowledgments

Thank you, Hagar, for sharing your life with me since the age of nineteen, and for supporting me in my travels to scary places. Only once did you ask me to say no to NBC. When I told my editors it was Iraq or my wife, they didn't hesitate, but I stayed at home anyway.

My sons, Guy, Daniel, and Jonathan: Wherever I've been, whatever I've done, you have been with me.

Then there's my second family: NBC News, especially the bureau in Tel Aviv, where I have often spent eighteen-hour days for weeks at a time. Gila Grossman, the most tenacious newsperson I have known, has become as close a friend and supporter as it is possible to have. Jeff, Amikam, Kevin, Yael and the gang, and numerous other past and present NBC staffers, especially Heather and M.L., Jim and Keith, Cheryl and Diane, Jerry, and, above all, Marc, have become much more than colleagues. For your friendship, I am grateful.

When I met Helen Rees on an airport bus in Cairo, her first words to me were "You must have a book inside you." She became my friend and agent, but it took twenty years for her to coax the book out of me. Fortunately, Marcia Markland, my charming editor at St. Martin's Press, and Thomas Dunne, the worldly publisher, made it a painless birth. But it was

Seth Schulman, my brilliant personal editor, who encouraged much of the soul-searching that makes this, I hope, so much more than an exciting adventure story.

I have been on fast-forward for most of my life, racing to keep ahead of the demands of a career in breaking news. Writing this book has given me a chance to pause and reflect a little on myself, but mostly on the dilemmas I have faced covering shattering events around the world.

I am grateful to the many people I have met who allowed a clumsy reporter into their lives. I think about them late at night when I cannot sleep. What happened to the abandoned boy with the harelip in the Sarajevo hospital? Did your mother come back to get you after the siege? And the hungry little boy who followed me all morning in Mogadishu asking for my pen. I wish I'd given it to you. I only had one. The Cambodian orphan I left studying by candlelight—did you become a teacher as you wanted? The boy in Gaza paralyzed by a bullet to the neck—did you get a wheelchair that would go through the sand?

If I could revisit the thousands of people I have filmed in the worst moments of their lives, I would apologize for having intruded on their suffering. I would share with them my belief that by telling me their stories they have helped in some small way to make the world a better place. Hopefully, they would agree.

Introduction

The phone rang at noon and the message was brief: "Is that NBC? Tell Martin to come to a wedding. Tell him to come now. He can be a witness. Good-bye."

I didn't rush out to buy a present. This was no invitation to join a happy couple in holy matrimony. This "wedding" was more like a funeral. The message was code to witness a murder. The al-Aksa Martyrs' Brigades in Nablus were going to kill a collaborator, and they wanted me and my NBC News team to film it.

Later I would get the details, and what a murky tale it was. The Israeli secret service had blackmailed a Palestinian man into becoming an informer. They knew he was having an affair with a married woman. The woman was married to a fighter with the al-Aksa brigades, who was hiding out in the Balata refugee camp with one of the top al-Aksa commanders. The Israelis wanted to kill them both.

The woman wanted to marry her lover, so she betrayed the hiding place of her husband and the militant leader. Israeli commandos stormed the safe house and found them crammed behind a false wall in a small room. In a hail of gunfire, the militants were killed. Case closed.

But al-Aksa knew there must have been a collaborator, and they quickly found him. And her. They videotaped their confessions against a plain white wall. The "wedding" was payback time.

When I got the call, I was shaken. How many dead people did I need to see? And I was confused. I understood al-Aksa's rationale: "The collaborators must be killed or they'll betray more people, and next time we'll be killed. It's them or us."

But I also understood the collaborators: "We have no life under the Israelis. Our lives are ruined whatever we do."

And I understood the Israelis: "Anything goes to stop the suicide bombers from killing more Jewish children. We're fighting a war."

As I put the phone down, I thought, I understand too much. I feel sorry for them all. But it occurred to me: If I sympathize with killers, informers, and blackmailers, maybe there's something wrong with me, too.

It wouldn't be surprising. After three decades covering war and suffering in every dark corner of the globe, anyone's brain would be fried.

So what should I do? Film the killing or not? I sat down and stared at the phone, wondering whether to summon the team and hit the road. Ethically, it was a no-brainer. No way am I going to witness a murder. But hey, I thought, it's going to happen anyway, if I'm there or not. It's not my fault. And this is my job.

Nobody owns the moral high ground: My role in life is to see and report, and maybe learn a little. So there I sat, looking at the phone, and needing to decide quickly—should we go film the murder?

This book is not a meditation on society, or a rant about how bad TV journalism has become, or a tell-all account of famous people I've met. It's something simpler and, I hope, more revealing: a series of true-life adventure stories that expose the haunting dilemmas journalists face as we help write that famous first draft of history.

Year after year, my work takes me to the world's most beautiful places at the worst of times. I visit with people at their lowest moments and tell their stories as best I can, while trying to cast light on the larger issues. At a time when the problems of strangers seem a world away, I try to answer the question: Why should we care? Sometimes the pictures tell the story, sometimes a word or two artfully mixed with a surprising juxtaposition does the job. Usually you can't do better than let a person reveal himself. But however I do it, my job is to help people care about other people.

Unfortunately, that isn't as morally clear-cut as it sounds. My work has led me again and again into pretty dicey territory. For instance, how callous can one be as a journalist seeking a story? I face that conundrum every day, and haven't always handled it with flying colors.

When Turkey invaded Cyprus in 1974, my soundman trod on a land mine just three feet from me and was killed in the explosion. Moments later, another of my good friends trod on another land mine and vanished in flame and smoke. When I overcame my astonishment that I was still alive, I realized I had filmed it all. I hadn't helped.

In a refugee camp in Wad Kowlie, on the Sudan border, I saw a man holding his starving infant. I happened to look into his eyes at the very moment he glanced down and realized that his child had just died in his arms. The man looked up, and our eyes met. Tears sprang to his eyes, as they did to mine. After all, at that time I had a child the same age as his. But I didn't move forward to comfort him or even make a consoling gesture. As the man began to wail and stumbled away with his dead infant, I instinctively rushed off to find my cameraman and told him to follow the guy until he buried the kid. Great sequence.

In Cyprus, I was filming people in a deep ditch digging out a mass grave. Parts of stiff bodies stuck out of the packed mud in grotesque poses, like one of those artworks where a head and chest emerge from a wall. Everything was gray and dark and monotone, and my only response as they uncovered a woman's body was to think, Oh good, she's got a red dress on, some color for the picture.

Getting a good story while maintaining one's humanity is difficult, yet it is hardly the only ethical challenge I've faced. For instance, how polite should I be when interviewing someone responsible for killing up to 2 million Cambodians? Is it wrong to stay in the home of a brutal Somali warlord, eating lavish food prepared by his Italian-trained chef, in order to report on, among other things, his theft of the same food from international aid organizations? And, critically for a young man with a growing family, how can one witness every imaginable horror and not take it out on the wife and kids?

This book does not offer solutions to these dilemmas, because there aren't any; all you can do is feel your way as best you can. And yet, if I continue to cover wars after all these years, it is because I believe that, all things considered, I've done more good than harm. Given the great challenges facing humanity today, as well as all the mindless distractions that impede us, it's critical to remind ourselves of what's really important— human beings and the dire struggles for survival so many face every day. And that's what war correspondents do.

The adventures in this book will, I hope, offer hours of entertaining reading. Yet I will have failed if in the very process of capturing readers' imaginations I have not also left them with a keener and more visceral sense of the world's pain. I will have failed if readers do not feel a new gratitude for the blessings they already enjoy, a sense that, as bad as life may be, it could always be a lot worse. That, in the end, is what I take away from all these years of murder and mayhem, which made me a connoisseur of sorrow.

I dedicate *Breaking News* to my father, a reader, who knew great sorrow. He would suck mints, stroke his Snoopy doll, and doze off among piles of open books. He would dip in and out of volumes on comparative religion, European history, modern psychology, Talmudic thought, fiction by Oscar Wilde and Goethe, and plays by Molière and Aristophanes, reading all in their original languages, including Greek. He wasn't a great listener, though, and he wasn't much troubled by the kinds of professional dilemmas I face. Whenever he asked me about the war in Kosovo or revolution in Iran or wherever I had just returned from, he would quickly interrupt and correct me, based on his vast knowledge of history, the editorials of the right-wing English press, and the philosophy of Attila the Hun. His solution to most conflicts was the same: Line up five hundred men, shoot them, end of problem. His idea of a compromise was: Okay, three hundred. When I tried to respond, he would nod for a minute, then in midsentence remove his hearing aid and pick up a book. Interview over.

Unfortunately, my father didn't live long enough to know about this book, let alone to spill coffee on it. Within two short years, my brother, Peter, died of leukemia; next my mother died following an operation; and then, about a year later, my father willed himself to death at the age of ninety. All this took place during the years 2000 through 2002, at the height of the second Intifada. Between suicide bombs and carnage in Israel, I flew to London, helping my dwindling family through sicknesses, intensive care, and funerals. Between reports for NBC, I wrote eulogies for my family members. My bosses were sympathetic, offering me all the free time I needed, for which I am grateful. But I was so swept along by the drama around me, at work and at home, that I had no time to mourn or reflect.

My father, a young lawyer, fled Vienna after escaping from a Nazi jail in 1938. Nine years later, two months after I was born in London, he changed his name to George Fletcher from Georg Fleischer, so that I wouldn't get saddled with his English nickname: Flyshit. When he discovered that Fletcher was an ancient Scottish name meaning arrow maker, and that it was linked to the MacGregor clan, he bought a tartan tie and wore it to work at the button factory. He tried to blend in with the British but couldn't. He never overcame the loss of his large extended family in the Holocaust; only he, a sister, and a niece survived. Nor did my mother, who along with her sister was her family's sole survivor. After sixty years living in London, all their friends were from Central Europe. They were still refugees at heart, and they passed some of it on.

When I was mocked in first grade for calling corn on the cob "kooka-roots," the Hungarian word we used at home, I told my tormentor to "hupfingatsch," Viennese dialect for "take a flying jump." I squirmed in embarrassment when my parents spoke in their thick Viennese accents to my English schoolteachers. I always felt something of an outsider, even as I progressed through school, captained the soccer team, and worked at the

BBC. It wasn't England's fault. England had sheltered Jewish refugees in their direst moment. But the burden of the Holocaust was too great for my parents, and they unloaded some of it onto me: a certain buried sadness, hatred for bullies, and sympathy for their victims.

But "one man in his time plays many parts,"* and it is only looking back that I see the connection between this inheritance and my career. I left the University of Bradford with a degree in modern languages and the offer of a job as a translator-interpreter in the Brussels headquarters of the European Community. It was the top of the translators' ladder and paid a high salary, almost tax-free. It also offered all the perks befitting an international civil servant. I could have had a cushy life, but instead I chose to roam the world, look for faults everywhere I went, speak rudely to people in authority, and evade responsibility at every turn. In short, I became a journalist. It took me a long time to understand why the glove fit so well.

I am proud to say that I have rarely interviewed a head of state or a chief executive officer. I don't care what the generals have to say. And don't get me started on the royal family. Nobody with a story to sell or a policy to spin interests me. What I care about are the people who pay the price, as my family did.

On the day that I write this, I spent an hour with a man and woman whose ten-year-old daughter was killed. They showed me her school dress, ripped and red with blood, which they keep wrapped in a shopping bag in their neighbor's apartment, because they can't bear to keep it at home. It isn't clear who killed their daughter, or why, but they want justice. I'm not a cop, I can't find out the answers, but I can help them ask the questions, and let them know that the world cares.

---

*William Shakespeare, *As You Like It,* 2.7.142.

BREAKING NEWS

One

Clueless

Today, when I watch reality shows like *Survivor* or *Fear Factor*, I have to chuckle. You think building a hut or sticking your head in a tub of worms is hard? Try treading through a minefield in Cyprus moments after your friend was blown up; or trekking through the Hindu Kush mountains into Afghanistan with the anti-Soviet Mujahideen; or sweeping through southern Zaire with the French Foreign Legion. When you are a war correspondent, the game you play goes like this: If you lose, you die, and if you win, you get to do it again, and again, and again, and watch as friends die, until you die or retire.

Every foreign correspondent I know can name half a dozen friends, at least, who have died on the job. Most would admit that it is all a matter of luck. As far as survival is concerned, you don't get better at being a war correspondent; you just keep getting lucky. Experience doesn't matter. My two most experienced friends, Neil Davis in Asia and Mohamed Amin in Africa, each a legend for his decades of front-line reporting, finally died in the silliest ways. Neil was killed by shrapnel from a tank shell fired in an immediately forgotten coup attempt in Thailand. Mo first lost an arm in a bomb explosion in Ethiopia, then died in a hijacked plane that crashed into the Indian Ocean.

My old mate Allen Pizzey, the CBS correspondent who knows the field as well as anyone, put it this way after two CBS friends were killed by a roadside bomb blast in Baghdad and another correspondent was badly wounded: "For journalists who cover wars, luck is like a blind trust fund; you can make withdrawals but not deposits, and you have no idea how much is left."

You don't study to be a foreign correspondent. You just do it, and grow into the role. My own introduction to war came suddenly, with no learning curve. I began in the deep end, literally. It was a hot Saturday, and I was swimming a hundred yards off the Hilton beach in Tel Aviv, doing a leisurely backstroke in the glare of the Mediterranean sun, wondering what had happened to my new friends Hugh Alexander, a UPI news photographer, and his Israeli girlfriend, Batia Grafka. We were supposed to meet at midday, and they were more than an hour late. Hugh was a gentile and Batia a hilarious, godless Jewess. I knew almost nothing could stop them from enjoying the quiet of Yom Kippur on the beach.

Two nights earlier I had dined with one of the Israeli army spokesmen, Captain Amnon Paldi, whose family manufactured clothes for Marks & Spencer. He talked in passing about the chances of war, but with no sense of urgency. None of us at the table knew that the Israeli army would declare a general alert the next day, Friday, October 5, 1973. They called it a precautionary measure in the face of exercises by the Syrian and Egyptian armies. War? The new Israeli army head of intelligence called the chance remote.

Since I had recently arrived in Israel, Captain Paldi's aside that he would be spending Yom Kippur in his army office didn't ring any alarm bells. But now, floating on my back, languidly enjoying the midday sun upon my face, it suddenly all added up. Amnon sleeping in his office. Hugh, a UPI photographer, not showing up. Those planes I'd heard flying along the coast during the night of Yom Kippur. War! It had to be. Nothing else would have stopped Hugh coming to the beach on this day.

I rolled over and struck out for shore. I ran to my clothes, slipped on my sandals, and, still dripping, raced past sunbathers and up the steps to

Hayarkon Street. Already I saw the first signs. There were cars on the street, unheard of on this one holy day of the year when driving in Israel is forbidden. Uniformed men carrying guns and helmets lined the road, waiting for lifts to the front. Egypt wouldn't open fire at the Suez Canal until 1:55 P.M., but word was already out. Soldiers were to join their units immediately.

Israeli intelligence had warned the government overnight that Egypt and Syria would invade that day at 6:00 P.M. The army had ordered a partial call-up of reserves, and the air force had demanded a preemptive strike against enemy airfields, which had worked so brilliantly for Israel in 1967. But Prime Minister Golda Meir rejected the generals' advice and went with her political advisers. They believed it imperative that Israel should appear to have been surprised. The country would need to absorb the enemy's first blow if it was to keep American support for the rest of the war. Israel must not look as if it had started the fighting, as it had six years earlier. So when war erupted, the only real surprise for Israel was that the attack came at 1:55, four hours earlier than predicted.

I ran past the soldiers and down Jabotinsky to my flat at 224 Dizengoff. The nephew of my colleague Rolf Kneller stood at my door, ringing the bell. "War," he shouted when I turned the corner. "We're at war!"

"Who with?" I shouted back. I was clueless; I'd arrived in the country less than a week earlier and moved into my apartment the day before. It was a fancy place, with two bedrooms, air-conditioning, and a large living room with a glass door leading onto a terrace. My biggest dilemma so far was where to buy shower curtains. War? What did I know from war?

"Call Rolf," he said. "He'll tell you what to do." Then he ran off to join his army unit.

I took the stairs two at a time, put my spare camera batteries on charge, and phoned Rolf in Jerusalem. "Go to the Golan Heights, I'll come down to the studios," he said. "Don't waste any time, you must go now."

What was he talking about? What should I do on the Golan? He just said there was a war. It seemed dangerous. Anyway, I had another question.

"Where are the Golan Heights?"

"Ach, du lieber Gott!"

I told Rolf dear God couldn't help me now; what I needed was a road map. But in fact, I needed far more than that. I had never worked as a war correspondent. I hadn't even been a Boy Scout, let alone had military training. The nearest I had been to combat was playing soccer in London. I didn't know the roads, or the people, or even the issues. Why was Israel suddenly at war? I had no idea.

War hadn't been on my mind when I stepped off the boat in Haifa in October 1973. I was a twenty-six-year-old news agency cameraman with only the slimmest of journalist credentials. Two years earlier, I had bluffed my way into becoming one of the youngest writers ever on the staff of BBC television news in London. I was on the fast track, but it didn't take me long to realize I was headed in the wrong direction. The post of writer was an in-house job that led to production and management. I never wanted to produce a show, or be an anchor. I wanted to be a foreign correspondent. Those were two magic words to me, glamorous and exciting and full of promise: free travel!

I have to admit that I was not a young man with a mission to save the world. Rather, I wanted to save money and see the world. I could not have been more naïve about the misery and the hardship I would witness, and the toll they would take.

In the BBC newsroom, I felt hopelessly bored. A dozen journalists sat around a large, U-shaped table, each with a more senior person to his right. As the junior subeditor on the flagship broadcast, the *9 O'Clock News,* I sat at the far left. Next to me sat the subeditor. On his right toiled the senior subeditor, and so on until, opposite me, sat the assistant editor, who ran the show. Each person was about three years older than the man on his left. If I plodded on, I could maybe sit opposite myself in another eighteen years.

On one particularly black day, when I got a soccer score wrong and most of England phoned to complain, Derek Maude, the assistant editor, took me to task. "Fook me, Fletcher," he yelled, "you'll never be a journalist!" Maude wore an eye patch, but you can hardly say he lacked vision.

After a year of frustration and insults from Maude, I decided I couldn't wait any longer to get into the field. I didn't have the patience to train to be a BBC reporter, and it wasn't clear I'd ever have the opportunity anyway, so I made a choice only the young would dare to make. While studying books on film, light, and sound that I borrowed from the local library, I talked Visnews, the world's largest news film agency, into lending me a film camera. Three months later Visnews agreed to take a gamble and send me out in the field as a cameraman. Despite the considerable drop in status and salary, I handed a one-line resignation note to the Beeb and never looked back.

My first foreign assignment for Visnews was to replace their Brussels veteran, Maurice De Witte, an eighty-two-year-old cameraman who wore a suit and tie on every assignment and brought along his black miniature poodle on a red leash. He was a dear old man but angry at being replaced, and he couldn't have been more delighted when I blew my first job. It was the first day of British membership in the European Community, and the best way to illustrate this for television was to film the Union Jack being hoisted for the first time alongside all the other national flags at the entrance to the EC headquarters. It was my first-ever job as a cameraman and I got there too late. I missed the story. I think a girl was involved. Maurice was delighted. Maybe this young whippersnapper would not be shunting him off into early retirement after all.

What Maurice didn't know was that three years earlier I had interned for six months as a languages translator at Berlaymont, the star-shaped community headquarters building in front of which the British flag now limply hung. Showing the "rat-like cunning" that one famous British reporter, Nicholas Tomalin, called the key requirement of journalists, I went straight to the office of the chief doorman. Fortunately, he remembered me. To Maurice's consternation, I persuaded the man to lower the flag and raise it again for me, while I filmed the historic moment redux. Today, I could be fired for that. Then, it may have saved my job. Maurice finally understood that it was time to move aside graciously for the new generation, and my career was born.

As it turned out, though, I was far from happy. In Brussels I suffered more than in London, barely emerging into daylight, filming stuffy committee meetings and conferences in the European Community headquarters. Overheated rooms, cigar smoke, mussels, and beer were about all I knew of working in the field.

Nine months later, when Visnews appointed me bureau chief in Israel, I was delighted. I rushed to share the good news with a new friend, the Israeli TV correspondent in Brussels. Ron Ben-Yishai tried hard to dissuade me. "This is where the excitement is, here in Brussels," Ron told me, "the struggle for a united Europe. Don't go to Israel. It's too quiet there. The story's over."

He should know, I thought. Ron was an Israeli paratrooper, a former military correspondent for Israeli television, and a rising media star. But I'd had my fill of winter in Europe, and bitter clashes among commission bureaucrats over controversial farming issues like how many hens a cock should mate with a day, ten or twelve. I decided to move on to warmer and more peaceful climes.

That September, Israel was in a summer stupor. The temperature was in the nineties. The glory of its stunning victory over three Arab armies in six days in June 1967 had led to social complacency, military arrogance, and, six years on, political inertia. Israel was resting on its laurels. And so I arrived on October 1, 1973, with little on my mind beyond sunny days and sultry girls. Five days later, Egypt and Syria invaded.

The next time I saw Ron Ben-Yishai was two and a half weeks into the war, on the Egyptian side of the Suez Canal. He drove a military jeep and wore paratrooper gear. His face was blackened with smoke and grime, and an Uzi submachine gun was slung across his chest. He grinned sheepishly. "Well, maybe the story isn't over yet," he said.

Nobody understood why Visnews decided to assign me to Israel, least of all Rolf Kneller, who had been the Visnews man there for decades. As far as he was concerned, I was just a young pest who threatened his job. He had sent a series of nasty letters to management asking why they were being so considerate as to finally send him help after having overworked and underpaid him for so many years. What was the real reason behind my arrival, he wondered, and as bureau chief no less? *Nu?* What did Fletcher know from Israel?

Clearly, not a lot. Now, putting such resentments aside, Rolf impatiently explained how to get to the Golan. "Drive northeast," he said. North I knew, but east was a problem. "*Ach!* Just follow the cars, they're all going to the Golan."

I hopped into my proudest possession at the time, a Mazda RX2. It was a sleek orange sports coupe with spider wheels and a rotary engine, the only one of its kind in Israel. The rotary engine was incredibly fast and quiet. I'd driven the Mazda from Brussels to Marseille, then crossed the Mediterranean by boat to Haifa with a trunk load of spare parts. Now my main concern, as I drove past citizen-soldiers kissing their families and heading to war, as I passed people painting their car headlights blue for the blackouts, and as I hid in a storefront when the air-raid sirens sounded, was my car. If it got damaged, I wondered, would Visnews pay?

Luckily, I had a full tank of fuel, and by now my camera batteries were partially charged. I got lost a few times and spent hours crawling in traffic jams, but by the next morning I was approaching the Golan Heights. The first days, when Israel was almost defeated, I couldn't get close to the action, and didn't really want to. The roads were clogged with private cars carrying soldiers and their gear, giant flatbed trucks transporting desperately needed tanks and armored personnel carriers, long columns trundling up the narrow, winding roads from Lake Galilee and Kiryat Shmona, and me in my orange Mazda, along with dozens of other pressmen.

After three days of filming the Israeli buildup on the ground and warplanes screeching overhead, I finally made it to the Heights. It was a rocky, hilly plateau forty by fifteen miles, with fabulous views over Lake Galilee to the west, while to the east was the snowcapped Mount Hermon, scene of some of the fiercest battles as Israeli and Syrian paratroopers duked it out for control of the strategic peaks. Whoever controlled the top had a straight line of sight over Damascus to the east and across most of northern Israel to the west.

As I entered the war zone, I was still well behind what I expected to be the main thrust of the Israeli troops, so I kept on driving east. Each time I stopped to film, I did a rueful check of the damage to the Mazda. The army vehicles along the rough tracks of the Golan sent chips of earth and stone smashing into my orange paintwork. In places it was beginning to look like a pineapple. In my head I composed a letter to Visnews requesting a new paint job on expenses.

I passed still-burning tanks and ambulances ferrying back the wounded. Dust clouds marked the progress of distant troops heading for the front. Knots of infantry rested at intersections. I tried to interview them, but mostly they were too tired or uninterested to talk. The only thing that sparked their interest was my car, especially the damage. They couldn't believe I had brought such a snazzy car to the front, and neither could I. Overhead, Israeli and Syrian warplanes were locked in dogfights, with puffs of white the only clouds in the blue sky. Sometimes a plane would suddenly spout black smoke and crash in the distance. Mobile artillery pieces fired and moved, fired and moved, to escape Syrian targeting. I wondered whether in this drab, gray landscape of rock, earth, and battle vehicles a Syrian gunner would find it easier to focus through his crosshairs, if they really had such things, on a bright orange car and take it out.

I decided to ask for directions. Seeing a car stop on the side of the road a few hundred yards away, I drove over and struck up a conversation with one of the occupants, who turned out to be Nicholas Tomalin, the London *Sunday Times*'s top reporter. He was very kind and helpful and gave me sound advice. "Don't get ahead of the Israelis," he said. "And don't stay in one place for too long. Also, don't start driving around in a convoy of cars." Whereupon Tomalin and his friends drove off, leaving me wondering whether to follow, even though he had just warned me against convoys.

I stood by the Mazda for a few minutes, looking at a few white trails and puffs in the sky, hearing muffled booms. Then I decided to drive after Tomalin and look for the forward Israeli infantry. I had just opened the car door when a flash of flame and black smoke rose behind the next low hill. This was followed instantly by the clap of an explosion. Moments later, other journalists whom I hadn't seen before turned up with the news. It was Tomalin's car. He'd been trying to turn around on a narrow track after realizing that the Israeli forward line we were looking for didn't exist. We were way too far forward. Later I heard it was a shoulder-fired, wire-guided Sagger missile that had done Tomalin in. Carried by Syrian commandos, it was one of the new Soviet weapons that would surprise the Israelis in this war. Five minutes after advising me how to stay alive, Nicholas Tomalin was killed by an antitank missile.

That was it for me. I got into the Mazda, turned around, and raced back to safety. But there was no safety on the Golan Heights. It was a madhouse. Total war in an area the size of Portland, Oregon.

In those first days, Syria threw almost 1,500 tanks at the Israelis, who had 177. Syria had 150 artillery pieces against Israel's 11. Syria's new SAM-6 and SAM-7 missiles were decimating the surprised Israeli air force. Golda's wish to be attacked first cost Israel hundreds of lives, and only frantic and heroic resistance saved Israel from losing the war quickly. But by Day Three the reserves had made it to the Heights, with their ammunition and vehicles. Now Israel was ready to fight back. The infantry were at division strength, backed up by brigades of tanks and artillery, and the Israeli Phantoms and Skyhawks took growing control of the skies. The Syrian army began to face a withering counterattack, with the vanguard of the press in hot pursuit.

I spent the next few days learning the unfortunate truth about being a war cameraman. The best stuff is the closest. No barroom briefings, no late-night note swapping, no exaggeration or plagiarism for the man with the camera. Either you were there, up close, or you weren't. You either shot the pictures or you didn't. As Robert Capa said: "If your pictures aren't good enough, you're not close enough." That worked for him until he trod on a land mine and died.

As Israel fought for its very survival, dozens of cars beetled around the battlefield carrying the world's press. Sometimes these broke down and held up army convoys ferrying men and vital ammunition to the front. No wonder that, after a week of battlefield anarchy, the army took control and banned the press from the Golan unless accompanied by an army escort officer. But by then Israel had smashed the Syrian tank divisions and was chasing the bloody remnants back toward Damascus. The threat to Israel from the north was over, and the only question was how deep Israel would advance into Syria. Would they occupy Damascus? If so, I thought, it would be without me. At this point, exhausted and filthy, I steered my battered Mazda RX2 back home to see if I had replacements for the smashed sidelights, to buy those shower curtains, and to have a long soak and a rest before going on to cover the southern front.

Back in Tel Aviv, all the world's major television news outfits had turned up and were sharing the same understaffed and overworked facilities at Herzliya Studios. Most of its male staff had gone off to war. The remaining personnel were working around the clock to accommodate the many time zones of the world. Each TV station or agency had one small edit room if they were lucky; otherwise they had roped-off space under a tree in the yard. CBS, ABC, NBC, BBC, ITN, the Germans, the French, the Japanese, the agencies—everyone fought, screamed, and cheated. The CBS bureau chief, Dan Bloom, was unbeatable because he knew all the low-down tricks. Whenever someone found a flat tire on a cameraman's car, he'd shout out, "Bloom!"

At the end of each day, when dozens of TV crews raced into the studios with their film for the night's show, producers would rush the cans to the film lab. If you were at the end of the line, you had no chance of getting on the air that night. It took close to an hour to develop a four-hundred-foot roll of film, and there were dozens of rolls. Cameramen would risk their lives and not even get their film developed. Producers screamed at one another and came close to fistfights. In the beginning, Dan would insist his film crews get back early, even if they missed some of the story, in order to get the CBS rolls of film first into the lab. Then he put in a few empty rolls, too, just to slow down everyone else. When the others got wise, a rule was introduced that a network could put only one roll in the bath at a time. Later, if Dan shared a charter plane with other U.S. nets, he would insist they wait for his man to arrive, delaying them all at small airports around the country. Meanwhile, Dan would have secretly chartered his own plane, which had already taken off with the CBS package.

Dan infuriated the other U.S. network producers, but I looked, laughed, and learned. On the Golan Heights I had first tasted war; now I was learning there was another war in the TV world—getting on air. Each station or network had ten minutes to feed all its pictures on the satellite. If one producer took a minute too long, the next producer up lost that time. This led to nightly screaming, cursing, and threats of violence, as Dan Bloom of CBS and Ken Lukoff of NBC pushed and fought over machine time, while the Herzliya manager, the portly Itzhik Kol, sweated, pleaded, and cajoled with the Hebrew equivalent of "Gentlemen, please!"

This was my introduction to the U.S. television networks, and I loved the intensity of their competition. The British correspondents and producers of the BBC were much more gentlemanly with their competition at ITN, reserving their true hatred for each other. One man, though, stood out: Keith Graves.

I knew Keith's fearsome reputation from my time writing for the BBC's *9 O'Clock News.* Although only about five years older than I, he was a true veteran, a former Fleet Street foot-in-the-door print man turned television fist-in-the-face type. Keith was over six feet tall, with a jutting jaw, a booming voice, black hair, and big black glasses. He threw telephones in the newsroom. Slammed down typewriters. Ran over the foot of a doorman who wouldn't let him into the BBC parking lot. At one time or another, he threatened to beat up many of the other BBC correspondents.

Like everybody else, I dreaded Keith. So I reacted instantly when Jerry Lamprecht, the Visnews producer who had come to run our operation, said to me, "Martin, we've got a great assignment. The army wants us to send a cameraman to be the world pool on some secret trip in the south, and that's you. You're going out with a BBC correspondent—"

"Okay, so long as it's not Keith Graves," I said.

"—Keith Graves."

"Are you kidding?" I said.

After a week of war on the Golan Heights, I had no problem facing battalions of Egyptian commandos or tank divisions. After all, the Israeli army stood between them and me. The only thing I was scared of was working with Graves. I couldn't know that Keith and I were about to go through the bonding experience from hell that would make us lifelong friends.

Yet Graves wasn't the only thing wrong with the proposed secret trip. Being the world pool cameraman was intimidating, too. It meant I was to represent all the TV stations of the world.

I had been a war cameraman for only two weeks. I couldn't tell Jerry I didn't feel up to it, but I hoped the assignment would be a minor one. And, in fact, this was a reasonable hope, since most of the organized army junkets were a waste of time. They were propaganda trips to film some captured weapons, or interview prisoners of war who didn't speak English, or pay rapt attention to a general praising himself.

I met Keith at the Government Press Office, and after a quick briefing from the spokesmen about where to meet our army escorts in the country's south, we set off at 10:00 P.M. in my dirty, chipped, but robust Mazda. As I had hardly slept the night before after filming in the south and was now beginning a six-hour overnight drive back again, I needed help staying awake. I turned to Keith to chat. "I've had a long day," he announced. He pushed the seat back as far as it went, pressed on the handle so it reclined, stretched out his long legs, folded his arms, touched his chin to his chest, and slept till dawn.

The way out of Tel Aviv wasn't too bad, but south of Ashkelon the road narrowed until El Arish, and then it was just a tarmac track through the Sinai desert all the way to our destination, Bir Gafgafa, the southern headquarters of the Israeli army, about fifteen miles north of the Suez Canal. It must have been a beautiful night, with clear, star-spangled desert skies and the moon casting long, palm-tree shadows over the wavy sand dunes, but I wouldn't know. I was just trying to stay awake at the wheel. All the way I had to wait in long convoys, maneuver around broken-down army trucks, and avoid animals on the road. But at least all the stops and waiting gave me a chance to stretch my legs and get some air. I wondered where this secret trip was headed and began to get excited. It had to be something special. I started to look forward to the challenge, and even Keith didn't look that scary, sprawled over half the car and snoring.

In my week on the Golan Heights, I had survived my baptism by fire, and after almost another week of covering the southern front, I thought I knew what to expect. In the Sinai there was no chance of escaping the army roadblocks. Whereas the Golan was full of connecting roads and hard dirt tracks, and it was impossible to block the press, who, often aided by their gung-ho army escort officers, could always find an alternative route to the front, the Sinai had only two tarmac roads going north-south. So if you were stopped, you were stuffed. There was no way to drive off-road in an orange Mazda. The sand was too soft. And all the fighting was around the canal, far out of reach. The most interesting pictures anyone had gotten in the south were of naked soldiers frolicking under field showers. But with these permits from the Government Press Office, we sailed through the roadblocks all the way to Bir Gafgafa.

As I finally rolled into the Israeli HQ around four in the morning, Keith stirred, stretched, yawned, and asked, "Where are we? What are we doing?"

"I don't know yet," I said. "I hope it's down to the canal."

An army spokesman found us right away. No doubt my orange Mazda, even in its sad state, stood out like a beacon among the dusty jeeps. He gave us a quick briefing. On this same day, he told us, October 21, 1973, sixteen days into the fighting, the Egyptian military had given their first press conference of the war. It was a total rout, according to General Izzidin Mukhtar in Cairo, a forerunner of the Iraqi spokesman Comical Ali in Baghdad years later. The Egyptian forces, he said, were inflicting heavy losses on the collapsing Israeli defenses. Mukhtar claimed Egypt had shot down 303 Israeli warplanes, as well as 25 helicopters, destroyed 600 tanks, 400 armored vehicles, and 23 naval vessels. A reporter had questioned whether the combined Egyptian and Syrian claims of knocking out more than 600 Israeli aircraft might be exaggerated, given that the Israeli air force had only 488 planes. Did Israel have no planes left?

As for Israel's expeditionary force across the canal, Egyptian officials called it an "adventure" that was suffering "heavy losses" as the Egyptian line held. In fact, earlier in the war the Egyptians did inflict heavy losses on the Israelis, who had been surprised by the supereffective Soviet-made SAM missile batteries that defended the Egyptian side of the canal, as well as by the antitank Sagger missiles that Egyptian infantrymen, like the Syrians, carried on their backs. On the Egyptian and Syrian fronts, Israel lost fifty warplanes in the first three days of war. The Egyptian troops killed and captured hundreds of Israeli troops and managed to astonish the Israeli defenders by transferring their entire Third Army across the canal into the Sinai desert, preparing the way for a thrust north into Israel's heartland. On the war's second day, Israel's defense minister, Moshe Dayan, declared on television, "We shall smite them hip and thigh," but off camera it was a different story. Deeply depressed at the dreadful news from every front, Dayan had advised his generals in the south to retreat. "What will happen, will happen," he said. He believed Tel Aviv was in danger.

Israel needed to go on the offensive, and quick. The country's war games had always posited a counterattack across the Suez Canal, and all preparations had been made. Before he had retired only three months earlier as commander of the southern front, Reserve General Ariel Sharon had marked with red bricks exactly where to punch through the barriers along the canal, and where to lay down bridges across the two-hundred-yard waterway.

But now Sharon, usually petulant and always controversial, was livid. He had been arguing furiously for days with the army leaders. His scouts had discovered a narrow gap between the Egyptian Second and Third armies, and he wanted to launch his fighters through it and across the canal before the Egyptians discovered the gap and sealed it. Sharon insisted this would win the war for Israel.

Two days were lost as his superiors equivocated. They were afraid that the general wanted all the glory for himself and was falsifying or exaggerating his reports. They were terrified that moving Sharon's division might leave the way open for the Egyptians to break through to Tel Aviv. And they also feared that Sharon was plain wrong and that his vanguard across the canal would be isolated and massacred.

Then, when Sharon finally reached the canal, he still couldn't cross. His giant fording equipment was blocked in snarling military traffic jams.

Sharon was like a bull on a chain. An army, he knew, needs to move, attack, keep the initiative, or it becomes a sitting duck. As he waited and cursed, the Egyptians mounted a furious assault on his forces massing by the canal. Warplanes screamed in, dropping bombs and strafing Sharon's vehicles at the beachhead. A machine gun on his command car swiveled around and smashed Sharon on the head, drawing blood and knocking him down. Briefly his men thought he was dead, but Sharon soon opened his eyes. Now, to the annoyance of his rivals, the gray-haired general looked even more glamorous, with a blood-flecked white bandage wound tightly around his head.

They accused Sharon of insubordination, scheming behind their backs, ignoring or misinterpreting orders, giving misleading information, competing with other generals, and, crime of all crimes, using his military position to lay the groundwork for his entry into politics. But finally the order came, telling the Jews for the first time since the exodus: Go to Egypt. It was Sharon's moment. Because the fording equipment still hadn't made it, the first tanks and infantry floated across on dozens of rubber pontoons. Then engineers strung together a couple of narrow, rickety roller bridges and poured three divisions of men and equipment into Africa, as Israel called the Egyptian side of the Suez Canal.

Now, although vastly outnumbered, the first Israeli force of twenty-seven tanks was punching forward in Egypt, destroying those killer SAM missile sites that had shocked the Israeli air force and conquering a narrow sliver of land along the Suez Canal and the sweet-water canal that led to Ismailiya in one direction and Suez city in the other. The desert lay flat and invitingly open all the way to Cairo. But as Israel built up its forces in Africa, Egyptian artillery had their range and were pouring mortars and heavy shells on the Israeli troops while commandos hiding in burned-out buildings hit the Israelis with devastating bazooka fire. It was a mess.

The army spokesman finally ended his briefing. My head was spinning. What a hellhole it must be over there, I thought. Glad I'm here. So what are we going to do, talk to some prisoners? Then came our world pool assignment. It was straightforward enough. "Hop in a vehicle, cross the canal, and find Sharon in Africa."

What? Keith smiled at me. We could hear the rolling thunder and booms of tank and artillery war from ten miles away. There was no letup. A helicopter swooped in blowing dust and dirt as medics raced forward carrying stretchers. Three trucks loaded with soldiers rushed past.

Two other journalists would accompany us: Hugh Mulligan, the legendary AP writer, and his even more legendary photographer, Horst Faas, who had won two Pulitzer Prizes, for his war coverage in Vietnam and Bangladesh. I'd been doing this for only two weeks. I felt hopelessly out of my depth, and it must have showed. Keith patted me on the shoulder and said, "Don't worry, you'll do fine."

He helped carry my camera gear, understood what was happening around us, and asked all the right questions, while I was dumbstruck. For two weeks everything that had happened to me was a first-time experience. I was making it up as I went along. Now I was going to cross the Suez Canal and join what may well become Israel's greatest military maneuver ever. Or its bloodiest defeat. But with Keith next to me and surrounded by tanks and soldiers, I was determined not to chicken out. Not that I had the option. There was no way back. As we reached the canal, clattered across the rickety metal bridge in our vehicle, an armored half-track, and turned right toward the Great Bitter Lake, with the crump of explosions behind and in front of us and the occasional bullet whining by, I resigned myself to fate.

It was dawn, and the sun was rising over Egypt. Our field of vision grew by the minute, and it revealed a frightening landscape. On the Golan, the vista had often been limited by hills, clumps of trees, stone houses, and twisting roads. Here in Egypt it resembled a grotesque tableau laid out endlessly before us: sunken commando speedboats upended in the canal, destroyed armored vehicles billowing black smoke, puffs of white in the blue sky as warplanes streaked high overhead, columns of tired infantry flashing victory signs as we drove by. In the distance was the immense desert, but close up, along the sweet-water canal, were green fields with orange orchards and palm trees, and among them devastated villages and homes pocked by bullets and shells. Wounded men lay by the side of the road, and blindfolded prisoners sheltered in the shade of the embankments. Sharon's punch across the canal had surrounded the Egyptian Third Army, cutting off their food and ammunition supplies. Now Israeli artillery in captured Egyptian bunkers poured mercilessly accurate fire on the trapped Egyptian tank division. The horizon was dotted with burning hulks. An Israeli commander called it a massacre.

But the Egyptian high command was still calling the crossing a failed Israeli adventure, and the Israeli government still refused to confirm or deny it was even happening. One man wanted the story out, though—Ariel Sharon. We came across him eating oranges with a bemused Egyptian farmer while Egyptian corpses still lay on the ground. "Tell the world," Sharon instructed Keith, "that Israel has crossed the canal. Two Egyptian armies are trapped." Keith pointed out that the nearest working telephone was probably in Cairo. That didn't stop Sharon. He told his radio operator, who in real life was a London taxi driver, to get through to the BBC. Within minutes Keith had the astonished foreign desk on the line. The connection was too poor for a live broadcast, but Keith got the information across, telling the BBC that he was in Egypt with the Israeli army, and that the Egyptian denial was, to use Keith's word, "bollocks." It was a world scoop. Keith confirmed Israel had invaded Egypt, and Sharon became a hero.

Then came an offer we could refuse. Five miles from the canal in the direction of Cairo, an Israeli tank division was hotly engaged with the main Egyptian defense force, which was trying to destroy the Israeli marauders and block their access to the capital. It became the biggest tank battle of the war. Military historians later called it the biggest tank battle since Stalingrad. The offer: Did we want to film it?

"Sure," we said, "but how?" It was flat desert, and each tank kicked up its own sandstorm. Close-up visibility was nil, but from a distance I could film the general action. We thought it should be safe enough if we went out with an observation half-track—an armored vehicle covered with antennae and long-range binoculars and all kinds of electronic devices to track the battle and send guidance information to the blinded tanks. It kept at a safe distance from the enemy tanks. Hugh Mulligan, the AP writer, was smart. "I don't need to go," he said. "I have a pen with a range of ten miles." But Keith said to me and Horst Faas, "I'll go with you."

What we didn't realize was that, because the observation vehicle is the eyes of the tank force, it is the enemy's key target. Knock out the vehicle we were on and you'd blind the entire Israeli tank force.

We climbed inside the vehicle, arranged ourselves as best we could on the hard metal bench, and fought for breath in the hot, musty, diesel-smelling space. The driver set off smoothly, seeking a strategic spot far from the battle. He settled on a small ridge. But before I could arrange the camera, we came under furious mortar attack. Shells rained around us with terrific booms, shooting clouds of sand into the air. As we fought to hold on in the cramped interior, the driver shot off the ridge and down onto the dunes, zigzagging at top speed while the commander shouted out, "Mines, mines, watch out for mines!" We were thrown about the inside of the metal hull, hurled into one another and into the sharp edges, everyone screaming and shouting over the roar of the engine. Shells continued to smash into the soft sand, which fortunately absorbed the shrapnel or we would have been goners. It was incredible war action, and I didn't shoot a frame.

We came to a breathless halt right next to a small, closed-off barbed-wire compound. There was a sign in Arabic. Fortunately, we had an Arabic reader onboard. "What does it say?" someone asked. "Danger. Ammunition dump," he answered.

"Oh shit," the commander said, "let's get away from here." The driver revved up, turned, and headed for another so-called safe spot to observe the battle. Now I was sitting half out of the vehicle turret, my legs dangling in. I didn't want to miss all the action again. Keith supported me around the waist to stop me from being thrown off as the half-track bounced along. Next to me, the gunner manned a fixed machine gun.

Only a minute later we heard a distant rumbling from the sky. It quickly became closer and louder. We looked around nervously. Where was it from? I rolled the camera just in case. It was an Egyptian jet. It roared by so low it half-filled my lens, and as the machine gunner whipped around shooting at the plane, the rat-a-tat of his rapid fire came close to bursting my eardrums. Again the driver took off, jerking the vehicle from left to right, leaving a crazy trail of sand cloud as we sped away. Then the plane, a MiG fighter-bomber, roared back and began dropping bombs on us. As we raced across the desert, the first bomb landed about fifty yards away and then a second bomb just in front of it hit and then a third. I swung the camera away from our gunner, who was yelling and shooting, to the first bomb and the next and the next, catching each explosion on film.

Keith gripped me tightly, although I couldn't make out if he was helping me to stay balanced or stopping me from ducking for cover. The MiG was gone! We were okay. Not for long. Now he was screaming back at us from the horizon, heading right for us a second time, guns spitting into the sand. But before the fighter pilot could send us into oblivion, he suddenly jerked upward into a steep climb. An Israeli warplane was on his tail. There was a brief low dogfight, fighter jets wheeling and swooping and shooting, and the MiG, trailing black smoke, turned on its nose, its wings shaking. It smashed into the ground just over a hillock about a mile away. There was an explosion and a flash of flame. Dark smoke billowed into the sky.

I had it all on film. It was incredible. Horst Faas, the Pulitzer-winning Vietnam veteran, didn't shoot a frame. He picked himself up from the floor of the vehicle and said it was the most dangerous situation he had ever been in. Me, I didn't have time to think about it. I just filmed it as if it were on the movie screen.

It was weird. I wasn't scared or shaky. I didn't think about the danger. I had no options, so I did my job. Everything on the film I shot was in focus, although the gunner was up close, the bombs were in the mid-distance, and the planes were on infinity. I must have been pulling focus all the time. The exposure was perfect, although the gunner next to me was in shadow, and the desert and sky were bright light, so I must have adjusted from about f5.6 to f16 or f22 even as I swung from the gunner to the plane.

I don't know why I wasn't scared. It seems unnatural. Certainly, I was too excited. But I think seeing death through the camera lens made it unreal. The lens acted as a filter. The attacking plane and the bombs seemed several steps removed from my own space. As the Egyptian roared over us, my attention was focused purely on swinging the camera around fast enough to keep the plane in the middle of the frame, and I remember trying to keep the gunner in the left side of the frame for better composition. The fact that I could have been blown to bits just didn't play a role. I was on automatic.

In war, automatic is a dangerous place to be, and I knew it even then. About four months earlier, a Swedish cameraman called Leonardo Henrichsen had shot some extraordinary footage in Chile. His pictures were still fresh in my mind. He had been on automatic, and it had killed him.

Henrichsen's film shows a national guardsman who seems to be pointing at the cameraman from a distance of about twenty yards. But as the seconds tick by, it becomes clear that the soldier is in fact aiming a pistol. The camera does not flinch. Then there is a bang as the soldier fires straight at the camera. Still, the camera doesn't waver, and after a pause of a second or so it pans slightly to the left, where another soldier aims a rifle straight at the camera and fires. He misses, too.

Seven seconds tick by. Henrichsen has ample time to understand the threat and retreat. But the cameraman has become an extension of his camera. He does not feel his own presence. He is not there anymore; he is no longer a cameraman but just a camera, an artificial eye. The lens has removed him from the action. The view through the viewfinder is square, like watching television. And it shows the action in black and white, not color, which distances him further. It does not register in the cameraman's mind that he is holding a camera and could die; if instinct kicks in at all, it is fight or flight, and Henrichsen subconsciously decides to fight. But he isn't holding a gun to fight with, just a camera. Doesn't he understand the danger? By now the television viewer is silently screaming to the cameraman to put the camera down, but it's too late. The soldier takes a few steps forward, still aiming his rifle. He shoots again. The camera microphone records the sharp crack. The picture whirls giddily and goes to black. Leonardo Henrichsen filmed his own death.

With bombs falling and machine guns firing, how close had I come to that? Hadn't I understood the danger I was in? Clearly not. My adrenaline was pumping, and I have rarely felt so alive as when Keith yelled, "He's crashed!" and the plane exploded into the desert.

That night, we caught up with General Sharon in his desert headquarters. He was standing at the center of a circle of armored vehicles, using a jeep hood as a table, feasting on caviar and champagne that his wife, Lily, had packed for him. He looked the very picture of a warrior, with his bandaged head and his company of generals and soldiers. They were silhouettes in the half-moon, with the occasional jeep's headlight lighting the scene further and throwing long shadows.

Sharon greeted us cheerfully but was deep in discussion. At this point in the campaign, he was berating the officers in southern command about the need to continue along the sweet-water canal to attack the Egyptian town of Ismailiya and cut off the Egyptian Second Army, after he'd already surrounded the Third. But pressure was growing on Israel from the United States and the Soviet Union to stay in their current positions and cease firing. Sharon openly cursed his commanders for delaying his cross-ing of the canal. If they had moved when he had demanded, he said, he would have conquered Ismailiya the day before.

It was freezing at night, as the desert can be. The desert deceives you. The hot sun, the warm sand, the clear sky, the zillion bright stars—how pleasant, you think. Then, suddenly, the temperature begins to drop. The call to the world pool had taken us by surprise, and Keith and I hadn't known we would be at the front line overnight. We had brought no clothes or bedding, just a bag with film and camera batteries. I was wear-ing only a thin cotton T-shirt, and Keith had a safari shirt. We slept on the sand, half-sheltered from the wind by an armored personnel carrier, cov-ered by a piece of flat cardboard we'd scavenged. But I fell asleep with a smile on my face, and it wasn't because of Keith next to me. That MiG! I was thinking. Great stuff!

We were in the middle of nowhere, so we couldn't ship the film back to Tel Aviv for broadcast. That would have to wait till we got out of Egypt. I couldn't wait to look at the film.

The next day, October 22, 1973, to our incredible disappointment, a cease-fire was declared. The savings in lives and property didn't occur to me. This was a disaster, I thought. What good would great war film be if there was peace? Who would care, except the archives? The story had moved on. Now the TV stations would want film showing peaceful scenes of soldiers waiting by their tanks, praying, calling home, smiling, joking. They would want images of convoys of armored vehicles returning across the canal to Israel, happy soldiers giving victory signs and smoking ciga-rettes, relieved Egyptian fellahin offering oranges and tea to the departing invaders. The tank battle was history. Peace! Keith and I were devastated.

We went to Sharon and told him we needed to get a flight back to Tel Aviv immediately. Could he arrange a jeep and a military flight from the desert airfield? We needed to get our film back now!

It was then that I got an insight into Ariel Sharon that stayed with me forever and informed all my subsequent reporting on this controversial army general who became an even more controversial defense minister and then prime minister. When we anxiously told him we needed to get out right away because the fighting was over, Sharon laughed. "Cease-fire?" he said. "Not yet. Stay here. Come with me to Ismailiya."

"But the government has agreed on a cease-fire," I said.

He laughed again and raised an eyebrow.

As it turned out, the general was right. The cease-fire broke down immediately. It was never clear who resumed firing. I can only say it was no surprise to Sharon. He led his men in a last charge along the canal to the very entrance to Ismailiya, but two days later, on October 24, another cease-fire was declared, and this time it stuck. By now, though, we were back in Tel Aviv with our scoop.

What I understood about Sharon was that he would never get enough. He would always want more, another mile, another success, another victory. He was winning, he wanted to keep fighting, and everybody above him, the army commanders, the government leaders, was holding him back. This was Ariel Sharon. An inspiring leader, a bulldozer with no brake pedal.

Later, Israel's defense minister, Moshe Dayan, who called Ariel Sharon the Israeli army's number one soldier, told Keith that if the crossing of the canal had failed, Sharon would have been court-martialed for disobeying orders. Instead, Dayan said, Sharon was a hero, and after that war Israel needed a hero very badly.

I was beginning to learn the awful exhilaration of the battlefield, where careers are made and lives are ruined or lost. I enjoyed the anarchy and the adrenaline, but I never went as far down that dangerous road as Tim Page, the Vietnam photographer. After being seriously wounded for the third time, he was offered the chance to write a book that would, once and for all, take the glamour out of war. He turned it down, saying: "Jesus, take the glamour out of war? How the hell can you do that? You can't take the glamour out of a tank burning or a helicopter blowing up. It's like trying to take the glamour out of sex. War is good for you."*

War is good for you? How dumb is that? Today I'd ask, What about the victims? Sure, we film them, even feel sorry for them, but who are they? After we take their pictures, do we even bother to think of them again?

Back then, however, with no preparation for war, I was swept along by the drama and asked few questions. I was slow to understand the import of what I was witnessing. When an Egyptian soldier surrendered to our jeep on the pool trip, he lifted up his robe, and at first I had no idea what he was holding in the hand that was cupped to his stomach. It was something red and streaky-pale and mushy. It looked like raw meat. It was his guts spilling out of a bullet wound. Soldiers used my T-shirt to blindfold him. I put my arm around his shoulders to steady him as he bounced up and down on the jeep. He had an IV drip in his arm that ran dry. He kept nodding at it with wide, terrified eyes, telling me, "Finish, finish." There was nothing I could do but keep filming. Keith helped the medics take him away, but soon we were told he had died. I felt I had landed in another world, a third or fourth dimension. I didn't know things like this were possible, yet I was in the thick of it, filming, staying calm, aloof even, doing my job.

Looking back, I can't say I enjoyed the horrors of war, but I do believe war engaged the senses in a way I had never experienced. I had never seen a warplane drop a bomb before, except in the movies, and I'd never felt a barrage of mortar shells shake the ground, or heard the whine of a shell overhead or the crack of a bullet close by, let alone seen or smelled a smoking body next to a burning tank. I'd never imagined what a man's guts look like when they spill through a hole in his stomach, or the expression on his face as he holds them in his hands and asks for help.

Since my initiation in the Yom Kippur War, I have met desperate people all over the globe—people without choices and without solutions, people to whom the platitude "Don't worry, it'll be all right" has no meaning, because it won't be all right, and they know it. The more I have seen of such people, the more distorted my youthful view of war has come to seem. What was I thinking anyway? Were my perceptions part of an extreme zero-sum game, in which another person's misfortune means you value your own life more? Or were they just plain stupid, like the comment by Tim Page, which shows just how far removed young men can be from what war is really all about—pain, needless suffering, and mindless hatred?

Two

When Luck Ran Out

W hen seen through a lens in black and white, danger feels distant, almost unreal. Your camera seems to have a magical power to protect you and separate you from events. At least my camera did, as I covered war in the Golan and the Suez.

During the summer of 1974, however, my camera lost its power—forever. I was covering a tin-pot coup d'état by a former assassin on the little island of Cyprus, off the coast of Israel. I was exhausted after ten grueling months covering the Yom Kippur War and its aftermath and thought the little coup would be a good break. I had never been to Cyprus before. I took a luxury room in the Ledra Palace, the storied colonial hotel that sits on the Green Line dividing the Turkish and Greek halves of the capital, Nicosia. I expected to film a story or two, take in the tourist sites of Paphos and the Troodos mountains, swim, drink, and in general conduct myself lewdly on the island of Aphrodite. I didn't realize what a minefield I had entered.

For all its rugged green beauty and its lascivious legacy as the birthplace of the Greek goddess of love, sex, and passion, Cyprus is a troubled place that has been under almost permanent occupation. First, the Greeks conquered the little island in 1500 B.C., followed by the Egyptians, the

Romans, the Byzantines, the English under Richard the Lionheart, the Turks, then the British again. In recent years, the Greek Cypriot call for *enosis,* union with Greece, had terrified the Turks on the island and alarmed their mother country. Even more alarming was the nature of the Greek Cypriot who had seized power in the coup—Nikos Sampson.

In the fifties Sampson had been a killer for the notorious Greek-Cypriot EOKA-B, a right-wing underground militia fighting for independence from Britain. He made his name as a photographer who always seemed to be first on the scene after terrorists murdered British policemen in the streets of Nicosia, in a place dubbed Murder Mile. It didn't take Sherlock Holmes to figure out that the only way a photographer could routinely film soldiers being murdered was if he pulled the trigger while snapping the picture. As EOKA's chief executioner, Sampson killed, by his own account, at least fifteen British policemen and civilians. The British sentenced him to death. But he was a free man after only three years. First the death sentence was commuted to life in jail, and then, when Cyprus won independence from Britain, in 1960, Sampson was freed in a general amnesty. He had then turned legit, if being a journalist can be termed legit, by running his own newspaper.

I met Sampson one night when he swaggered into the Hilton bar in Nicosia and invited the journalists for a drink. Hacks crowded around as the word quickly spread—the president is buying. He said he wanted to brief the media, to make sure we got the story right.

Sampson was of medium height and build and looked like a pimp, with black hair, black trousers, and black shirt. It's amazing, I thought, what a few neckless goons at your side can do for your stature. Yet on this night I found Sampson a witty man, full of jokes about the British press. Rubbing shoulders with him at the bar and toasting his presidency seemed harmless enough, even flattering. I don't remember being appalled at the character of my drinking buddy, or even thinking much about it. He was now president, after all, and probably not much less savory than many world leaders.

Sampson was to last only eight days in office. When the coup broke out, the minority Cypriot Turks appealed for help from Turkey. Then the Greek military government, having provoked a pointless confrontation with its NATO ally, quickly collapsed. This left the courageous assassin to face Turkey's wrath on his own, backed by only a few thousand poorly armed Greek-Cypriot national guardsmen. Sampson hurriedly resigned, but it was too late. The coup gave Turkey the excuse it had long sought. Within days, "Operation Attila"—the Turkish invasion of Cyprus—was under way.

My timing, again, was impeccable. I'd come for a break and found myself back on the front line. This time I had some experience; I thought I knew what I was doing. Boy was I wrong.

It was Nick Tomalin who'd first told me never to drive in a convoy. Although it's routine in war zones for reporters to stay together, and they'll even sneeringly call themselves the hack pack, the term *safety in numbers* is an oxymoron. Journalists are just too curious. If the first car in a press convoy stops, the last car will inevitably overtake to see why. Then the other cars will pull out so they don't lose their places in line, even if there is absolutely nowhere to go. And that is how my soundman, Ted Stoddart, died on a narrow Cyprus road lined by olive trees and fields of flowers. And how Paul Roque lost an eye and half his nose, and how Simon Dring and Chris Morris were wounded by shrapnel, and how Lefkos Christodoulides had his stomach blown open. Because the hacks in the back had to know why my car stopped.

After another evening drinking with Sampson's goons and a crowd of journalists, I was asleep in my room in the Ledra Palace when I got an early morning call from Hugh Alexander, the UPI photographer. It was July 20, 1974, a day that has since gone down as one of the blackest in the histories of Greece, Turkey, and Cyprus. "On your bike, mate," Hugh said, "the party's over. The Turks are coming. I've got a car. Let's go."

"What time is it?"

"Five thirty. Come on, we're late."

We had only been warned the night before that the Turks might invade. I jumped out of bed, grabbed my camera and bag, and ran to

Hugh's car. It stood almost alone in the parking lot. We were late. Most journalists had gotten the word even earlier and were well on their way to the coast. Another stills photographer shared the car with us, Michel Laurent, a dapper, baby-faced Frenchman wearing a white suit and a white straw hat. He was clever and friendly, a lovely guy with freckles, sensitive eyes, and full lips. In Bangladesh he had worked for AP and shared a Pulitzer Prize with Horst Faas for pictures of four men being bayoneted to death. We became friends, but not for long. Less than a year later, Michel would become the last journalist killed in Vietnam. He died the day before the war ended.

Together we raced from Nicosia through the Kyrenia Mountains to the island's Turkish part, toward the port of Kyrenia, where we expected the Turkish navy to put in. The roads were deserted, and it was only about fifteen miles away. Should arrive in plenty of time, I thought. We were halfway there and had just reached a plateau when we heard the drone of airplanes growing louder and louder. We stopped the car, and suddenly we saw them, so many transport planes and helicopters that they appeared to darken the sky.

A figure leaped out of one of the planes, then many figures, little dark shapes with parachutes first trailing, like black smudges in the sky, before they abruptly spread in puffs of white. Holy shit! We were just passing a little old village. Hugh pulled the car off the road and slammed on the brakes next to a farmhouse. We jumped out and grabbed our gear. I quickly set up the tripod, locked down the camera, pushed my eye into the viewfinder's rubber cup, set the exposure to f16, focused on infinity, and zoomed in to begin a pullout showing thousands of elite paratroopers floating earthward. But before I could press the little red record button, I felt a sharp jab in my ribs.

Whirling around, I saw a fierce Turkish Cypriot with a ratty yellowing mustache and cigarette breath poking me with an old .22. He made it clear he would prefer that I refrain from taking pictures.

The old partisan believed that the success of the entire Turkish invasion rested solely on his ability to stop us from working. No amount of pleading and cursing and begging, or even crying, could persuade the peasant to stop threatening us. I thought if I ignored him there wasn't a chance in hell he'd actually shoot me. But his bloodshot, wide eyes and trembling trigger finger persuaded me not to take the chance. More Turkish Cypriots emerged, and at gunpoint they forced us back into our car. They were kind enough, bringing us tea and dates, but they made us sit inside for an hour until this made-for-television parachute invasion was over and the paratroopers had marched away.

Then they lowered their guns and allowed us to leave. Cursing, we continued toward Kyrenia, hoping we hadn't missed the navy landing, too. Soon we came across a tired-looking group of Brits trudging down the road back toward Nicosia. They carried a television camera, tripod, bags, and, strangely, a pillow. One of them was Mike Nicholson, the star ITN correspondent. He brightened up considerably as he regaled us with his scoop that would win his team the Royal Television Society news film of the year award. He had left the hotel with the rest of the press, ahead of me, but his car had broken down. Everybody else reached the coast before the paratroopers jumped. This time they were ahead of the story. "You won't believe it," Mike gloated, "the Turks landed right on top of us. I interviewed an officer as he landed. It was fantastic. He just fell right into the frame, feetfirst, then his body, then his head, so I asked him why he came, and in perfect English he said, 'To kill Greeks.' Great stuff! And we were alone with the story!" Nicholson got the scoop that I had seen but couldn't film. I could have throttled him.

Nicholson's pictures were historic images of a full-scale parachute assault in a modern war. Of all the TV news crews in the world, Nicholson belonged to ITN of London, which shared its footage with the UPITN news film agency, Visnews's biggest rival. I was screwed. UPITN would satellite their exclusive news footage to television stations around the world, and Visnews would have nothing to offer. It was the agency man's nightmare. Not only had I missed the story but I didn't have anything to offer in its place. By the time I returned from Kyrenia, whatever I managed to film would be old hat compared with pictures of the actual invasion.

Pictures of slow-moving boats would never compete with paratroopers dropping from the sky.

Visnews would be furious. UPITN would clean up on Eurovision, the European news film exchange, where news editors from across the continent swap footage. Eurovision was the most important client for the agencies, their one way to measure their competition. The more Eurovision acceptances you had, the better you were doing. It was like a soccer score, and today's would read, UPITN 1, Visnews a big fat zero.

I squirmed as Nicholson related his success and perked up only on his final sentence: "Then our car broke down, so we started walking. But there are no bloody cars here to give us a lift." As we wished him luck and continued on toward Kyrenia, I fervently hoped Nicholson would have to walk the whole way back to the capital. It did cross my mind to double back secretly and get my old Turkish partisan to confiscate Mike's film at gunpoint, but I couldn't bring myself to be that devious. Even the wily old CBS producer Dan Bloom wouldn't have stooped that low. I think. But Mike and his crew soon got a lift, and their historic footage was broadcast the same night, destroying the competition. That would be me.

The Cyprus war lurched from cease-fire to shoot-out and back again for weeks. Gas stations ran dry, and most journalists were reduced to walking, which limited the stories we could cover. There was a war going on and no way to get to it, apart from fighting in the capital. As I worked with no soundman, I had to carry my camera, tripod, and bag with spare film, batteries, and a small light. It was heavy, hot, and tiring. Until my luck turned.

Getting shelled by mortars would not normally be considered very lucky, but luck for a foreign correspondent comes in many shades. The barrage began as a group of reporters trudged past a gas station on the edge of Nicosia. As rounds slammed in with a whoosh and a roar, we rushed to what we thought was safety, until somebody remarked that sheltering in a gas station, even one that had run out of fuel, was like sitting on top of a bomb. But we were trapped. So were two Austrian United

Nations peacekeepers who had abandoned their white UN jeep and flung themselves into a ditch by the gas station office. It had been hard to get a phone call out for weeks, so when Michael Keats, a UPI reporter, saw a phone in the office, he automatically picked it up. To his astonishment he heard a dial tone. He quickly dialed headquarters to file a dramatic report under fire. The other journalists lined up for their turns. But I wasn't interested in phoning the news desk. I had my eyes on the abandoned UN jeep. When the shelling stopped, the UN soldiers stood up to leave, only to hit the deck again as another barrage burst nearby. Then gunfire began.

Everyone had his nose deep in the earth except for me. Peering through the smoke and the dirt thrown up by the explosions, I focused on the UN jeep with its engine still running, half off the road. I noticed two large jerricans strapped to the back, probably full of precious fuel. I looked around. The two young Austrians were shaking. But all I thought was: Transport! Not giving myself time to reconsider, I jumped up, ran through the smoke and the dust to the jeep, threw my camera onto the passenger seat, leaped behind the wheel, and hit the gas. Three kinds of screaming: The wheels. The Austrians. Me.

I drove the hijacked UN jeep around the war zone for the next week, with photographers, TV crews, and print reporters all hanging on like passengers on a Pakistani bus. It was exhilarating and exciting, and it didn't occur to me that I had just stolen a car. I was in an extremely competitive situation. Transport was the key to covering the war, and I didn't want to find myself beaten by ITN or anybody else again.

There had been two other Visnews cameramen covering the war. One was our local freelancer, Phanis Papaeyiris, a charming Greek Cypriot who gave me a few phone numbers when I arrived, briefed me on the main characters and the location of the local TV station, and then promptly disappeared to his mountain hut for the duration. The second was Paul Nazarian, one of the agency's hot shots. After three days of war, he found himself aboard one of the evacuation planes and turned up among a crowd of refugees in London, unable to return. That left me alone covering both sides of the war. So when I stole the UN jeep, I felt no remorse, only gratitude that Mother Luck had thrown me a bone at last.

Today I feel sorry for the two Austrian soldiers. Did they walk shame-faced back to their base? How did they explain the loss of $25,000 worth of UN equipment? Were they punished? What an unkind thing I did. But in situations of anarchy like war, revolution, or even a tsunami, the goal-posts move. Values shift, and dilemmas demand instant solutions. A reporter spends only 5 percent of his day writing, maybe less. The rest is logistics: getting into the right place at the right time and staying there long enough to know what's going on and to make a few notes or shoot some film. For that I needed the UN jeep.

War reporters face moral dilemmas all day: Is it reasonable to film a crying woman two feet from the lens? How about a lost child screaming for its parent? Should one film him or take him by the hand? If a man is to be executed and the soundman's gear suddenly doesn't work, what do you do? Delay the execution? That's what the BBC's David Tyndall did in Biafra in 1970, when he yelled, "Hold it, we haven't got sound," and the quivering man about to be killed had to suffer that much longer while the soundman sorted out his gear. Later, Tyndall was mortified by his instinctive response to the dilemma, as was the BBC, which severely reprimanded him. But every move in this job poses a different dilemma, and nobody can be right all the time. In fact, the most critical question is usually not moral in nature but practical: How far down this road can I drive and stay safe?

Thus far, I'd found the Cypriot conflict exhilarating but also risky and scary. Despite the frequent cease-fires, the front lines between the Turkish and Greek Cypriot forces changed so often that reporting on the battles demanded a daily foray into no-man's-land. Every day was a brush with death. Once I teamed up with the BBC reporter John Bierman in his car. As we bumped across a tilled field to skirt yet another roadblock, gunfire erupted. John floored it, and the car leaped into the air on each furrow, our heads crashing into the roof, cameras flying. John screamed, "What shall we do, get out, go on, what?" I realized that the shooting was coming from the hills on John's side of the car and that if we got hit, John, being a big guy, was likely to shield me. He'd get it before I would. "Keep going," I yelled. "Let's get out of here. I should make it," I shouted. "Don't know about you though." We laughed and sped away.

Another day, John and I were racing around a bend on the winding coast road leading from the east to the Turkish-held area west of Kyrenia when we ran straight into a roadblock. John screeched to a halt some twenty yards from a wavering bazooka pointing at our solitary car. Turkish paratroopers lay behind the shoulder on both sides of the road with their guns trained on us. Past the bazooka-bearing soldier lay the smoldering wrecks of three destroyed cars with a choking stench of burning rubber, burning bodies, and cordite. The smoke was black. There was a hill with another unit of men with a machine gun aimed at us.

"Oops," I said. They weren't here yesterday.

John got out of the car, put his hands in the air, and walked slowly forward. I sat in the car with my hands on display on the dashboard.

The Turks had advanced a mile overnight. Before we arrived, three civilian cars had stopped here. Two young Turkish soldiers had sauntered up to check the cars and were killed in a hail of fire from the Greek Cypriots inside. All the men in the cars were killed immediately by the return of fire, the commander of the roadblock told us. And then we arrived, Union Jacks flying and shouting, *"Basin, basin"*—"Press, press."

"Lucky you stopped so far from us," the Turkish officer told John, "or we'd have killed you."

For almost three weeks this hope-for-the-best reporting paid off. Until it didn't. It sounds trite, but that's the way it is with luck. You're lucky, until very suddenly, you're not. On the evening of August 7, at dinner in the Hilton Hotel on the Greek side of Nicosia, the young BBC correspondent Simon Dring said his cameraman, Keith Skinner, was feeling tired, and he asked me whether I would work with him and his soundman, Ted Stod-dart, the next day.

I liked to share my car with another journalist, if only to split the driving. But I never worked with a soundman. First, and critically, the Visnews budget didn't allow for a soundman. Second, I preferred it that way. I was barely responsible for myself and certainly didn't want to be tethered to a soundman by a cable. Nothing is worse when mortars fall than to run in one direction and feel the cable go taut as the soundman runs the other way; you both jerk backward like cartoon characters while shrapnel and earth fly past.

I worked with a CP-16A film camera with sound recorded automatically on a magnetic stripe built onto the film. The microphone was fixed to the top of the camera, as was a small light. I carried all the spare film, batteries, changing bag, light meter, condoms, and moldy sandwiches in a Billingham shoulder bag. It was a Visnews innovation that enraged the usual two-man union crews, who disparagingly referred to me and my ilk as one-man bands. It was a lean and mean way to work, and it helped if you had the build of a mule, which I didn't. Still, it worked for me. Above all, I was free to make my own decisions, without worrying about someone else's fears or bravado. By now, after ten months of daily challenges in Israel, the Golan, and Sinai, I was learning to trust my own judgment. I had come a long way since that moment when I looked at Nick Tomalin driving into the distance on the Golan and desperately wanted him to tell me what to do.

But this time, I agreed. I had known Simon for only a few days. He was superkeen, usually a danger sign in a war, but with his blond hair, penetrating eyes, and sharp features, he had a dash and glamour made for television. For me, a young agency cameraman from Visnews, it was an honor to work for my old colleagues at the BBC. Visnews didn't interfere in how I chose to work in the field, but I knew that it always liked to win brownie points with the BBC, one of its top clients. So if I helped out Simon, Visnews would be happy, Keith would get a day off, and I didn't much mind either way. It would make for a nice change. I knew Ted from his earlier assignments in Israel. He was a stocky young Englishman with brown hair and mustache and a weathered face. I told my friend Paul Roque, a roguish half-French, half-Welsh stills photographer with the Associated Press, with whom I'd been covering much of the war, and he agreed to follow in the car we'd been sharing. Two cars. That's okay, I thought, two cars isn't a convoy.

We set out early the next morning in the big BBC Mercedes. Paul followed in our little Fiat, stopping only to pick up a stray black-and-white kitten, which he stroked as he drove. An hour or so outside Nicosia, we reached a shuttered café with a group of armed men and cars outside. It was the last Greek position before no-man's-land. We slowed to get the vibes and asked about the road ahead. Scruffy soldiers of the Greek National Guard, dressed in a variety of military-type T-shirts and jeans and sneakers, were listening to bouzouki music and breakfasting on watermelon and ginger cake. Two carloads of journalists were waiting by the café, taking the advice of the soldiers not to continue. The soldiers gave us some cake and warned us that the road ahead was not safe. But as it was August 8, the first day of renewed peace talks in Geneva and we needed to show what was happening on the ground, we said thank you and drove off. Nobody's going to shoot just when their leaders are sitting down to talk, we thought. And we were right. Nobody shot. But we didn't think about land mines.

Dawn had been cool when we set out, but by now the sun had risen. It was already hot and muggy at 8:15, with the faintest breeze from the nearby sea. All the car windows were down to catch the wind. I looked around. The two carloads of journalists who had been waiting at the roadblock were swinging out onto the road and following. "Not good," I said to Simon, who was driving. "We got a convoy."

He glanced in the mirror. "Safety in numbers, old boy."

"I don't think so," I said.

Ted, in the backseat with the camera and sound gear, looked out the window.

The main road along the coast of northern Cyprus has many gentle bends, with fields on both sides and occasional narrow slip lanes to the right that lead to villages on the slopes of the low Kyrenia mountain range. It is a beautiful drive, with cows grazing in green fields, sweet-smelling bushes with butterflies and birds, and ancient gnarled olive trees. Nearby in the hills was the old stone village of Bellapais, with its narrow cobbled alleys and cafés, its old men with black berets who sip the local dry white wine and play backgammon all day long. Here Lawrence Durrell made his home and under a sweeping lemon tree in the village center wrote much of his famous book *Bitter Lemons*.

As we drove slowly along the roads, looking for trouble, Bellapais seemed most ineptly named—beautiful peace. For Cyprus had seen precious little peace in recent days. Thanks to Nikos Sampson, who had torn the veneer of quiet off the island, the Turkish army had seized a bridgehead with an army of 240 tanks, 400 armored vehicles, and some 30,000 troops, including an elite regiment of paratroopers. Against them the Greek Cypriots put up a surprisingly robust defense, but they had no chance with a few thousand national guardsmen plus young volunteers who had rushed home from Europe and America to join the fight. These men were dressed in sneakers and jeans and barely had bullets for their old rifles. Close to 5,000 people, mostly from the Greek side, had died in the fighting. Now here we were, in no-man's-land, looking for the first Turkish lines.

Simon slowed at a sign that said "Lapithos," the next village up the side road. "Let's go right," he said, "what do you think?"

"No," I said. "There's nothing going on, it's all quiet, no point. Anyway, it may be mined."

"We were here yesterday," Simon said. "It's perfectly safe. All the minefields are signed and wired off. Let's go see what's happening in Lapithos. Maybe the refugees are coming back again." Earlier in the week the Greek Cypriot residents of the village had abandoned it after two days of heavy Turkish shelling. Simon, Ted, and Keith had filmed some of the fighting.

"Ted?" I asked.

Ted shrugged.

"Okay," I said.

I wanted to say no, but I figured, What the hell, I'm working for the Beeb today, let them decide. I didn't feel good about taking that right turn to Lapithos, and I've never let anyone else decide anything for me in the field again. I handed over responsibility, and it was a fatal mistake. All we wanted to do was see if the refugees had come home yet. Who cared? What difference did it make?

Simon drove slowly, no more than fifteen miles an hour. All three of us scanned the road for mines and peered into the bushes ahead for Turks. I thought, This is really stupid. In the car behind us came Paul Roque and his kitten. Behind him in the third car were Chris Morris of BBC Radio and three Fleet Street reporters, and in a yellow car at the back, a reporter and a photographer from *The New York Times*.

This time there was no barbed wire, and there were no warning signs. Simon and I spotted the mounds pushing up on the tar road at exactly the same time, and we shouted almost in unison: "Mines!" They were about a foot apart, arranged in 3-2-3 formation, and stretched forward as far as I could see. Some were just bumps in the earth, others were in plain view.

Even at such a slow speed, there was no time to jam on the brakes. Simon, with incredible cool, turned the wheel to avoid the mines. He slowed and stopped. But the mines were everywhere, in front, beneath, in back. Horrid dark things peeking out of lightly packed earth.

Here I'd like to describe how I felt, but I have no memory. I went into shock almost immediately, shaking uncontrollably. I didn't even want to shift in my seat in case a mine went off. What did I know about mines? Nothing. Except I knew I really didn't want to be there.

I've since learned there are two main types of mines—antipersonnel and antivehicle. They are buried a couple of inches into the ground. It takes a weight of only about ten to forty pounds to trigger an antipersonnel mine and about three hundred and fifty pounds to trigger an antivehicle mine. If our heavy Mercedes had hit an antivehicle mine, it would have been blasted into the air and torn apart. Then there's the "Bouncing Betty," an antipersonnel mine that, when you tread on it or hit a trip wire, leaps into the air and explodes at chest height. It can blow your head off. Another kind of antipersonnel mine explodes at ground level so as to destroy soldiers' legs. If a soldier loses his foot, it then takes another two soldiers to carry him to safety. That's three soldiers removed from the battle.

It turned out the Turks had laid both antipersonnel and antivehicle mines to stop the Greeks from reaching the village. But the Greeks were smart. They didn't come. We did.

Simon leaned out of his window and started shouting. Then I leaned out of my side, and we both shouted, "Mines! Stop! Wait!" We sighed and sat back in our seats for about ten seconds. I had already stopped shaking. My mind cleared. We were in a minefield and this wasn't a movie. What to do? "Not a problem," I said. "We just walk out. We just have to stay calm."

"Yes," Simon said, "we can see the mines. We just walk out." Neither of us was convinced, but we didn't have wings and the Greeks and Turks weren't going to help. We were on our own.

Today, I know that it isn't hard to get out of a minefield, so long as you don't panic. Just lie down with a long thin thing like a sewing needle and gently poke it into the ground at an angle, making sure there is no metallic object buried there. Crawl forward over the area of ground that you have just checked for safety. However, one thing I didn't have in my Billingham bag was a sewing needle. Today I always carry one.

Simon and I leaned out of our windows again to tell the others to wait. They weren't in the minefield, we were. Even Paul Roque's car had stopped before the mines. Only we were in danger.

As I opened my mouth, the yellow car at the back pulled out. "What's up? Why'd you stop?" the *New York Times* guy yelled. He began to overtake the car in front, heading toward us and the mines. There is no word I know to describe that instant of sheer terror. The fucker was going to kill us all. Then the car stopped. But the photographer, Lefkos Christodoulides, got out and started to walk forward. He was maybe thirty yards away when the third car started to empty as curious hacks seemed incapable of understanding our shouts. They all began to walk toward the unmarked minefield.

Then Ted opened his door and got out. He held up his arm and shouted a warning, telling them to get back. That's when Ted trod on the mine. It was a Bouncing Betty, and the explosive pierced his heart. There was a short, dull blast and a ball of fire and a whoosh of smoke and hot air. For an instant it was hard to breathe, as if the air had been sucked away. I flew onto Simon and knocked my head on the door. The smoke cleared quickly. There must have been a breeze. Ted appeared through the smoke, one hand clutching his chest. His eyes glazed though he seemed calm, stunned, as he looked at Simon and me. Ted knew he would die and so did we. We watched in shock through the open car window as he stumbled and tried to walk but fell to the ground. Ted's last words were "I've got it. Please look after my wife."

Later in London I visited Ted's wife and family in mourning. It was the most uncomfortable experience of my life. His family was large and close, and when I entered the living room, they were all seated against three walls, forming a horseshoe shape, and I sat against the fourth wall, as if I was being interrogated, which in a sense I was. Ted had three children. I don't remember anybody crying. Everybody was shocked and angry, and I bore the brunt of it. Because I was the only member of the team not killed or wounded, it seemed as if I had some blame to bear.

I tried to describe what had happened, but I couldn't convey the futility of the moment, the stupidity and the senselessness of it. Because if a family member dies, it has to be for a reason, otherwise how can you accept his death? Something must make it worthwhile.

"Ted was a hero," I said. "He died trying to stop the others from getting hurt." That was certainly a possibility. I had no idea why Ted got out of the car. I don't know whether Ted's wife and family were comforted by the thought that his death had some value. I doubt it. Journalists always discount the danger and assume if something bad happens, it will happen to someone else. Maybe, like me, they have Walter Mitty fantasies of saving their colleagues and being heroes, of sweeping a child up and running to safety. Maybe today I would have the courage, or the experience, or the coolness, to attempt to help somebody in the line of fire, but probably not. Only a very highly trained person can act rationally and effectively at such a desperate time, and none of us had any training at all, not even in basic first aid.

I have always been a fatalist. In Egypt, they say it is *"makhtoub"*—"it is written." Whatever the response to danger, it all boils down to one thing— luck. And luck will run out one day. Maybe I could have said some of this to Ted's family. But I didn't. I listened to their anger, nodding dumbly, glancing at his small children. Was there any reason they should lose their father? Was there any point to his death? I don't think so. It was a painful thing to describe their father's last moments.

Now Ted was lying among the mines about five yards away. Simon opened his door and walked quickly toward his colleague, who looked lifeless on the ground. Another explosion. Simon collapsed. Blood flowed from his arms and legs, but his hands automatically went to protect his balls.

Paul got out of his car and went to help Ted and Simon. I was also out of the car, standing by the open door, dumbstruck. Everybody was. There was no yelling or screaming, no calling for help or shouting advice. I knew only one thing. No way was I moving my feet. I wasn't going anywhere. I wasn't going to help anyone. I wanted to shout at everybody to stop moving around among the mines. But I couldn't. I was muted by the awful finality of our plight. This was life or death.

By now, somehow, I had the camera in my hand, and I had turned it on. I was on automatic again. I was doing my job. Paul, on his way to help Ted, left the road to get away from the mines, and I followed him with the camera as he took long strides through the grassy undergrowth. He was wearing an open short-sleeved shirt and dark shorts below his knees. He looked at me and saw me filming him. Then he looked down to see where he was treading and was thrown into the air by the force of the blast from the land mine he'd trod on. Paul vanished in a ball of flame and smoke that sent a blast of hot air rolling over me. I heard the smack of shrapnel flying around me, smashing and burning pockmarks into the cars and the trees. Paul was down. He got it in the face, legs, arms, feet, everywhere. He didn't scream. It was silent madness, quiet carnage. Since then I've read that, in times of ultimate stress, the brain narrows and focuses, cutting out sound and even slowing down the action. I don't know if that's why it all seemed so quiet and deliberate. I do remember a single cow mooing in the field.

Once again, incredibly, the burning shrapnel missed me. I put the camera down. I wanted to go to help Paul, but I couldn't move. My brain was racing. Simon wanted to help Ted and got blown up. Then Paul wanted to help Simon and he got blown up. Helping didn't help. I wasn't going to make that mistake. I was going to get out of this. I was not going to die or get hurt. I wanted to go home. The number of thoughts that flew through my head—flashes and particles of thoughts and ideas and people—was extraordinary, yet these existed alongside a blank, a tunnel of focus and determination. I was not going to make a mistake. I would stay calm. I would not help Paul. Do! Not! Move!

Somehow Paul was back on his feet, bleeding and staggering around. He shuffled back toward his car. I turned on the camera again and filmed him leaving. I looked down the road. Lefkos had been hit by shrapnel; he had a gaping hole in his stomach and was cradling it in disbelief. Chris was pouring blood from the arm and wrist. One of the Fleet Street guys, in terror and panic, ran blindly through the minefield, brushing against me as he passed, then ran back out again. He reminded me of a headless chicken. We were both lucky, because if he had trod on a mine, surely this time I would have gotten it, too.

Then everyone who was still able piled into the last two cars and raced back to the Greek roadblock by the shuttered café, calling for help. I filmed them leaving and then turned to see the damage. Of ten journalists, one was killed and six were wounded. Ted was dead on the ground. Simon lay three feet from him, propped up on one elbow, bleeding heavily from his arms and legs. I stood by the car. I hadn't moved an inch, apart from filming everything. Only now did I notice there was a land mine by my right foot, three inches from the tire.

It was quiet again, apart from the mooing cow that was probably up-set by the bangs. I stood there, transfixed, wondering what to do. Simon was also silent, breathing heavily, looking at Ted. A minute or so went by until we heard a motor and tires on gravel. A jeep appeared around the bend, driving slowly toward us from Lapithos. The car stopped at a safe distance, and a Turkish officer inched forward in full combat gear, shak-ing his head. He spoke in Turkish, but I didn't need a translator. What could he be saying apart from "What the fuck are you doing here?"

The officer and a couple of his men edged toward Simon. They crouched with their arms outstretched, like crabs, as if that would help them if they trod on a mine. They helped Simon to his feet and, holding his arm, guided him step by step past the mines to safety. There was no way to move Ted.

As for me, I was on my own, surrounded by broken sunglasses, streaks of blood, burned shoes, and land mines. So far I had survived by standing still. But the moments ticked by and it became time for me to make a move. The Turkish soldiers were waiting by their jeep, where they had laid Simon across the back on a stretcher. They were all looking at me, expect-ing me to join them. I looked down and began to count the mines that I could see, but I knew there must be more. I knew Ted's mine was not an antivehicle mine because he wasn't heavy enough to activate one. Paul's mine had been a small one, too. I could see the big mines, about twenty of them, but I couldn't see the small ones. Maybe there were trip wires across the road as well?

I lifted my right foot and edged it forward, keeping it in the air while I hesitated and scrutinized the earth ahead. Then, with as little weight as possible, I put my foot down again, a few inches forward. I lifted my other foot and examined the ground. Even though I could see the mines, I steeled myself for the blast with every step. Each time I put my foot down, I felt the pressure on my toes, then on the arch, and finally on the heel. Each step took forever.

Those were lonely minutes. The mines had a mesmerizing quality. I felt queasy, as if I were at a great height and were being drawn out into the abyss. The mines pulled me toward them, like sirens. My skin was clammy in the heat and with the fear, but I breathed easily and regularly. I didn't panic. One by one I passed the mines. Some were round, some had little sensors sticking out, others were just telltale mounds of earth. I kept away from the shoulder where Paul had gotten blown up. There were probably more mines hidden in the earth and grass. I had to stop once or twice. I was trembling uncontrollably again. Over the next fifteen years, details would suddenly erupt from my memory, surprising me and filling in more pieces of the puzzle. The way Simon and the Turkish soldiers tilted their heads as they watched my snail's progress. How they flinched when I put my foot down. How I held my camera in front of me as some form of protection. How I felt each breath, and heard it, which helped calm me. The cow mooing. The sun glistening off the drying blood.

Edging past the mines to safety, past Ted's body, and Simon's and Paul's blood, I registered the blood drying on Ted's chest and his calm face, but I couldn't bring myself to look directly at him. I was afraid I'd get light-headed and collapse. As I passed the spot where Simon had fallen, I didn't want to tread on blood, but even more I didn't want to tread on a mine, so I stepped in Simon's blood and left a bloody footprint as I moved slowly on. Looking back on it, I wish I had filmed my feet as I walked past the mines. It would have been a great shot. But I wasn't that cool. I knew this was life or death. As I neared the end of the minefield, my total concentration was broken only by Simon's words: "Hey, Martin, can you get my bag?" He had left it in the car.

"Sure," I said and turned slowly around and inched back to the car. We must both have been in shock and didn't know what we were saying or doing. But luck was on my side.

When I finally reached the jeep, Simon said, "What took you so long?"

"How are your balls?" I answered. He was still clutching them as he lay on a stretcher across the back of the jeep. "Fine, thanks for asking."

"That's good," I said. The Turkish officer offered me a cigarette. "No thanks," I said. "I don't smoke."

As I climbed into the jeep next to Simon, I paused to look back at Ted.

He lay flat on his back with his arms straight down by his sides. His shirt was off, exposing his bloody chest. Suddenly I realized, as I was about to leave, that I couldn't be sure Ted was dead. He looked dead. He must have been dead. But nobody had felt his pulse. Nobody had even checked the wound, a small hole in the chest, by the heart. Maybe he was only wounded and unconscious. Maybe he was still breathing. He didn't seem to be. I didn't want to leave without checking, but there was no way I was going back into that minefield. I paused, then pulled myself up into the jeep. That moment when I left my friend has haunted me ever since.

As we drove away, I turned the camera on again and filmed the Turks evacuating Simon. I panned from the road to show Simon on his stretcher, and when he noticed the camera on him, he suddenly started talking and did a forty-five-second piece to camera about the dangers of the front lines and the need for better UN policing of the cease-fire. When I saw it later on television, I remarked that, if Simon had had half an hour to write it, he wouldn't have changed a word.

With the Turkish officer clucking sympathetically at Simon's wounds, we drove through the deserted streets of Lapithos, which had been our destination. I said to Simon, "Well, now we know—the refugees aren't back yet." He grimaced weakly and took deep draws on a cigarette, while I held his stretcher to cushion the bumps. A medic in a dark room in a burned house dressed Simon's wounds, which to me seemed extensive but not too deep. Then we all drove off to a field hospital.

The Turks wanted to prepare Simon for an operation. He and I immediately protested. No way was Simon going to be operated on in a Turkish field hospital in the middle of a war. Although the medics and soldiers were exceptionally caring and friendly, everything was filthy. We quickly agreed that I would make my way back to Nicosia to ship the film, which, after all, was why we'd come in the first place. It must be pretty dramatic, we decided, and would lead all the news bulletins. Then I would get back as quickly as I could with a jeep to pick up Simon and take him to the British army hospital in Akrotiri, on the other side of the island.

I left Simon lying bandaged on a dirty bed, surrounded by wounded

Turks and looking exceptionally forlorn. I set off with the one roll of film. It was another adventure. I got a short ride with a Turkish convoy and then began to walk and hitchhike toward Nicosia. There was shooting across the Green Line, but I made it to the Hilton Hotel.

Things then remain a blur. I handed the film over to a BBC colleague for satelliting, then went to reception to take my room key while friends greeted me: "Hi. How are you? Where have you been, any good pix?"

What could I answer? It was surreal. I was in a parallel world. My soundman had just died, my correspondent was wounded, and I was being offered a drink in a five-star hotel in the center of town by people who had no idea what had happened. In a daze I took the elevator, walked slowly to my room, and soaked myself under a cold shower. Thirty minutes later I opened the door to go downstairs and found a group of journalists waiting respectfully in the corridor for me to talk. Word had gotten out. Maybe the other wounded guys had returned. I was touched that they hadn't knocked on the door, or even beaten it down. I gave them a quick rundown of what had happened. Then I went to Simon's room to get his shoes but couldn't find any. I asked if somebody knew Simon's shoe size and could lend him some. Someone pointed out that he couldn't walk and wouldn't need them. "Yeah, right," I said.

By now the other BBC journalists had swung into gear and were trying to help. They found a British soldier with a jeep who agreed to drive me back across the Green Line to collect Simon. Before we left, I suddenly remembered to call Visnews and tell them what had happened. They already knew of Ted's death and some of the details. It was on the wires. I told them of the extraordinary pictures I had shot. Like it or not, I thought, we had just become the story. "Incredible, incredible," the desk editor said and then added apologetically: "But I'm afraid there won't be much interest in your film today. President Nixon just resigned."

Simon spent several weeks in the British army hospital. His wounds were mostly superficial, and he recovered fully. Paul, however, faced months of surgery and rehabilitation. He had lost an eye and half his nose, had serious wounds to the feet and legs, and had damaged his elbow.

After three weeks' more work in Cyprus, I returned to Israel, and Paul and I lost touch. That's the way it is in the news business: Deep friendships form for short periods in intense times, and then you move on. Still, I felt bad. Paul and I had been so close during the war, up until the minefield, and I felt guilty that, when it really mattered, I hadn't been there for him. I didn't go to help him in the minefield, and afterward I wasn't there to help him to recover from his wounds.

I had come out from the minefield unscathed, and in fact my professional career was in great shape. Dan Bloom, the CBS bureau chief, called the minefield report the best war film he had ever seen. It was the real thing, he said, up close and personal. In Britain it won second place in the Royal Television Society news film of the year awards, beaten only by Mike Nicholson's film of the Turkish parachute drop. But like most news film awards, the success was bittersweet. It had been won on the back of everyone else's tragedy, and I felt guilty at my prize.

So I knew why I hadn't called Paul. But I didn't know why he hadn't called me. Maybe he was angry because I had filmed him getting blown up. I couldn't imagine that, though, because the first thing he said when he woke up in the British army hospital in Akrotiri was that he wanted to see the film. But after almost a year of silence, I feared the worst.

I began to torment myself. Why should I feel guilty? I'd just done my job. After all, that was what we were there for, to film the war. The nature, if not the purpose, of war photography is to exploit the pain of others, for a good cause. And when the tables were suddenly turned, and we became the victims, I didn't feel I had any right to stop shooting just because my friends were the casualties. If we filmed the injuries and deaths of strangers, then I felt it would be hypocritical not to turn the camera on our own.

I let it pass and continued with my life until one day, on vacation high up in the French Alps, while attempting to ski the world downhill racing course at La Daille in Val-d'Isère, I had a sudden vision of Paul Roque, his blown-off nose and destroyed eye. I felt the need to see him. He had been my friend, a buddy in war. We had a bond. I skidded to a halt and gazed at the mountains and the fir trees covered in snow and thought more about Paul. He must have had lots of plastic surgery. What did he even look like? With one eye, was he still a photographer? And what had happened to that kitten? I decided to find Paul and confront him. I skied back to the rented chalet and told my long-suffering girlfriend, my future wife, that I wanted to leave early. The next day I took the fast train to Paris, where I found the phone number of the Associated Press and called the bureau.

My heart was pounding. *"Bonjour,"* I said. "Can I speak to Paul Roque please?"

"Un moment, s'il vous plaît."

"Okay."

Long pause.

"Bonjour, ici Paul."

"Hey, Paul, great! It's Martin Fletcher!"

Dramatic pause. My stomach churned a bit.

Paul: "Oh, hello."

And then silence. But I didn't waver. I resolved there was no way I was not going to see Paul and have it out. If he was pissed off, I wanted to know why. It seemed really unlike him. He was a nutter. Once there'd been smoke from a fire across the road in Cyprus, and instead of stopping he'd just floored the pedal. "I used to be a rally driver," he shouted. He gunned the car, and we sailed right through the flames. Mad. So what did he have to be upset at me for? Just because he got blown up? He was back at work, wasn't he? What was the big deal?

"Well, hello, Paul," I said. "I'm in Paris for a couple of days. I thought we could get together, you can show me around, we can have a couple of drinks, a chat. Okay?"

Paul was frosty to the point of unfriendly: "Uh, I'm really busy right now."

"That's okay, just for an hour or so, any time that fits you."

"Well, okay, I suppose so."

The next afternoon, a small blue Renault pulled up outside Café Roma on the Champs-Élysées. I had already paid the bill and was waiting nervously. I tugged on my jacket and walked to the street, smiling and happy to see my old friend.

Paul reached over, pushed open the door. "Get in."

I sat down and said, "Hey, it's really good to see you."

At first I just kept my eyes on the road. I think I was a bit scared about what I'd see. When I had last seen Paul, his face had been swathed in bandages. One leg was cased in plaster and suspended by a pulley. His hands were wrapped in thick gauze and plaster, and in general he looked like a cartoon. Since then he must have had numerous operations, including cosmetic surgery to put his nose together, fix his eye socket, and God knows what else. Maybe he limped?

So I was hesitant to look too closely. As we drove down Rue de Rivoli, Paul launched into a tedious description of the sites. Place de la Concorde, a gift from the Viceroy of Egypt to Louis Phillipe, Jardin des Tuileries, the Louvre, the Louvre des Antiquaires, an upmarket antiques mall, hang a right and a left along the Seine, past Notre-Dame, note the gargoyles, construction began in 1163 . . . Even with a natty scarf around his neck and wrapped against the cold, I could see that Paul looked heavier. Must be a bit sedentary after the injuries, I thought. He even seemed taller than I remembered.

"You've put on weight," I said.

"Yes, I have," he answered, glancing at me strangely. He sounded different, too, but I put that down to the surgery. He had caught the blast in his face and had no right to be alive. So he looked and sounded different? He was lucky to still be on the planet.

As we continued our tour, Paul drove slowly and defensively in the thickening rush-hour traffic. At least he isn't such a crazy driver anymore, I thought. I stole glances at him and was surprised not to see any scarring or injuries. I couldn't work it out. He just looked so different. But then he's basically got a rebuilt face, I thought. Of course he looks different. The plastic surgeons did a really good job.

After more than an hour of discomfort and similar musings, I finally summoned the courage to speak frankly. I laid my arm around the back of Paul's seat. "Let's park the car a minute," I said. We were back on the Champs-Élysées. "We've got a lot to talk about."

"Have we?" Paul answered. He pulled over on the inner road, close to the shops. As he found a parking spot and began to maneuver into it, I looked closely and for the first time made a prolonged examination of his face, looking directly at his eyes, his nose, his skin, his hair, and then sharply back to his eyes. Holy shit, I thought. He's got two eyes!

"You're not Paul Roque, are you?"

"No, of course not," he said. "I'm Paul Treuthardt."

"What! What happened to Paul Roque?"

"How should I know?"

"But when I called I asked for Paul Roque. . . ."

"They just said there's a call for Paul, and I took it."

"You've got no idea who I am, have you?"

"No—I don't."

"Fuck me! You've been driving me around Paris, showing me the sights, for one and a half hours, and you don't even know who I am?"

"I thought you were a friend of my son's. I often get calls like this and drive people around."

I was so pissed off that I got out of the car and walked away. I couldn't trust myself to talk to him. Normally I'd just have laughed at such a ludicrous mix-up, but because my emotions were so mixed at seeing Paul Roque again, and I was carrying around such guilt, I was furious. What a waste of time! But I was also relieved. I still didn't know how Paul Roque would react to me. Maybe he'd be happy to see me after all? So I went straight to the nearest phone booth, pushed in a token, and called AP again.

"*Bonjour,* can I speak to Paul Roque please?"

"*Un moment, s'il vous plaît.*"

"Okay."

Long pause.

"Bonjour, ici Paul."

"Paul Roque?"

"Oui."

"Paul Roque?"

"I just said so!"

That was better. I grinned. "Paul, it's Martin Fletcher," I said.

Pause. "Fuck me. Martin Fletcher?"

"I just said so."

And Paul Roque let out a whoop of joy so loud and long I had to hold the phone away from my ear. When I put it back, he was still yelling in excitement. I went straight around to AP. We hugged, went out for a drink and another and another. Then we ate, and he drove me home, racing like a rally driver. He lived in a lovely little house on the outskirts of Paris. His roommate was a beautiful French fashion model. That's my Paul, I said, as he organized a date for me. He pointed to a silver can on his bookshelf. It was one of his proudest possessions—my film showing him getting blown up.

We had a splendid weekend. We didn't dwell on what happened in Cyprus. We didn't talk about why we took these risks or whether it was worth it. We didn't discuss the dilemmas or analyze our actions. We just had a great time, savoring our lives. We were young and happy to be alive, and as you spent time with him, you stopped looking at the scars and the one empty eye socket.

I have always felt that I owe a great debt to Ted, Paul, and Simon. Their tragedy was a wake-up call for me, one that has affected my career ever since, possibly even saved my life. Before Cyprus, it didn't occur to me that I could get hurt. After leaving that minefield, however, I knew that I could never again enter a war zone without care for the consequences. The end of Ted's life, the damage done to Paul and Simon, everybody's panic, all this taught me: Staying cool saves lives. I learned to take time out to judge the moment and the risk, and never, never to put my life into the hands of someone else.

Every reporter in a war zone is familiar with that nagging and growing fear: Have I gone too far down this road? Why is it so quiet? Where is everybody? Why are those kids in the distance looking at me with their hands clapped over their ears? Do they know there's a bomb on the road? An ambush around the bend? But I also developed what I think of as an alternative threshold of danger. Just because something, like a roadblock of men in Somalia aiming guns at you, looks dangerous doesn't mean that it is. On the other hand, the most innocuous detail can be an alarm signal. If it is close to evening and the armed men at the roadblock are smoking, then you know it's their drug, khat, and you'd better get away quick.

Before Cyprus, I was young enough to believe that experience would keep me safe. Luckily, I survived long enough and became experienced enough to realize that experience has nothing to do with it. Experience can prolong your career as a war correspondent, but luck will end it. In the end, luck runs out. Avoid hubris, my father would warn me, beware the gods—the gods don't like it when they are challenged by mere mortals.

Three

Salad Days

When I met Willie Burns, he was a happy man. Several months earlier, he had been surviving off government unemployment checks in a cramped tenement apartment in dreary Dundee, Scotland. Like hundreds of thousands of Brits before him, he hungered for a better life in the colonies, in one of the far-flung properties of the empire where the sun never sets. By 1975, however, colonialism had entered its twilight years, and there weren't many options. So Burns moved his family to Rhodesia in Southern Africa, where Rhodesian Railways needed workers—or, rather, white people to supervise the black workers.

Puce-faced, his skin peeling from the unfamiliar constant sunshine, he greeted me at the gate and guided me around his big new house to the sundeck. Pointing out the colorful foliage and exotic fruit trees, he offered me a seat in the shade of a purple bougainvillea bush in full, glorious blossom. A black servant in white livery brought us whisky sours as we settled down to enjoy Burns's two little children splashing merrily in the swimming pool. Burns's wife gave dinner instructions to the fat black lady who was hanging the laundry and then strolled over to join us.

"Sorry about the lousy local Scotch," Burns said, grinning. "But you can't have everything."

I glanced around. "Looks like you've got most of it, though."

"Been here two months! Not bad, eh?"

"Not bad at all."

He chuckled and raised a toast: "Long live white supremacy!"

"Uh, cheers," I said.

Willie Burns was one of the first people I interviewed in Africa, but the stunning change in his circumstances told me everything I needed to know about white rule. I had come for two weeks to cover a minor war and wound up staying for four years and witnessing the end of a way of life. It was easy to sniff at people like Burns, but in truth I was torn between contempt for the imperialist whites and enjoyment of their lifestyle. I, too, had never had it so good. It was *Lifestyles of the Rich and Famous,* for the poor and heartless. Like other members of the media, I partook of the white man's paradise: bloodred sunsets, rainbow foliage, black servants, and that holy trinity of home comforts: swimming pool, sauna, and tennis court. Yet unlike most of the "Rhodies," as Rhodesia's whites called themselves, I could not deny the murderous, exploitative, and supremely immoral conceit of white supremacy that made the good life possible. Later, when I lived under apartheid in South Africa, the abuse became unbearable. My stint in Africa brought me considerable career success: I moved from anonymous agency cameraman in Rhodesia to NBC News bureau chief and on-air correspondent covering the continent. Yet as time passed, and I saw up close the evils of white supremacy, I was forced for the first time in my life to confront my own collusion in the injustices of our era.

By 1975, black power was sweeping through Africa, dooming the white colonial regimes, with Rhodesia and South Africa hanging on for dear life at the continent's southern tip. Rhodesia's whites had declared unilateral independence from England in order to preempt London's call for black majority rule; as a result, they were being punished by economic and political sanctions that prevented the country from trading with most of the world. Black freedom fighters waging war inside the country to end white supremacy were spurred on by the triumph of liberation movements in nearby Angola and Mozambique.

Visnews had sent me to the country in March of that year, three days after Mozambique's new black Marxist president, Samora Machel, threatened war by closing the Rhodesian border and declaring his support for Rhodesia's black guerrillas. Now Rhodesia's already hard-pressed security forces had to police another eight hundred miles of border with a hostile country that provided sanctuary and support for the guerrillas. It was an impossible task, as events would soon prove. Given the economic and military squeeze, the whites couldn't win, but neither were they losing. "Good old Smithie," as the Rhodesian white leader Ian Smith, a former British Royal Air Force fighter pilot, was affectionately called by his constituents, promised that "never in a thousand years" would black rule come to Rhodesia. And why should it? As Smithie liked to point out, we have "the happiest Africans in Africa."

If the collapse of white rule seemed near, Rhodesia's whites remained in almost complete denial. In the capital, Salisbury, a quaint etiquette prevailed, with great emphasis on the maintenance of social "standards." Signs in hotels and restaurants demanded proper dress code, like "No Tackies," which meant no running shoes. Jacket and tie were often required in the most modest of establishments. In the venerable Meikles Hotel, a colonnaded colonial mausoleum, white ladies with rinsed hair sat stiffly on each floor, like guards in a museum, to protect the morals of residents. At the stroke of 9:00, the aging dining room pianist would play "Tie a Yellow Ribbon Round the Old Oak Tree." It was a tradition, and in the empire's twilight years, you didn't mess with tradition. Although Rhodesia's climate was most conducive to growing grass, you weren't allowed to sit on it. To be fair, schools were excellent, manners impeccable, sports remarkably developed for teams with no international competition, and the standards the Rhodies wished to maintain rivaled the Europeans' in every respect. Except for one little problem. They existed mostly for whites in a country where two hundred and fifty thousand whites lorded it over 6 million blacks.

The Rhodesian capital was a remarkable contradiction. Armed ladies pushing prams were the only sign of war. Heavy, sweet fragrances of mauve jacaranda blossoms and white and yellow jasmine wafted delicately across Cecil Square. The central garden of this rebel capital had once been planted by patriotic landscape artists in the exact outline of the British flag, with red, white, and blue bougainvillea bushes, lawns, trees, and shrubs forming a floral duplicate of the Union Jack. Low white colonial buildings with verandas and wrought-iron latticework lined the main streets. Wide avenues fanned out to leafy green suburbs with large, luxurious homes, whose semitropical vegetation burst into the colors of the season, offering calm and serenity. Black nannies wheeled white babies in the streets, chattering without an obvious care in the world. The air was dry and clean, the sky clear blue. At nearly five thousand feet, Salisbury had none of the muggy oppressiveness of the African lowlands.

True, sanctions meant new cars were almost unavailable, the shops stocked only the oldest fashions, and locally produced alcohol burned the throat. But this just seemed to unite the white colonials in their true-grit struggle against the effete degenerates back home. Rhodies felt that they were the last true Brits. Their children went around in pressed school uniforms with caps and ties. The place resembled a color postcard of an idealized British suburb circa 1950. The joke was that when your plane landed in Rhodesia you set your watch back thirty years.

After covering Mideast mayhem for two years, I was impressed. In my first letter to my parents in London I wrote, "Salisbury is really a lovely place—so green with beautiful flowers and fountains, wide streets—built by Cecil Rhodes so that a team of oxen could turn round without a three-point turn. It's hot and sunny but not oppressive, it rains once a day for a few minutes, and there's no sign of the 'situation.'" Presciently, I continued, "The people are so calm it amounts to complacency and are confident that if the Africans did ever try to fulfill their slogan of 'we will take Zimbabwe with the bazooka' they would blow themselves up with it. They have no idea."

All you needed to get the message was an open mind and a week or two. The numbers said it all. Twenty-four out of twenty-five Rhodesians were black, yet they had no genuine political role. South Africa excepted, the world was lined up unanimously against the rebels, who refused to relax their grip on white power. The whites had had a good run since Cecil Rhodes led a pioneer column from the Cape coast in 1890 to seize this beautiful land in the name of queen and country, as well as profits for the British South Africa Company, but now they were on the wrong side of history. How long could that last? Mike Sullivan, a BBC reporter with a cutting sense of humor, once smashed his fist down on my kitchen table and yelled, "Today am independence day!" Everybody laughed, but I caught the look on the cook's face, and it was grim. Despite our liberal values, to the black servants we journalists were every bit as bad as the colonialists, maybe worse for our smugness.

I was right about another thing, too, when I reassured my parents in that first letter: "This is one place where you certainly don't need to fear for me. The Rhodesian authorities try to stop the press doing anything worthwhile so it seems as if we'll all just sit around." One of the many bonuses of being a war correspondent in Africa in those days, I discovered, was that there was little risk to life and limb. The continent is so vast and impenetrable that, by the time we arrived in some distant land to report on the latest outbreak of fighting, it either was over or had moved elsewhere. Fighting in these bush wars rarely involved tactical battles or artillery duels or even land grabs. They were mostly a series of impromptu looting, rapes, and tortures followed by massacres, performed indiscriminately by each side as they marauded into enemy territory and then retreated. I covered wars in Rhodesia, Angola, Mozambique, Uganda, Ethiopia, and Zaire as well as sundry revolutions and attempted coups d'état, and rarely heard a shot fired in anger. The nearest I came to being killed was when our truck hit a bump and an escort officer from the Rhodesian Ministry of Information accidentally fired his rifle next to my head.

In Rhodesia I couldn't find the war, but I did come across a cast of characters that made up one of the world's most eclectic and eccentric press corps, all gathered to record—and enjoy—the end of an era. We met over and over again, for years, in every troubled corner of the continent. I was living Hemingway's "moveable feast." It was the only place and time you could fly two thousand miles, take a train another three hundred miles, hire a taxi through the jungle to a ferry, ford a river, hitch a ride on a buffalo-driven cart to the most remote corner of the region, check in at the local derelict hotel, go to the bar for a drink, and meet thirty people you knew.

Everything became a shared joke. In Kenya, where the Masai tribe drank cows' blood and cut off their daughters' clitorises, Christian missionaries strongly influenced the names given to the girls at birth. In one brief stay, waiting for Idi Amin's fall in neighboring Uganda, I made the acquaintance, in the biblical sense, of girls named Mercy and Hope. A competition began among the bored hacks to find a Faith to complete the trinity of the charities. AIDS was no deterrent, but only because it went by a different name. *Slims* was the label given to a wasting disease that turned people into walking skeletons and destroyed their immune systems. It became common in central Africa and Uganda in the days before it was renamed AIDS, but no connection had been made with sex. So, blithely, we partied on across the continent.

In Salisbury, the carousing centered on the legendary Quill Club, on the first floor of the Ambassador Hotel. Attendants were constantly washing its staircase clean of blood from the heads of drunken hacks tripping down the uneven steps and smashing against the walls on the way to dinner. Here I became acquainted with the questionable charms of many of my new colleagues in Africa. The Quill, also known as the Swill Club, was my first stop in Salisbury after I checked into the Meikles Hotel. Little did I know that this innocent search for company would set the pattern for the rest of my four unruly years in Africa. Everything that followed spun out of those first twenty-four bawdy hours.

It was five o'clock when I met Alex Morrow-Smith at the grimy wooden bar. I had just ordered a whisky ginger, an admittedly girlie drink and my favorite of the time. Alex, a Scottish correspondent of the Argus

Africa News Service, overheard and took immediate exception to mixing venerable Scotch whisky with lowly ginger ale. Now, most people, if offended, may at most pass verbal judgment, but Alex Morrow-Smith was unlike most people. "You fookin' poofter," he said to me, by way of introduction. I was about three inches taller than Alex, but that was as far as my advantage went. He had a pugnacious face and stance that spoke of years of brawling. He was built, as the British say, like a brick shithouse. And, as I was to discover, he was a former soldier in one of Scotland's toughest regiments, I believe it was the Black Watch. It was said that he had routinely been confined to the slammer for smashing up soldiers, officers, and civilians, and in general causing mayhem. He was also exceptionally literate and kind, but right now that was yet to be discovered.

My whisky ginger, to my consternation, arrived quickly. "Go on then," Alex said, "pick oop the fooker." That I was not about to do. I looked around nervously but had been in town only two hours and knew nobody. Behind Alex I noticed the only person in the room who looked able to take care of the aggressive Scot. This man was huge, well over six feet, and also built like a prizefighter. He had a big, open face and was clearly studying my reaction to Alex. Some latent survival instinct inspired me to recognize him as an Afrikaner, although I had never met one before. He had that friendly, farmhand look of the simple giant, although this also was totally deceptive. He turned out to be the Argus Africa News Service bureau chief, and Alex's sorely tried boss. As an amateur linguist, I had studied a few chapters of basic Afrikans, under the mistaken impression it was spoken in Rhodesia. Deon du Plessis, as was the big guy's name, was indeed a South African Afrikaner, and when I said to him, trying to ingratiate myself quickly, *"Hoe gaan dit, my ou maat?"* he boomed with laughter and slapped his great arm around my trembling shoulders, answering, "I'm fine, my old friend, how are you?"

I was in. The threat passed. I sipped my poofter drink, and Alex and Deon instantly became my firm friends and protectors. Being Alex's friend didn't mean you wouldn't get thumped, though. He delighted in punching others, especially his close friend John Edlin of the Associated

Press, another notorious drunken hack throwing them back at the Quill Club that evening. John, a New Zealander, had a high-pitched cackle that penetrated walls. He routinely wiped blood from his nose and bought another round after Alex whacked him one. Alex never hit me, though. I probably wasn't that close a friend.

Next I found myself standing next to "Paranoid" Paul Ellman, who wrote for the London Sunday paper *The Observer*. I raised my second whisky ginger by way of friendly introduction and smiled at him, saying, "So?"

Again, not a brilliant gambit, but I found his reaction a bit over the top. "So? So! What does that fucking mean? So? You must work for television, you're all fools." With that he turned around in disgust and pushed through the crowd. I was to find that Paul was prone to such outbursts, but alone in Africa I was rather taken aback. Again, he later proved very helpful, explaining the confusing issues wherever we met across the continent. He happily wore a T-shirt his colleagues had made for him with "Paranoid? Who, me?" inscribed on the chest.

Then there was James MacManus, a young reporter from the London *Guardian,* whose blond curls, blue eyes, and handsome features assured him of an endless supply of Salisbury housewives whose husbands were out fighting the "terrs." James was the next person I tried to engage in conversation, but in midsentence his eyes suddenly glazed over and he walked away. I wasn't doing very well. Is it me, I thought, or could it be them? Where have I landed? By now the bar was seething with bodies, drunken laughter, and shouted conversations. I glimpsed Alex pushing a large man against the wall. A dark-haired woman had attached herself to James. Ellman was back, drinking alone in a corner.

Then Bill Mutschmann tapped me on the shoulder. "I'm told you're saying you're the new Visnews man in town."

"Yes," I responded, "and you?"

Mutschmann, or "Mutters," as he was known because of his habit of eating alone at restaurants and muttering to himself, was the lamentable, or so he had been described to me in London, Visnews cameraman whom I had been sent to replace.

"I'm the Visnews man here. Not you. Me," Bill said. He was a short, stocky, middle-aged American with deep wrinkles, scraggy eyebrows, and a menacing stare.

"Oh really?" I answered, looking around for my new giant friend, Deon du Plessis.

It turned out that Visnews had failed to inform Bill of his dismissal. In those days telexes got lost and letters didn't arrive. Visnews would not have sprung for a phone call. "Well, maybe the letter's in the mail," I said lamely. It did indeed arrive the next day, which diverted Mutters's rage from me to Vis London, but among his mates in the Quill Club I became known as the guy who took Mutters's job. So many undercurrents of jealousy, intrigue, and drama swirled around the beleaguered Rhodesian capital, though, that my personal dilemma didn't last long and was quickly drowned in drink as Mutters and I became firm friends, united in the hacks' traditional scorn for head office.

That first night in Africa remains stamped on my memory not only because of the bizarre people I met but because of the evening's trailblazing conclusion. While I was still reeling from my encounters and wondering what else could possibly go wrong, things, as they tend to do, went right again. Next up in my evaporating list of drinking buddies was a Cockney in tight-fitting black trousers, a black shirt, and a quiff of brown hair, with a disconcerting, sudden, loud laugh. "So you met Mutters then, did you?" He grinned. "Don't worry about him, he's a nutter, everybody here is."

Peter Jordan had driven overland from Britain several years earlier. When we began chatting in the Quill Club, he was a freelance stills photographer, though he went on to become *Time* magazine's top photographer in Africa. His Billingham camera bag was always slung over his shoulder. We hit it off immediately. Like all foreign correspondents who routinely trashed the white colonials in our daily reports, Peter and I would go on to rent a succession of spectacular colonial homes, complete with black cook, gardener, and cleaners, while the owners holidayed in Blighty. We took the fullest advantage of the mandatory swimming pools, tennis courts, and saunas, filling them with a trail of lechery and debauchery. My reputation back home in head office took a severe blow when the foreign editor called urgently to send me off to Ethiopia to cover the latest clashes in the Ogaden desert. Sunday, our cook, took the pressing call: "Who are you? No, you cannot talk to Mr. Martin," he informed my appalled boss at three o'clock in the afternoon. "The master is sleeping."

But that first night, after drinks and dinner, Peter was to help me recover from my initial bruising encounter with the Old Africa Hands in the Quill and introduce me to the seedier side of town, which we would find a lot more welcoming, too welcoming, in fact. Our destinations were the Elizabeth and then the Queen's hotels, gloomy drinking and dancing pickup joints that served the local colored community.

Colored, in this racially strained kaleidoscope, meant neither black nor white but people of mixed parentage. Coloreds were less than whites but more than blacks. The definition seemed fluid—not like in South Africa, where strict laws governed human labeling. South African nonwhites could be Black, Colored, Indian, or Chinese; if a nonnative Chinese businessman needed to mix with white business executives, he could be given the appellation *honorary white*. In Rhodesia, relations were never so severe. Whites could wait behind blacks in the post office, sit next to them in the cinema, or drink with them in many bars. Nonwhites couldn't sit on all park benches, or go to the whites' swimming pools, let alone buy houses in white neighborhoods, but relations were never as bitter as in South Africa. Many white Rhodesians were appalled at the strict race laws of South African apartheid. On the other hand, women carrying automatic rifles over their shoulders and pistols on their hips, unheard of then in South Africa, were normal in Salisbury's genteel suburbs.

That first night, Peter Jordan showed me one way to while away the time we didn't spend covering the war. With a few other tipsy hacks, we reached the dance floor of the Queen's Hotel around closing time. The music was loud, couples gyrated closely, and sweaty waiters hurried around taking last orders. We flopped onto sofas, ordered beers, and our number promptly doubled. The newcomers were very pretty, too; or at least they appeared so in the dim light and our happy state. Soon Peter and I found ourselves in a cab with two of the "colored" ladies. It had been dark at the Queens and it was dark in the cab and it was dark outside as we stumbled up the stairs to their flat. Only inside, when the light came on, could I survey the full attractions that awaited me.

Deirdre was tall, beautiful, with a lovely young face and unusually soft, straight brown hair. Oh, Africa, I thought, I am in heaven. I hadn't even been in the country for twelve hours and . . . Yes, this is my kind of war. But my smug reverie was quickly interrupted by Peter's loud "Oh shit!" Let's just say that he was less impressed with his date. Peter's girl was probably very nice, maybe even very intelligent, but his forced grin said it all as he went to pick up his camera bag. "It's late, I'm going," he said. "See you tomorrow at the Quill."

Not so fast. In the cab Peter's new friend had had occasion to check out the goods, and she wasn't going to let him off the hook. She was squat, heavy, and clearly very strong, with glaring brown eyes. For the second time that evening, I had found someone who, if necessary, I could call upon to protect me from Alex Morrow-Smith. She, too, had drunk a beer or two too many. Perspiring, smelling of musk, Peter's date grabbed him by the arm. Although Peter stood close to six feet and was wiry and tough, he didn't stand a chance. His last words, as he was ferociously yanked and lost his desperate grip on the doorframe, were a muted shriek from behind the slammed bedroom door: "Martin, look after my cameras!"

I fared somewhat better, although my new lady friend's hauteur took a dive when she removed her shoes. They turned out to be four-inch plat-form heels, and in their absence she shrank considerably. Then she took off her wig, revealing a close-cropped skull, which shrank her by another six inches or so. I hope that's all she can remove, I thought. Luckily it was, and Deirdre proved a memorable introduction to the Dark Continent.

When I groggily presented my press credentials at the Rhodesian Ministry of Information the following morning, I felt well on my way to becoming an Old Africa Hand. The official who took my forms asked how long I'd been in the country. Looking at my watch, I said, "Oh, almost twenty-four hours." What a day, I thought. If it goes on like this, I'll never last two weeks.

The party went on for four years. Poolside get-togethers with Paul Harris and Bruce Palling lasted through the weekend. One house I rented boasted a large bucking leather bull of the kind found in Texas saloons. It stood outside the sauna, encouraging lewd late-night frolics. In another memorable mansion, Peter and I decided one afternoon to go skinny-dipping. The servants were off, it was hot, and we had a couple of hours to blow before Quill time. Peter dove in, and I ran across the lawn to follow him. I heard a shriek from a passing schoolgirl, who with perfect timing glanced through the only gap in the hedge. Then the doorbell rang and a Rhodesian friend joined us. She elected to go topless. Then it rang again and another friend dropped by unannounced. Peter and I felt that, as this was our place, and we had wanted to swim nude, there was no reason to get dressed. Then the bell rang yet again, and again, as about two dozen friends as well as visiting journalists from London dropped by without warning. The way to feel even more naked than naked is when everybody else is fully clothed, and so it went for hours. But Peter and I were too drunk to care.

I owed Peter a lot, especially for the rabies jabs he gave me in the stomach. Peter and I, along with Mutters; another good friend, Paul "Dirty" Harris, whose nickname was shrouded in mystery but was reputed to derive from either his pornographic language or a foul act performed on him by a lovely Greek girl; and several more hacks, spent a few days on a farm in Chipinge, by the Rhodesian border with Mozambique, in yet another futile attempt to report on the growing guerrilla war. Between boozy lunches and frightening drives along the war-torn border, we repaid the farmer by helping him dig trenches. A cute mongrel licked our hands and played with us for hours. The dog then died. After his brain was sent to Salisbury, it was confirmed he had died of rabies. The health authorities hurriedly contacted us. As our gentle hands were un-used to manual work and were now covered in cuts and blisters from the digging, doctors feared that the dog's saliva may have caused our own brains to become inflamed with the always-fatal virus. To survive, we re-quired treatment before symptoms developed. The doctors beseeched us to go straight to the hospital for two weeks of injections. We hurried there, although in typical fashion Mutters refused—he wasn't having his stomach stabbed for any reason. We all agreed that rabies might improve his difficult disposition.

After seven injections on the first day, we needed another injection a day in our stomachs for the next fourteen. This meant we couldn't leave Salisbury. However, Peter and I had been invited to a weekend party in "the sharp end," the northeastern Mount Darwin area, which had become the front line in the war. Farmers were attacked almost daily, and we reck-oned we could have a great time accepting the Rhodesian farmers' leg-endary hospitality, and if we were lucky we might get attacked to boot. But what about the rabies jabs? To break the daily treatment could prove fatal. We solved that problem by persuading the doctor to give us the serum, which came in two vials, to be combined before injection, and promising to inject each other daily. Not that either of us had any idea how to do it—but this party was not to be missed.

We rode horses, oblivious to the possible presence of guerrillas stalk-ing the farmers, ate and drank tremendously, and engaged in riotous de-bate with the farmer and his friends on the prospects for Western democracy. As the Rhodies saw it, the West's future was limited, not their own. They did not regard their struggle as a last-ditch fight to protect white supremacy. Rather, they thought they were defending Western Christian civilization against Soviet expansionism, and their wives and daughters from rape at the hands of the natives—"the lootin', shootin', burnin', and rapin' that's goin' on all over Africa," as "good old Smithie" put it.

But we had come to party, and political talk soon yielded to dancing and singing. When bedtime came, Peter and his girlfriend turned in, leaving me to find a place to put my head down. No beds remained. I had danced and talked a little with a pretty Rhodesian friend of Peter's who had joined us for the drive from Salisbury, and she, too, had nowhere to sleep. Together we stalked the corridors of the vast farmhouse until we poked open a door and finally found an empty single bed. We dove in and began to introduce ourselves, but a minute later the door swung open. The farmer's scary sister filled the doorframe, arms crossed. In a booming voice, she demanded, "What are yooooou doing in myyyy bed?"

"Nothing! Sorry!" we cried and leaped out in terror. Clutching our clothes, we returned to stalking the corridors, which by now reverberated with snores and other sounds. But no beds were available, all the sofas were taken, too, and we were getting cold. Eventually I pushed open the door to Peter's room, told him and his girlfriend to move over, and my new friend and I climbed in. It was the beginning of a beautiful relationship. Not with Peter, I hasten to add.

The next day brought the moment of truth for the rabies jabs. Our hands shook, and each of us urged the other to go first. I called Peter a coward. In the end, neither of us could go through with it. The farmer's scary sister offered, insisting she had plenty of experience with horses, but we were not persuaded. Instead, we decided to drive to a Rhodesian army base five miles away to find a medic. He'd know what to do. Off we set, over dirt roads that we knew could be mined. The guerrillas in that area liked to assault farmhouses by night, firing machine guns and throwing hand grenades. As the farmers shot back, the guerrillas would run, but only after they had laid land mines along the tracks that provided the farms' only access. We kept our eyes peeled for guerrillas in the distance and mines on the road. It was a nerve-racking trip, during which we chastised each other for not daring to give the injections and, more pleasantly, compared notes on the previous night.

When we finally found the medic, he knew little more than we. First he asked which arm we'd like it in, not knowing the serum needed to be injected into loose flesh, preferably the tummy. Then, when he poured the contents of one test tube into the other to form the serum, he contaminated it by covering the vial opening with his dirty thumb and shaking hard.

The next day we injected the serum ourselves. Or rather, Peter did. Gritting his teeth, he pinched together some flesh from his skinny stomach, slowly thrust the needle in, and gently squeezed. Then it was my turn. Pinned to the floor by the laughing party guests who were sitting on my arms and legs, I clamped my eyes shut and called out, "Do it gently" as Peter injected the rabies serum into my stomach. Maybe I owe Peter Jordan my life, but Mutters had the last laugh because he was fine while we suffered for two weeks. Neither Peter nor I had an ounce of fat on our bodies in those days, so after seven days of jabs we had to inject into the same tender, inflamed area. On the plus side, Visnews showed great concern about my brush with such an awful death and offered to fly me back to Europe for a checkup. I accepted and promptly went skiing in Switzerland for two weeks.

Upon my return, I found that the genteel and good-natured competition among the agency cameramen had been overturned by the arrival of Lord Richard Cecil. A charming, tough, and energetic young man, Cecil possessed all the advantages of the British aristocracy and every qualification to penetrate the heart of the Rhodesian establishment. Although the British Labour government remained at virtual war with the Rhodesian whites, large portions of the opposition Conservative Party, as well as the aristocracy and senior ranks of the British army, supported the white colonialists, who they felt were being abandoned by an opportunistic Britain in the face of black power. The Rhodies saw Cecil as a link with Britain's traditional power base. Rhodesia's defense minister would later describe him as "possessing everything that made Britain great and built the British Empire."

Cecil was the second son of the Marquis of Salisbury, after whom the Rhodesian capital was named. An Oxford graduate, a former officer in Britain's elite SAS regiment with combat experience in Ireland and tours of duty in the Middle East, Cecil was just the kind of friend the Rhodesian whites wanted. Personally, he was a modest, friendly man who did not trade on his heritage. A beautiful receptionist at the Monomatapa Hotel, after whom everybody vainly lusted, immediately succumbed to the handsome young man who had come to gain his spurs as a reporter. But she discovered her lover's true identity only after he lost his wallet and advertised in *The Rhodesia Herald* that anybody returning the contents would receive a handsome reward from Lord Cecil, who was residing in room such-and-such in the Monomatapa Hotel. She proclaimed herself very upset with his failure to disclose his aristocratic background, but somehow their relationship withstood the strain.

Professionally, however, Richard was ruthless. He used every family contact possible to ingratiate himself with the Rhodesian military and quickly became a regular on combat patrols as well as with the "fire force," the elite helicopter fighting units Rhodesia maintained, which flew anywhere to help ground troops when they reported "contact" with the terrs. His war film was distributed by UPITN, Visnews's direct competition, and, to put it mildly, he was wiping the floor with me. Richard was covering the war, while I filmed army parades. Soon, I was reduced to writing begging letters to the army PR office, but to no avail. Lord Cecil was the only foreign reporter to see any real action in the Rhodesian bush war. Repeatedly.

One day I received a rueful message from my boss at Visnews, wishing, tongue-in-cheek, that the terrs could take care of Richard. Unfortunately, his facetious comment was tragically to be fulfilled. With his cameraman, Nick Downie, also a former British army officer, Cecil parachuted into the Mtoko area with the Rhodesian African Rifles, an army unit with black soldiers and mostly white officers. They gathered their gear and set off on what should have been a surprise attack on a guerrilla base. Richard was behind the soldier walking point on the right flank, moving carefully through bush and tall grass. Suddenly an insurgent popped up and unloaded his AK47 on full automatic into the body of the nearest white man, who was Richard. His body was ripped open, and he died within minutes. It was a tragic end to the promising life of a thirty-year-old British lord who had hoped to follow in the footsteps of Winston Churchill by gaining experience in an African war and then entering politics. He was the only journalist to die covering Zimbabwe's liberation.

I'd been Visnews's man in Rhodesia for a year when Irv Margolies, NBC's gangly, eccentric and lovable, fast-talking London bureau chief, invited me to lunch while I was vacationing in England. Later we repaired to his bizarre office, which was furnished in purple and chrome. He said he had an offer I couldn't refuse. "You know Neil Davis, how he works in Asia?" Irv machine-gunned at me. "That's what we want you to do for us in Africa. Great job. Fantastic. We need you, you need us. It's yours. We'll double your salary. What do you make?"

Neil Davis was without exception the nicest man I have ever met. He was also the best combat cameraman, the sharpest reporter, and, I mention in passing, a babe magnet—tall, lean, handsome, his lush hair falling over his face in loose blond curls, his mouth permanently raised at one corner as if about to smile. He had been the Visnews cameraman in Asia, as I was in Africa, along with Mo Amin in Kenya. For more than a decade Neil had worked in Vietnam and Cambodia, where he specialized in front-line fighting with the local troops, leaving the cushy briefings and American helicopter facilities to everybody else. He was the only man to film North Vietnamese tanks smashing down the gates of the American embassy in Saigon, the defining image of the end of the Vietnam war. When a Korean colleague was captured by North Vietnamese troops, an experience from which few returned alive, Neil crossed the lines, alone and unarmed, to find him. And, unknown to his colleagues, he blew most of his savings by setting up an orphanage for South Vietnamese children.

Neil finally left Visnews and joined NBC News as the first network "one-man band," a new concept of cameraman, soundman, producer, and reporter, all rolled into one modest pay packet. That Irv now wanted me to serve as a one-man band for NBC News was thrilling, if not entirely unexpected. During the Portuguese revolution, NBC had had three crews there, yet almost all the footage they used was mine from Visnews. It had been the same everywhere in Africa for the past year. And Irv had offered me a job as a cameraman earlier, when I was based in Israel. I had always answered that I didn't want to join NBC as a cameraman but would love to come as a producer. This was even better. As a one-man band, I'd finally have a chance to report on the air. I had set myself a time limit of five years to work as a cameraman, see the world, make some money, and then return to London to continue my career as a producer, an editorial post that was the extent of my ambitions.

The solitary nature of the one-man band appealed to me. I loved being an agency cameraman, working alone, in charge of my own time and beholden to nobody. I loved never knowing in the morning where I'd be by nightfall, when the telex would come to life in the middle of a tennis game and clatter, "Proceed Angolawards soonest" or "Need you urgentest infill Nairobi" or "Coup rumors in Equatorial Guinea, advise travel plans immediate," and within the hour I would be in the cab to the airport, with no further instructions, covering the story as best I could. Have camera, will travel. Working alone.

On the other hand, the one-man-band arrangement was unrealistic. Even with all his gifts, Neil was miscast in the role. He couldn't pull off the workload of four men, especially the grind of traveling alone with twelve heavy cases of camera gear. In Africa, where every palm had to be greased and the simplest task took on its own crazy logic, the challenge was even greater. I once tried to buy a last-minute plane ticket out of Accra in Ghana. The ticket officer told me the flight was full but winked that, for an extra hundred bucks, he could swing it. I paid the bribe, boarded the plane, only to find it half empty. On another occasion, we were left stranded in Tanzania when a flight was canceled because President Nyerere had commandeered the plane to fly to a conference of African leaders. So I knew that working in Africa as a one-man band would be just too hard.

"Thanks for the offer," I told Irv. "I'm flattered, but I have to decline."

"What? Are you nuts? Why not? How much do you want?"

"It isn't about the money. I do know how Neil works. And it's impossible. Nobody can work like that. The proof is that Neil hardly ever gets on the air, and he's the best there is. If he can't, I certainly won't. Make me a producer and I'll sign right now."

But he didn't, and it was obvious why. Irv thought it important to cover Africa, but nobody else at NBC did, and, as a result, he didn't have the budget. Astonishingly, at that time not one American network had a staff member based on the continent. Africa was the black hole of American television. The continent was considered dangerous, expensive, and disease-ridden—a hardship post. This struck me as laughable. Certainly Africa could be very dangerous. While the Rhodesian war was as comfortable as war could be, exceptionally pleasant for the press, in fact, elsewhere in Africa journalists were routinely arrested, beaten, even tortured and killed. Africa was also expensive, certainly as reflected in the hacks' expense reports, as well as disease-ridden. In addition to the rabies jabs, my body was pockmarked by inoculations against sundry fatal illnesses and plagues. However, a hardship post? I was having the time of my life.

But within weeks, I regretted having turned down Irv's offer. First, as much as I loved being a cameraman, I was beginning to get frustrated with the anonymity of agency work, where I was "just" the cameraman. Second, Visnews usually preferred quantity over quality. And third, to paraphrase Hemingway on journalism, agency work is the best training possible, as long as you get out of it soon enough. Irv's one-man-band offer presented a way out, as well as an opening into a world to which I aspired, that is, reporting stories for a real broadcast rather than distributing raw film footage to stations around the world—footage that would then be reedited, rewritten, or, even more likely, rejected. And another minor consideration: The money was more than double my Vis salary.

Two months after I'd turned down Irv's offer, I called him back. "Hello, Irv, it's Martin Fletcher." After a few pleasantries, I cut to the chase. "About that one-man-band job in Africa? I'd like to take it after all. Thought it over, and I know I can do it. I'd love to work with you."

"Too late, the offer's off the table."

By now I knew how Americans worked, but I still felt like I'd just been stabbed. "Oh. Okay."

"Got another job for you, though. Great job. Glad you called. Was just about to call you. You'll love it. You're just the guy. You'll be fantastic. We need you, you need us. Not quite the same as the job you . . . turned . . . down. But it's a perfect fit."

The fit was too good. It was exactly the same job as I had with Visnews, only worse. At least with Vis I was my own boss.

Irv continued. "Cameraman. In Africa. You'll work with a correspondent. I told New York what you said about it being impossible to be a one-man band in Africa, and they agreed. Got more money out of them. Owe you. Well done. You want the job?"

"Who's the correspondent?"

"Tom Ackerman."

I knew Tom from Israel, where he served as an NBC Radio correspondent. A very good young radio reporter, with almost no experience in television.

"How much?"

Irv told me. It was more than I earned at Vis, but not by much. "What happened to the last offer? That would be fine."

"You turned it down. You said no. Now the money, plus a bit, is split between two people. You want the job, it's yours. You don't, good-bye."

Even though the job wasn't perfect, I took it. I did so because I had seen the future. As an experienced fixer as well as a cameraman, I had previously been farmed out by Visnews to help NBC with their first-ever live broadcast from South Africa to New York. The network's State Department correspondent, Richard Valeriani, was accompanying the secretary of state, Henry Kissinger, on a swing through Southern Africa aimed at persuading Ian Smith to work toward black rule.

Having ensured that everything was in order for the feed from SABC, South African television, I went to the airport to greet Richard and brief him on the latest developments. He descended the steps in what appeared to be tennis whites and was whisked away in the press bus, not to be seen or heard from again until he appeared in the studio the next morning to be interviewed by the *Today* show. Something had gone wrong in New York, though, and they were almost out of time before the broadcast began. The question posed to Valeriani was, roughly, "Richard, the Rhodesian leader is known as a wily negotiator. What are Secretary Kissinger's chances of success in this mission?" Richard spoke for a few seconds and then summed it up: "Oh, I'd say about fifty-fifty." He was cut off, and satellite transmission history, however modest, had been made.

In the control room I listened, agog, to Richard's potted and rather inaccurate analysis and heard New York congratulate him in his earpiece: "Good, well done, Richard, great job, thank you." I said to myself, "That's it? I can do that!" Thus was born my ambition to be an NBC News correspondent.

Now, hearing the reduced offer from Irv, I was disappointed. But, I calculated, if cameraman was the way in, so be it. I was twenty-nine years old, and time was on my side. Then Irv sweetened the pot a little. "I've only got a small budget for this Africa operation," he continued, consoling me. "Make it work, get Tom on the air a lot, and I'll get more money, hire a camera team, and you can be the producer."

In the summer of 1977, I took up my first position with NBC News, as their Africa cameraman. All my possessions fit into the back of a car, which a friend drove the six hundred miles from Salisbury to Johannesburg. The move cost NBC less than a hundred dollars in gasoline expenses. Irv was delighted. "We budgeted four thousand. We're saving money already," he crowed. His heart was in the right place. He was anxious to demonstrate to New York how successful the new Africa operation would be, so that he could expand the tiny bureau and get Africa the coverage it deserved. "Now get on the goddamn air!" he said.

Easier said than done. Despite Irv's enthusiasm, American networks still maintained a legendary disinterest in things African. This contrasted dramatically with the European stations, which had, if not an insatiable, then at least a responsible, appetite for African news. This partly owed to Africa's status as practically a domestic story in many European countries.

The African colonial heritages of Britain, France, Portugal, Spain, Italy, Belgium, and Germany ensured that their correspondents could invariably find a local angle that would interest their editors. In Namibia, the question to German immigrants was always: "Did you come in 1939 or 1945?" If the answer was 1939, it meant the interviewee was Jewish; if 1945, a Nazi. America had no such political or cultural shorthand. America's main link to Africa was slavery, which it preferred to forget.

For nine months, Tom Ackerman and I slogged on, Tom writing and reporting, I filming and producing. He was learning television, I was learning the American network way. We roamed Southern Africa, covering the news, such as it was, in Lesotho, KwaZulu, Bophuthatswana, and Mbabane, unspellable tongue twisters for our show editors, who had no idea where we were or why. It was upsetting. The only stories that got us on the air were in Rhodesia and South Africa, because they involved whites. The sorry lives of the blacks held little interest for our editors, while they were what I cared about most. Irv's plan to expand airtime and then the size of the bureau was going down the toilet, and with it I could see my career plans gurgling round the S bend. It couldn't be denied. If South Africa was racist, so, in a certain sense, were the American news shows. This, however, led to my breakthrough in a way that could never happen today.

By now Peter Jordan was *Time* magazine's photographer in South Africa. We were again sharing a house, although he was rather disappointed in me, as I had struck up a regular relationship with a tall, elegant South African girl and had largely removed myself from his ambitious party plans. Nevertheless, Peter called me one day from his office in Johannesburg to tell me he had just been ordered to Zaire. "Let's go," he said. "This could be big."

Katangese exiles had invaded the southern Shaba province of Zaire for the second time in fourteen months and were advancing upon the regional capital of Kolwezi. The region's rich mineral deposits were the prize—important because they could form a power base for the secessionist rebels, threatening President Mobutu Sese Seko's pro-Western

regime, which depended on the mines' billion-dollar exports. It was rumored that Cuban soldiers supported the Lunda tribesmen who were
spearheading the insurgency. Visnews would have been all over it, but if
ever a story would provoke the automatic yawn reflex in New York, this
was it. Lunda tribesmen? Who the fuck are they? Where? Tom had no interest. I tried to persuade him that he should call the NBC assignment
desk in New York and convince them this was important. In a few days,
ten thousand blacks had been reported killed and the insurgents hadn't
even reached Kolwezi. The story was just beginning. It looked like a
bloodbath. He declined. So I tried.

It wasn't up to me, the lowly cameraman, to call the assignment desk.
But I sensed a huge story, even if no whites were involved, so I called New
York for the first time since joining NBC about nine months earlier.
Louise Gersen took the call. "The second . . . Katangese . . . invasion
of . . . Shaba?" she pronounced deliberately, in her cutting, humorous
way. "I didn't know there was a first one. Where is it and why should we
care?" My explanation that so many dead blacks in less than a week
spelled a slaughter and we should be there to report on it was received
with a definitive "Forget it! Nice talking to you."

It was an American variation of McClurke's law. McClurke was a long-
retired editor at BBC Radio who once formulated an equation to measure
what scale of disaster was needed to get on the air. It went something like
this: A hundred thousand Bangladeshis killed in a flood equaled ten
thousand Africans killed by famine equaled five hundred Egyptians eaten
by crocodiles on the Nile equaled five British soldiers killed in Northern
Ireland equaled two of the queen's corgi dogs run over by a bus. I was
learning that, for American network television, the bar was even higher.
Ten thousand Africans didn't register on its scale.

Then Peter called again as he left for the airport. "This is the only direct flight to Kinshasa for a week. You coming or not?"

By now I'd had it up to here with no interest in Africa. I made one
quick phone call, to Mike Kaufman of *The New York Times,* who knew his
way around the world better than anybody. He gave me a short list of

Kinshasa contacts to get me started, plus a word of warning: "It's probably the hardest place to work in Africa, and therefore the world. Contact
Josie." I ignored the NBC assignment desk, quickly packed, and raced to
meet Peter at the airport. It was my first story without Tom. There was
one other journalist on the plane, Serge Schmemann of the Associated
Press, who later won the Pulitzer for his coverage of German reunifi-
cation.

I had never covered Zaire before, so I spent the plane ride reading Peter's research on the country and quizzing Serge. With an hour to go, I
flicked through the list of names Mike had given me. I didn't need the
translator's help, because I spoke French. There was the name of a driver,
a hotel phone number, a couple of government contacts, and, most important of all, the money changer, to take full advantage of any black
market. His name was Josie. Mike had specifically repeated that this was a
man who could be trusted and who could fix anything.

At that moment a man plopped himself down next to me and asked,
"Why are you going to Zaire? It's dangerous now."

"That's why I'm going," I said, nodding at the camera, which was
strapped in across the aisle.

"Do you know anyone there?" he asked. "Kinshasa is a difficult place.
Nothing works and everybody cheats. Just getting a phone call from your
hotel room can take a day. You need help?"

"I don't think so," I said. "I've got this list of contacts, I'll be fine, really,
thanks." I didn't want any government agent cramping my style, and this
man looked just the sleazy part. He was tall, with crinkly light brown hair
and a Levantine nose.

"Let me see," he said and grabbed my list. I was just beginning to
protest when he threw his head back and roared with laughter. "Ha! Josie!
That's me! Josie! I am Josie!"

We got on famously. He was a youngish Lebanese businessman based
in Kinshasa with a finger in every pie, as well as, it appeared, a top contact
in every government department, all of whom owed him, and all of whom
he was willing to mobilize on my behalf. He never asked for anything in

return except one little thing. I should direct the international press, when they came, to change money through him. He had been doing some business in South Africa, which he interrupted as soon as he heard the rebels had invaded again. Whenever there's a war, there's a Josie, and he always gets rich quick.

An hour after we landed, the government closed Kinshasa airport. It became a military site. We had flown the last plane in. Josie took us to the InterContinental Hotel, where he negotiated good rooms at cheap rates. While Peter and Serge checked in and tried to prevent our bags from being stolen, Josie surreptitiously took me behind the reception into the hotel's telephone exchange, which consisted of one man sitting in front of a wall of exposed cables, different-colored plugs, and numbered holes. A brief chat with the operator, an exchange of room numbers and banknotes, and we were set.

Josie's deal was this: Each time I needed to make a phone call abroad, instead of the regular eight-hour wait, I would get the call through within a minute. After every call I would come straight down and slip the operator twenty-five American dollars. He would keep half, and half would go to his friend at the post office exchange. I would not be charged for the call itself, which could easily run into hundreds of dollars, because it could not appear on a list of requested calls. I could file for NBC Radio for hours at a flat rate of twenty-five bucks. The network would save thousands. Everybody won, except the post office and the government budget.

Such an arrangement today would fall well afoul of most of NBC's policy handbook, apart from being morally wrong. Then, however, it struck me as a perfectly fair and natural way to benefit from a rotten system. If I thought about it at all, which I probably didn't, I was simply reducing the amount of money available to be stolen by officials of the corrupt and murderous president, Mobutu Sese Seko Kuku Ngbendu wa za Banga, a name he officially translated as "All-powerful warrior who, because of his endurance and inflexible will to win, will go from conquest to conquest leaving fire in his wake." His real name, I might add, was Joe. Mobutu had already stolen half of the budget, and most of the rest evaporated in bribes, corruption, and incompetence. Mineral-rich Zaire was virtually bankrupt.

But now I had to make my first corrupt $25 phone call. I had to break it to NBC News that they were about to have exclusive coverage of something they didn't want: the second Katanga invasion of the Shaba province of Zaire. As I sat on my hotel bed and looked at the telephone, familiar nervous pangs cramped my stomach. Lunda tribesmen? Who the f——? By now I was beginning to have second thoughts about the value of this exclusive. Kinshasa was dead quiet, there was no sign of war, and even I was beginning to think, Who cares? We had seen nothing to film in the streets, and I would probably get nowhere near the fighting. I had flagrantly disobeyed the instructions of the foreign desk and could possibly be fired for spending NBC money so recklessly. What's the point of saving hundreds of dollars a call if nobody wants to speak to me? What happens if there's a big story in South Africa and I'm not there?

I hoped to speak to Louise, who had appeared kind and sympathetic. I might need all the sympathy I could get. Could I claim I'd misheard her? When I'd asked her if I should catch the Kinshasa plane, she had answered, "Forget it!" Could I say that I thought she had said, "Get it!" That was my only chance to save my job. Oh well, I thought, as I placed my first black-market call from Kinshasa, lucky I left Visnews on good terms.

But another desk editor picked up the phone. A rather aggressive male voice. "Oh, hi," I began tentatively. "I guess Louise has gone home. Uh, it's Martin Fletcher and I—"

He interrupted quickly. "Where the hell are you? We've been looking for you. We need you to go to Zaire, but the Kinshasa airport's closed. Nobody can get in. It's a huge story. Two thousand whites are trapped, they're surrounded by the rebels in a town called Kolwezi. We're trying to get a charter organized . . . special government permission . . . maybe via Belgium . . . where are you?"

A huge grin formed on my face as I chuckled. "Well, that's what I've been trying to tell you . . . I'm in Kinshasa."

McClurke's law. Nobody cared about ten thousand dead blacks. Two thousand whites in danger and we were mobilizing the network.

I filed for NBC Radio, establishing that NBC had exclusive coverage from the world's latest hot spot. Then Peter, Serge, and I went into the streets and found a large rally in support of the president. I filmed the dancing and singing, the speeches and marching, and then handed the camera to Peter, who filmed my first-ever piece to camera for NBC News. Looking at it today, I see that it was truly awful. I emphasized the wrong words in a clipped English accent, and what I said could have benefited from a serious rewrite. I looked stiff, nervous, and my hair was sticking up. But none of that counted because: I was there. Reports flooding in about the whites trapped by the fighting in the mining town of Kolwezi and Serge's dramatic stories on the AP wire only emphasized the enormity of our exclusive coverage.

Now that I had the story, I had to grapple with the next great obstacle facing the press in Africa: getting the story out. I was broadcasting feverishly for NBC Radio, thanks to my new buddy manning the telephone exchange, but there was no satellite feed from Kinshasa, and the airport was closed. I couldn't get the film out. I was stuck, TV scoop in hand.

Josie!

I called him with my dilemma. Moments later he called back. "There's a military flight to Brussels leaving in two hours. Go to the military side of the airport, tell the guard on the gate you have an appointment with Colonel Maurice, and give him the film. Some dollars, too. The film will be in Brussels tomorrow morning, inshallah." I couldn't believe it. The guy was amazing. And he was my guy! I resolved to buy Mike Kaufman a big dinner next time our paths crossed.

I called NBC and asked them to get someone to meet the flight in Brussels. Arrangements were made to get the film to the London bureau for broadcast the same evening. After I made the airport connection, I ended the day by placing a thank-you call to Josie. I mentioned in passing that I really needed to get down to Kolwezi, in the war zone, where the story was.

The next morning Josie woke me up. "The president is flying to Kolwezi. You can fly with him on his personal plane. Would you like that?"

Would I like that? NBC couldn't believe their luck and good planning. They had flown somebody over from London to meet the Zaire military flight in Brussels, *Nightly News* was going to lead with my first-ever story, and the appetite for the story was huge. Among the American television networks, which was all NBC cared about, we were alone in Kinshasa, and now we'd be alone in Kolwezi. The saying that failure is an orphan but success has many fathers never rang truer. My illicit dash to Zaire, thanks to Peter, was history. I was reporting on NBC Radio every hour about the fighting, the large number of dead Africans, the success the government forces claimed in pushing back the rebels from Kolwezi, as well as on the threat to the vital copper mines in the south and the danger to Mobutu's regime. Yet maybe, fresh from Visnews, I still didn't have my finger on the pulse of my American editors and audience, because there was always the same live follow-up question: "What about the whites?"

On the flight to Kolwezi, I filmed over Mobutu's shoulder while he took the controls of the big C-130. The president was a short man even when wearing his signature leopard-skin hat, and his jolly demeanor belied his vicious past. The ambitious and wily son of a cook and a chambermaid, he had worked his way up to army chief of staff and then, in 1965, engineered a coup d'état to seize the presidency. In a classic African Cold War power play, Mobutu was backed by the West against evil communism, and this gave him license to murder his predecessor and institute a reign of terror and theft. Mobutu, who was barely educated, began to steal while young, and continued to steal, until it was estimated that, as president, he had amassed a personal fortune of $5 billion.

The sun glinted off his trademark sunglasses in the cockpit as he laughed and enthusiastically pointed at an accompanying jet fighter that flashed by. As we circled Kolwezi airport, he pointed out the homes of white men trapped in the town. Even Mobutu seemed to care more about the whites than the blacks, probably because he knew their fate was prompting worldwide concern for his country. Soldiers sent by Belgium and France to protect their nationals would save his skin, too. There were about a dozen journalists onboard, but aides wouldn't let us ask questions and insisted we maintain a respectable distance from the great man.

Mobutu made the trip that day to demonstrate that his troops had defeated the rebels and pushed them back from Kolwezi. When we landed, he did indeed briefly strut around the tarmac, past burned-out planes and destroyed trucks, while soldiers posted on the perimeter waved and saluted. The plan was to follow Mobutu into town to survey the damage caused by the defeated rebels, who had fled. But apparently they hadn't fled very far, because they began to pour mortar fire onto the president and his entourage. Explosions threw up dust and earth, fortunately some distance from Mobutu and his men. Twenty minutes after landing, bodyguards crowded around Mobutu and rushed him back onto the plane while calling on us to follow immediately. As soldiers hustled me away from the shelling and across the tarmac, I filmed the pandemonium while somehow also recording a breathless radio report on my tape recorder.

Later, in my Kinshasa hotel room, I listened to the taped report with horror. It was unusable. I was out of breath, I repeated myself, you could hear soldiers shouting at me to run away; what I said under such stress made some sense but not a lot. Then again, it had the most important thing going for it: I was there. Exclusive for NBC. It was embarrassing for me to hear, but a BBC Radio reporter, David McNeil, who listened to the recording with me, insisted that I send it to the network. "They'll love it," he said. "It's great radio, you're on the spot!" David was in my room because it was the only room from which he could get a phone call through in time to make his deadlines. Later, after the airport reopened and the press arrived, my room was to become like Grand Central, for everybody apart from ABC and CBS, of course. We were killing them. I had a complete lock on Zaire's international telephone exchange.

In case NBC Radio hated the breathless report, which was also quite short, I recorded a longer, calmer version describing the debacle at Kolwezi airport and called London, the center of the foreign operation. When they were ready to take in the feed, I unscrewed the telephone's mouthpiece, attached alligator clips to the correct wires inside the phone, and pressed my tape recorder's play button. London confirmed they had recorded the reports successfully, and I went downstairs to pay the operator his bribe. It was late, and finally I lay back, feet on the bed, tired and happy. On the same day, *NBC Nightly News* would run my first-ever film report, the one I had shipped to Brussels the day before. The anchor could introduce it with news about Mobutu's airport escapade. And NBC Radio would run the longer radio report describing Kolwezi. Maybe, if David was correct and it wasn't too terrible, radio would use the shorter, breathless version instead. And my competition weren't even in the country. Not bad for a cameraman, I thought.

But it got better. The next morning, when I checked in with the desk in New York, I was astounded to find that *Nightly News* had led with my embarrassing, breathless radio report on the president's narrow escape. They followed that with my longer, calmer summary, and then, after a brief Washington reaction spot, they ran my TV report of the rally that I had shipped to Brussels. The first time I was on television, I had three reports in the first ten minutes of the show. Nobody had ever done that before, and nobody has since. Over at CBS, Walter Cronkite shouted in the newsroom, "Who the hell is Martin Fletcher?" That was echoed by the NBC anchor, John Chancellor, who grabbed the phone when I next called. His first words were "Who are you, anyway?" The reaction to my initial foray onto network air was summed up in a telex from Walter Millis on the assignment desk:

Think you will be interested to know that you did segment one of Nightly News virtually alone. . . . I cannot recall this happening before and it is a considerable personal and professional triumph for you.

The story gained further traction on the strength of worldwide concern for the trapped whites, who included eighty Americans, and fear for the future of Zaire's vast mineral deposits. Three days later, as the fabled

French Foreign Legion parachuted into Kolwezi, another telex slid under my hotel door:

> We using everything you giving us. Apparently Zaire story ranking slightly below second coming and somewhat ahead of world war three in States at the moment.

By now the airport had reopened, and NBC crews and correspondents had arrived in force, but the network executives decided this was my story. For the first time I received my own camera crew, and I continued to send reports. Belgian paratroopers rescued the whites; the French Foreign Legion, with my crew and me in hot pursuit driving a looted Renault 4 with smashed windows and broken doors, swept through southern Zaire, killing and capturing insurgents and forcing the remnants to flee back to Angola, from whence they came. The foreign troops eliminated the rebel threat to Zaire, thus setting up President Mobutu for twenty more years of thievery to build up his billions in Switzerland and collection of villas in Switzerland and France.

Then came a telex from the executive vice president of NBC News:

> Congratulations on great material you been providing. Everybody here pleased and excited. When all cools down, will expect to see you in New York for talks.

On schedule, five and a half years after setting myself a five-year deadline as cameraman, I was promoted to producer. Somebody else could lug those deadweight aluminum boxes around. I set aside the heavy camera and made my pen my working tool. My back pains disappeared.

In quick succession, Tom Ackerman left Africa, I replaced him as NBC correspondent and then bureau chief, the budget grew, and I hired a South African producer, cameraman, and soundman, all tough and hilarious characters. The producer was Heather Allan, a tall, commanding young woman who excelled at arranging parties and later became NBC's best bureau chief, running one of the network's largest and most complicated bureaus, in Burbank, for a decade and a half. Only Heather, at the same time forceful and gentle, could have controlled George De'Ath and Tony Wasserman, the camera crew we put together. Both were unruly characters straight from the pages of a bad African novel. Tony would have been the rough, gruff farmer with a heart of gold; George, the lady-killing mercenary. Hard-drinking womanizers always ready to party, they filled every minute of the day with laughter, curses, demands on Heather, practical jokes on each other, and all-around crazy behavior.

Tony in particular smashed rules of decorum wherever he went. While he was covering the fortieth anniversary of the Normandy invasion, NBC executives and producers, who didn't know Tony very well, invited him to an exclusive seafood restaurant on the French coast. Declining the fine wines, Tony knocked back a few beers, stripped down to his underpants, brushed by the shocked maître d', and dove into the fish tank with the lobsters and crabs, then returned dripping to his table. After being introduced to an attractive American correspondent in another restaurant, he stunned her by disappearing under the table and biting her between the legs. Restaurants seemed to bring out the best in Tony. When six people ordered Irish coffees after dinner, he yelled out: "Each!" Twenty minutes later a line of waiters emerged, bearing thirty-six large drinks. Yet without fail, dawn the morning after would see Tony running off the excess alcohol, beard flying and elbows pumping. He never missed a call to work.

Neither did George, who matched Tony drink for drink and whose nights were just as challenging. His chiseled features, lean and muscled body, penetrating eyes, quick wit, and extraordinary self-confidence, enhanced by his love of fast cars and fine wine, guaranteed him a stream of gorgeous young women. George, in his gray Jaguar E-Type, and Tony, in his cups, were a team to remember. They argued, partied, and, ultimately, pushed the limits too far. If anybody appeared indestructible, it was George and Tony, yet they would both die young, after our little Africa team broke up. George, aged thirty-four, was clubbed to death by a mob while filming in Crossroads, a notorious black township near Cape Town. Tony, aged fifty-one, collapsed and died in, of all places, Heathrow Airport. Others in these pages died young, too. Neil Davis, John Edlin, Paul Ellman, Mutters—all died around the age of fifty.

It was an honor to know them. Those were great years in Africa for me, working with extraordinary people, sharing homes with close friends like Peter Jordan and later, Peter Kent, another tall, handsome ace reporter, apparently put on this planet to make me feel inadequate.

Still, I was not entirely happy. I was, after all, living under colonialism and its modern incarnation, South African apartheid. As the years passed, my fascination with the good life waned, and the injustice I witnessed became impossible to ignore. I once tried to help a black woman who had been knocked over by a car, and a white policeman threatened to arrest me for getting in the way of his interrogation while she lay bleeding in the street. He didn't care about her injuries. He wanted to know what she was doing in this white area. White supremacy was brutal and unfair, and doubly evil because it was so easy to ignore and enjoy. Even my South African friends, who knew the family names of their servants and paid for the education of their children, believed this purified their power. I never had that colonial tunnel vision, but my daily brushes with apartheid's practical realities took their toll. I knew my old cook in Rhodesia was right: I had become one of the "masters."

My collusion with the oppressors was brought home to me best when Peter Kent and I shared a grand house on the hopelessly misnamed Hope Road. Our gardener, Joseph, and his wife, Mary, the cook, gave birth to a boy child. It took a month or so for Peter and me, both classic bachelors, to notice the infant's absence. Under the Group Areas Act, blacks could live in white suburbs only as domestic servants; under no circumstances could they bring their children to live with them. So Joseph and Mary had had to send their first child away to their distant homeland of KwaZulu, where Mary's mother cared for the one-month-old. "What?" Peter and I said in unison, our liberal sensitivities scandalized. "Please, bring the baby to live with you here. We don't mind, and we won't tell anyone." Within days, the little family was reunited and living happily in the staff room around the back.

But informers were everywhere. A week later the doorbell rang long and loud. Two South African police officers politely explained the situation. "You are responsible for a gross violation of the Group Areas Act. You are being very kind to your people, but it will cost you . . ." We would have to pay a fine of several thousand rand, a few thousand dollars, for every day Joseph and Mary kept their baby at home. It didn't take us long to inform the poor parents that they would have to send their child away after all. The system had turned Peter and me into enforcers of apartheid in our own home.

Soon afterward we were dining with two girlfriends when we heard a noise in the garden. While I bravely volunteered to stay behind and protect the ladies, Peter ventured forth, fork in hand. Sounds of shouting, running, then silence, followed by a panting Peter collapsing onto a chair after he had chased two young black men up the street. The next night, I awoke in my bedroom, a tiny thatched cottage in the garden, to find two men standing next to my head. In my groggy state, I could only imagine it was Joseph, so I said, quietly and calmly, "What are you doing here?" But as I finished the sentence, I already understood my danger. If I panicked and yelled, they would shut me up for sure, and probably with knives. I pulled the sheets over my head and lay there naked and trembling for about twenty seconds, while the two burglars whispered in Xhosa, a threatening language of clicks and glottal stops. Then they climbed calmly out of the window.

The next night Peter and I went out, and the persistent thieves returned yet again. I was scheduled to leave for Uganda the next day. My bag was packed with all my best stuff, as well as my flute, $2000 in cash, passports, and documents. They nicked the lot. Four squads of police arrived. First the patrol car, then the detectives, followed by a fingerprint team, then more detectives. It appeared a team of black burglars was doing the whole area. The previous night a black maid had disturbed them, and with one blow of an ax they had severed her arm and part of her thigh. If I had shouted in alarm, I would probably have been axed, too. We asked the police what to do in the future. All four units gave the same answer: "They're robbing all the whites. Get a gun. Shoot them." We were not only reporting on the problems of apartheid but sharing them. I didn't want any part of it.

Looking back on it, apartheid was the end of what Shakespeare termed "my salad days, when I was green in judgment, cold in blood."* By now a veteran war correspondent, I could no longer claim youth, innocence, and inexperience, nor could I remain cold-blooded about the cruelties I witnessed daily. The pain of the Dark Continent was just too great to be concealed by the levity and cynicism of the Old Africa Hands in the Quill Club. It was great fun at the time, but it was also an act, a valiant attempt by young adventurers to stay sane among the tragedy, poverty, corruption, and abuse that we found in every country we visited. What the whites did to the blacks, the blacks did to one another, and much worse. We could find humor in the darkest moments, but in the end that didn't make it bearable, for me at least. One of the continent's nastiest tyrants, Zimbabwe's President Robert Mugabe, reminded the London *Sunday Times* in June 2000: "This is Africa. This isn't Little-Puddleton-in-the-Marsh. They behave differently. They think nothing of sticking tent poles up each other's what-not and doing filthy beastly things to each other. It does happen, I'm afraid."

Mugabe was right about Africa but wrong about Little-Puddleton-in-the-Marsh. Brutes do the same thing with those tent poles in Europe, the Middle East, Asia, and South America. It was becoming my lot to document these brutalities. I have never considered myself a war correspondent but rather a correspondent who covers wars, not by choice or design, but because conflict is the bread and butter of foreign correspondence for an American television network. In every African country, officials would complain that foreign correspondents never reported on progress in agri-

---

*Antony and Cleopatra, 1.5.21–22.

culture or the construction of new highways or advances in literacy. We turn up only when people are dying. We could only shrug and ask for a guide to the battlefield. So I continued to report on wars, famines, and revolutions in Africa and farther afield, but from a less compromising location: NBC rewarded me for my years of severe hardship in Africa with the plum job of reporter-producer in Paris.

Four

There Is No God but God

Paris, the jewel of foreign assignments, was my reward for years of hard labor in Africa. I celebrated my first evening with long-legged dancers at the Lido music hall, opposite NBC's plush offices at 73 Champs-Élysées, a few blocks from the Arc de Triomphe. Then I rented the first apartment I saw, four opulent rooms in Montparnasse, once bohemian Paris's artistic and cultural heart. My living room had three walls of glass and a wraparound balcony with a stunning view that stretched across Parisian rooftops to Montmartre and the Basilica of the Sacré-Coeur. In Africa I had lived Hemingway's moveable feast. Now I planned to continue at the source and promptly installed myself at the Café le Dôme at 108 Boulevard du Montparnasse, where he wrote part of his hilarious tribute to *la vie Parisienne*. I had worked hard, I thought, and I had arrived. *Garçon, un vin rouge, s'il vous plaît!*

I was sharing this bliss with Hagar, my girlfriend who became my wife. We'd met six years earlier, while I was still a Visnews cameraman. I was driving along an Israeli highway when I came upon a hitchhiker, a beautiful nineteen-year-old army sergeant whose regulation khaki skirt stopped several inches above the knee. Her long black hair framed a smiling face and sparkling eyes, and her Russian-Yemenite heritage gave her perfect olive skin. Although I was running late for an assignment, I skidded to a halt and picked her up. During the hour's drive she read the newspaper, and we barely exchanged a word. When we arrived at her destination, I was too shy to get her phone number. Cursing my British reticence, I watched her walk away and out of my life.

Fortunately, there was nothing shy about Hagar. Three hours later, when I had finished filming a demonstration outside the Knesset and was just turning the key in the ignition, I heard a tap at the window. It was Hagar. She had finished her business and had spent two hours looking for me in the crowd of twenty thousand. This time we didn't stop talking and laughing. When we arrived in Tel Aviv, I gave her the keys to my apartment, and a month later she moved in.

We lived together for a year and a half, but when my short assignment in Africa began to stretch on, we parted ways. Hagar left Israel to study photography in England. We remained close but for four years made the best of our separate lives. Until Paris. It's a cliché, but the city is made for love. I asked Hagar to join me. She promptly enrolled in a French class at the Alliance Française and studied at the École des Arts Décoratifs and the École des Arts Appliqués. It was party time! *Garçon!* Make that two glasses of *rouge!* In fact, bring the bottle!

NBC News, however, had other ideas. In the spring of 1980, the day after I signed the contract for our flat, they shipped me off to Tehran to cover the Iranian revolution for three weeks. From there I went straight to Poland to cover the first stirrings of the Solidarity revolution. And so it went; I became one of NBC's foreign firemen, parachuting into whichever trouble spot hit the headlines. In two years based in Paris, I worked there for only forty-five days.

From Afghanistan, where I covered the Soviet invasion and the Communists' spreading grip on the country, I flew to Iran to report on Khomeini's revolution, or to Iraq for the Iran-Iraq war, or to the Israel-Lebanon border whenever violence erupted. I dropped into Libya when American F-14 Tomcats shot down two Libyan warplanes over the Gulf of Sidra, and I spent three weeks in Algeria waiting for the release of the

American diplomats held hostage in Tehran. In between these assignments, I returned to Paris, paid Hagar's bills, filled out my expense sheet, and mailed it en route to the airport.

Challenging as it was to be away from Hagar, these assignments proved immensely valuable to me as a journalist. I didn't realize it then, but I was witnessing the birth of modern Islamic terrorism. Two explosions during the early 1980s let the Islamic terrorist genie out of the bottle: the Soviet invasion of Afghanistan, which actually began on Christmas Day 1979, and the Iranian revolution. I had a chance to experience both up close and gain deeper insight into the emotional and philosophical underpinnings of Islamic extremism. Today, groups like al-Qaeda and Hizbullah do not seem foreign to me; rather, I understand them as logical outgrowths of a phenomenon I saw unfolding gradually during the Cold War's waning years.

If I thought such frenzied travel would do my career any good, however, I was sadly mistaken. Reporting on air is a highly subjective task. Many people, including the great Les Crystal, liked my work. Unfortunately, he had just been pushed out as president of NBC News, replaced, to the dismay of some network stalwarts, by Bill Small, the former CBS Washington bureau chief. Small seemed ambivalent about my reporting, and he hated my British accent, I was told. His Parisian acolyte—my bureau chief, Becky Bell—didn't hate only my accent; I felt she hated me, period. For the first time I came up against NBC politics, and it was brutal.

Becky had wanted to be a network correspondent, but never made the grade. Her patrician Texan accent also impeded her. Now here I was, this limey ex-cameraman getting above his station. Moreover, I was hardly ever in the bureau. The New York desk would call me in the middle of the night and I'd be on the plane by dawn, leaving Becky fuming that she had been left out of the loop.

She frequently had been. In February 1981, Lieutenant Colonel Antonio Tejero Molina stormed into the lower house of the Spanish parliament, followed by a couple hundred members of the paramilitary Civil

Guard in funny hats. Brandishing pistols, the mustachioed colonel and his men took 350 members of parliament hostage in a doomed attempt to topple the government. The drama was caught by a robot television camera, which broadcast the action live around the world. Our Paris bureau moved quickly. We hired a private jet, flew to Madrid, and within three hours had rented an apartment overlooking the parliament. It gave a perfect vantage point for Fred Francis, who quickly joined us from Frankfurt, to report live on events unfolding before his eyes. It was news coverage at its fastest and most effective.

The next day herograms poured in from New York to the Paris bureau. We had killed the competition and provided fast and accurate reports of a breaking story under difficult conditions. Becky Bell was a heroine. Nobody was more surprised than she. As Becky, still standing by her desk in her coat at noon, read the pile of congratulatory messages, she yelled to the desk assistant Hazel, "What's happening in Madrid?" Becky habitually disconnected her telephone at night, a journalistic no-no, and she hadn't read the newspapers. At midday she still had no idea that her entire bureau had decamped overnight to Madrid. Her habitual sour demeanor was not sweetened by her undeserved acclaim, and she never forgave me for not somehow waking her up before we chartered the jet.

Becky was quite large and could be scary, especially when rampant. Once she pulled out a newspaper clipping from her drawer and waved it at me aggressively. She pointed to a word she had circled in yellow marker—*loyalty*. It was from an interview with Bill Small, in which he had stressed the characteristic he most required in a journalist. "Loyalty!" Becky growled. She leaned forward as if to grab my hair and pull it out in clumps: "Loyalty!" I had the perfect answer. "You can't demand loyalty, Becky. You have to earn it." Unfortunately, I only thought of it three years later.

I did myself even more harm when the American hostages were freed from their 444 days of captivity in the U.S. embassy in Tehran. I was the producer in charge of all NBC's coverage in Algiers, where negotiations to free the hostages were taking place. It soon became clear that the hostages' first stop after Tehran would be there. I was sitting on top of a huge story, but there was one slight problem: Algiers TV wouldn't allow Western networks access to their broadcast facilities without a telex confirmation of the satellite booking. The telex arrived, but the door to the telex room was locked and nobody could find the key.

The ABC, NBC, and CBS morning shows were all expecting reports. With the deadline approaching, hysteria in New York mounting, and two pretty ABC women alternately cursing and crying, macho Martin took matters into his own hands. I kicked the telex door down. Or rather, I tried to. My violent lunge yielded only a cracked door, a bruised heel, and an escort out of the building. In my defense, I was just trying to impress the hot chicks from ABC News, but that excuse didn't carry much weight at my network. For two days, NBC was banned from the studios. With the hostages about to land and NBC unable to feed live, Bill Small went apeshit, egged on by Becky Bell. I sat alone in my hotel room, head in hand, unable to believe my stupidity. Those chicks weren't even all that hot!

Credit goes to Yves Allard, our Paris engineer, for somehow persuading the Algerians that I didn't mean any disrespect, that this was not yet another example of a capitalist American riding roughshod over inferior Arab socialists. After Allard proffered our abject apologies to M. Abbas, the apoplectic station manager, NBC was permitted, fortunately for my career, to join the other networks in broadcasting the first pictures of the freed American diplomats.

So even as I worked my heart out, risking my neck all over the world, my on-air career, which appeared to be taking off splendidly, was actually on the skids. I wasn't overly upset about it, because I was already achieving my great ambition, covering world news as a producer and reporter, working with NBC's top teams. How long it would last, I figured, was out of my hands.

In the spring of 1980, Jerry Lamprecht, by now NBC's head of foreign coverage, called and asked me to go to Afghanistan to cover the war there. I had been to the country twice to report on the conflict from the Soviet side. This time, Lamprecht wanted me to report on the Islamic resistance. Would I go to Pakistan, he wondered, infiltrate across the Hindu Kush mountains, and travel with the Islamic Mujahideen inside Afghanistan? Oh, and by the way, would I do it alone, with a camera, working as a one-man band? I wouldn't have any of the moral and physical support of working in a team. We had no contacts among the rebels. I would be the first television reporter to go in, and I'd be on my own.

I might have declined, but that never occurred to me. Jerry is a close friend, a gifted producer, and one of the most knowledgeable journalists I have ever known. In his own quiet way, he was hilarious. He would end all disputes with colleagues, foreign dignitaries, and NBC executives by muttering, "I suppose a blow job's out of the question?" He was an old Visnews mate who became NBC's vice president in charge of all news coverage. Jerry was the reason it took Bill Small so long—about a year—to end my reporting career.

At first the Afghan assignment seemed quite a lark. Jerry had given me carte blanche to equip myself with the necessities for guerrilla war, so I headed straight to Au Vieux Campeur, Paris's top outdoor store. I bought myself a rain poncho, leather boots, yet another Swiss Army knife, a money belt, a water bottle, medicines and bandages, a fishing jacket with lots of little pockets for film and batteries, thick hiking socks, two hats, one for rain, one against the sun, and, as recompense for my anticipated discomfort, a handsome leather jacket, which went straight into my clothes closet. I managed to fit all the rest, plus mountain hiking clothes, into one medium-size backpack. In a second backpack, I carried a Canon Super-8 mm 814XLS film camera with a directional microphone, spare batteries, two dozen rolls of film, a tape recorder, and blank cassettes. To train for the trek, I climbed up and down the ten flights of stairs to my apartment while carrying Hagar on my back.

I had the gear, I was fit, but nothing could prepare me for what was to come. I arrived in Peshawar, situated nine miles east of the Khyber Pass, in June 1980. Peshawar was then a bustling frontier town in Pakistan's fabled North-West Frontier, the violent and mystical mountain land that defied the British Empire and inspired Rudyard Kipling to write the lines embedded in the memories of English schoolboys: "East is East, and West is West, and never the twain shall meet." Forbidding to outside powers because of its vast tribal patchwork of shifting loyalties, the North-West Frontier remains today one of the most likely hiding places of Osama bin Laden. Back in 1980, bin Laden was living somewhere in the teeming alleys and Afghan refugee camps on the outskirts of town. He was then a rich young Saudi looking for a way to fight Holy War, while I was a reasonably solvent young hack seeking a way to cover it.

Peshawar itself was hot, noisy, and dusty, its narrow streets clogged with foul-smelling old cars, donkey carts, and nervous, snorting camels. Barefooted men hauled barrows of goods, yelling their prices as they dodged the traffic. This little town was the main throughway for 1.5 million despondent and penniless refugees escaping the war in Afghanistan. The Red Army by now had spent six months destroying homes and villages, trying to force the Afghan people either into towns, where they could be controlled, or out of the country, where they would be somebody else's problem. Hundreds of thousands slept in the white aid tents set up in the dry plains on the town's outskirts, subsisting on the world's charity. Soviet spies circulated among them, as did Pakistani spies, Pushtun double agents, gunrunners, opium smugglers, and the leaders of seven Afghan rebel groups dedicated to fighting the Soviet army. These budding organizations were already jockeying for the power struggle they knew would follow the Communist invaders' inevitable defeat. From them would emerge the Taliban and the seeds of al-Qaeda.

Among the crowds, amid all the romance, intrigue, and danger of Peshawar, there I was, looking for someone to trust. I bought Afghan tribal clothes to blend in with the refugees and grew a beard. I called on the headquarters of the various rebel groups looking for English speakers, promising each group that I'd tell their story if they would take me with them inside Afghanistan. And all the while I tried to avoid the Pakistani secret police and the Soviets. Officials at the U.S. embassy had warned me not to cross into Afghanistan, and so had British diplomats and aid workers. The

Pakistani police were trying to keep foreign journalists out of Afghanistan and might not merely have turned me around; they could have jailed or deported me. Above all, I was told that I needed to beware the Soviets, since they wanted to make examples of any reporters they caught or killed to scare off other journalists.

I hooked up first with the Jamaat-e-Islami, an offshoot of the Muslim Brotherhood that eighteen months later would assassinate Egyptian president Anwar Sadat and that today is even better known as a forerunner of the Taliban. They proposed to take me to Jalalabad, one of the key towns in eastern Afghanistan, where daily battles erupted between the rebels and the Soviets. We would travel at first by bus, but then I would need to walk for a week across dangerous terrain. Would I be able to keep up? The Afghan fighters warned me that they couldn't slow down or cut me any slack, because they needed to evade Pakistani police, Soviet spies, and Afghan army units. No problem, I said.

On the day of our departure, my guide, who spoke some English, said, "If anyone asks where you're from, say Nuristan."

"All right," I said, "Nuristan. But how will I understand the question?"

"Nuristan," he said, "just say Nuristan."

I didn't get a chance to say even that. After a six-hour bus journey with my guide and several guards, the Pakistani police stopped us. Armed officers boarded the bus and walked slowly up the aisle staring into the face of each man until they came to me. I was wearing tribal clothes and hat, hadn't shaved for a week, and my chin touched my chest as I pretended to sleep. But a prod, a nod of the head, a flick of the wrist, and I was out. Clearly they were looking for foreigners.

I had mixed feelings. I wanted to get into Afghanistan, but on the other hand, if I couldn't, that wouldn't be so bad either. The closer I had gotten to this side of the war, the less enthusiastic I'd become. These were the early days of Islamic resistance, and it was amateur hour for the Holy Warriors. American money and CIA arms had not yet started to flow, nor had Arab funds from the Persian Gulf or Saudi Arabia. Poorly armed and disorganized, the Afghan rebels were taking heavy losses. Putting my life in the hands of these rustic fellows didn't seem so smart. Not that putting my career in the hands of Bill Small was smart either, I reflected ruefully, as we waited by the side of the road. Why am I going to such trouble, I thought, if my boss wants to fire me?

The bus back to Peshawar broke down, so we continued by hitch-hiking. Six Afghans and me, thumbing a ride. One had a seeping wound instead of an eye; another had a huge boil on his left cheek; another one, a long scar from his ear to his Adam's apple. Like them, I wore a long gray cotton shirt and an itchy woolen Chitrali hat that sat on my head like a pancake. I also wore enormously baggy cotton trousers that hung low to the knees. The Afghans believed that the Messiah would be born unexpectedly to a man whose pants would need to catch him.

Fortunately, a bus came by and picked us all up. It was so hot that we took turns sitting in the draft of the one window that opened. I was either terribly hot and damp or dry and cold. When I finally returned to the Inter-Continental Hotel in Peshawar after fourteen hours of fruitless driving, I was coughing and sneezing. A TV crew from ITN in London, led by John Suchet, an old BBC friend and colleague, had placed bets that I would fail, and they collapsed laughing upon seeing me stumble through the marble foyer. They had already failed twice to enter Afghanistan. It turned out I wasn't to be the first reporter to walk into Afghanistan. Dan Rather went in at the same time with his *60 Minutes* crew, earning himself the nickname Gunga Dan, although they came out much sooner. Arthur Kent, the brother of my flatmate in South Africa, Peter Kent, had gone in earlier.

A few illicit brandies restored my spirits, and two days later I tried again, this time with the largest of the guerrilla groups, the radical Islamic Hezbi Islami. Their leader, a hawk-faced, sinister man called Gulbuddin Hekmatyar, would become a hero of the anti-Soviet resistance and, later, a villain of the Afghan civil war. Gulbuddin lectured me on the failings of everything Western and the one path forward, total faith in Allah. Then he offered me guides and guards to witness his party's Jihad against the

Soviets. He made clear that he wanted me to communicate two things to America: Send weapons, and stay away. "Tell America we need antitank rockets and missiles to shoot down helicopters," he said. "Then we will defeat Communism alone."

The first part of our journey went well enough: eight hours in a Datsun pickup bumping along a dried-out riverbed until the rocks closed in and the driver turned back. Then the climbing began, and a storm whipped up around us. At ten thousand feet in the Hindu Kush, pounding rain churned the stone-and-earth precipice into mud. The slippery ledge, thirty inches wide, hugged the mountainside, with a drop into bushes and trees, then a sudden plunge to the valley far below. Biting wind howled and cut into my eyes. At one point, I slipped and desperately dug my knee into the *karez,* the low irrigation channel carved into the rock that funnels water from village to village. I grabbed a plant growing from a rock crevice and hung on for dear life as Abdul Sadr, my guide and new friend, gently helped me to my feet.

Abdul Sadr was about twenty-five years old, dark-skinned, with straight black hair and a slow smile. His hands were as soft and unused to manual work as mine. As we walked, he told me that his father was a mullah who'd joined the Afghan army and rose to the rank of major general before defecting, like many Afghan army soldiers, to the Mujahideen. Unlike many other parents, Abdul Sadr's father had demanded that his children pray and study. They could leave the house only with his permission. The strict regimen paid off. One brother was now a doctor, the other a university lecturer. Abdul had studied English, and somebody had evidently done a good job, for he spoke quietly, carefully, and fluently.

The storm slowed us down, but as suddenly as it came, it ended. Rays of white light pulsed through the dark clouds, and the wind dropped. A blue sky emerged, and the hot sun began to dry us as we climbed higher and higher, panting in the thin air, heading for the white peaks of the mountain wall that protects Afghanistan from invaders. Then a quick thudding echoed in the distance, becoming closer and louder: deadly M1-24 attack helicopters, the Soviet flying tanks. A patrol of two whirred up the valley, hunting the enemy. The Afghan Mujahideen, the Holy Warriors, fell to their knees, covering themselves in their earth brown shawls, and I did the same. All the Soviet gunners would have seen were a few dozen gray-brown boulders strewn along the mountain pass. When the choppers disappeared up the valley, the Afghan mountain fighters stood and resumed their climb.

The hours passed and turned into days. As the Mujahideen walked, they leaned sharply forward, the weight of their upper bodies obliging the lower halves to follow, wiry legs pumping at a relentless pace, almost running. They were sure-footed like mountain goats. Each carried a backpack of flour to make bread, a weapon, and ammunition belts. I followed, exhausted, stumbling and wheezing, disguised in drenched and mud-sodden tribal clothing, cursing Jerry Lamprecht and his harebrained scheme.

Our destination was a village called Naray in Kunar province. One of the key Soviet aims at this early stage of the war was to denude the border areas of people, depriving the insurgents of local support and preventing guerrillas from crossing from Pakistan. Naray had already been attacked eight times, and most of the residents had fled to the refugee camps in Pakistan. The group of thirty-five Mujahideen I was trying so hard to keep up with wanted to reach their homes and see the damage. They also wanted to kill as many Soviets as possible, as well as Afghan army soldiers, whom the rebels called "Afghan Communist collaborators."

Each man I walked with carried a weapon. Five were armed with Soviet Kalashnikov assault rifles with magazines of thirty rounds; the rest had a mixture of hunting rifles, single-shot bolt-action rifles, and pistols. Magazines of about fifty rounds crisscrossed their chests. They looked good on my film, with their beards, hooked noses, and fierce eyes. They waved their weapons as they walked, but they were no match for the Soviet tanks, helicopters, and machine guns, or the elite Soviet Spetsnaz mountain troops. On the other hand, there is an old Afghan proverb: "Oh, foreigner, do not attack us—attacking is our job!" What the Mujahideen lacked in firepower, they more than made up for in stamina and conviction.

We walked twenty miles a day, mostly through the night and the early morning hours to avoid the heat. From time to time, we stopped at the mountain peaks to rest and to pray. The Mujahideen prayed a full five times a day, although, since they were waging Jihad, the requirement to recite four Koran verses each time was reduced to only two. The men sang as they marched, tribal chants in praise of their land and their women. They were happy to be going home. I, meanwhile, struggled to keep up. Aside from Jerry Lamprecht, I cursed my smart new leather boots from Au Vieux Campeur. I had huge, painful blisters on my heels and toes. The Mujahideen walked in plastic sandals if they were lucky; most had only cow skin wrapped around their legs and feet, leaving the big toes and heels exposed. The cowhide was wrapped tight with thongs made from other parts of the cow.

I regret to say that I slowed them down and was a burden. Throughout this trek, I was bathed in sweat and at the limit of my strength. Two Mujahideen had to carry my backpacks. In one bag was all my camera gear, in the other my clothes. I had long since dumped most of my Paris bounty. As Abdul Sadr and I had sat down to our first meal, at a dirty roadside eatery still inside Pakistan and I picked at unidentifiable chunks of meat and fat floating in grease, he had asked if I'd brought antibiotics. "No," I answered, "but I do have painkillers." "Oh, good," he said, "you'll need them."

We carried no water, drinking instead from cold, fresh mountain streams. We also had no food, save flour with which to bake bread. We relied on ragged villagers, who would emerge from destroyed mud homes as we passed and provide us with a gruel of vegetables and animal fat. We slept in huts or under trees, spread out across the hillside in case of attack. I dreamed of home.

In his village, Abdul Sadr explained, his family was respected. They did not sleep with the animals. His father had taught him that bribery, embezzlement, and theft were bad traditions that should be punished, and that he should always tell the truth. Unfortunately for me, my Mujahideen guards did not receive the same training. When one of the fighters carrying my bags began to drop back, in my hyperalert state I immediately understood why. It was clear he didn't have to lag behind. He was short and squat with huge calves and strong as a horse. The idea that I could walk faster than he was laughable. He was carrying my personal stuff, and I knew he wanted to rob me. But what to do?

I didn't consult with Abdul Sadr. I knew he'd be outraged and would probably confront the thief. Then the thief would deny it and claim that Abdul had insulted him. Either way, it would end badly. If the porter was outed as a thief, I imagined he could have his right hand cut off. Or if he got away with it and felt insulted, he could demand satisfaction and fight Abdul Sadr. That was all I needed, to cause a war among my guards. So I kept quiet, but I knew I needed to let the porter find something worth having or I wouldn't sleep soundly again. If he didn't find money in my bag, he'd know I'd hidden it on my body, and I would not be safe. My life was in the hands of these simple folk. They were all killers, but they were my killers, and I needed to keep it that way.

I carried all my cash, two thousand dollars, in a money bag around my waist. That night I took out four hundred in twenty-dollar bills, wrapped it in a pair of socks, and slipped the socks inside the backpack. The next morning, the Holy Warrior lagged behind again, and sure enough, when I checked the bag that night, the money was gone. The next day he stormed ahead and the problem was over.

No wonder he had a bounce in his step. The average annual income of an Afghan peasant then was sixty dollars. I had bought my safety for four hundred. When I tried to claim the money back from NBC, they refused to pay, admonishing me for not having a receipt. I sensed in this the hand of Becky Bell, my bureau chief in Paris, who went through my expense accounts like Sherlock Holmes hunting for Moriarty. Any financial hanky-panky and she and Bill Small would have flung me over the Reichenbach Falls.

Despite the dangers, the trek through the Hindu Kush was one of the most beautiful experiences of my life. I climbed across wild and craggy mountain terrain, saw distant peaks like the knuckles of a fist, softened by lush hills in shades of green. Fields of flowers spread out before me, alive with the squalls and croaks of wheeling birds. Leaves and pine needles carpeted the paths, and the waterfalls and rushing streams sparkled in the sun, changing colors as the clouds moved. We crossed a fast-flowing river on a raft of a dozen cow skins pumped full of air like hairy balloons tied to sticks and branches. We passed refugees heading for safety in Pakistan, prodding cows and goats, carrying wooden logs on their heads and babies on their backs, and we exchanged news and gave advice. We stopped for tea at every abandoned village, for everywhere one or two people had stayed behind, as if to bear witness. When we passed a cemetery, the Mujahideen took off their shoes in a show of respect for the dead. They said a quick prayer, made a slow wiping gesture down their faces, and walked on.

One night we stayed in a large hut overlooking rolling, billowing mountains. A thunderstorm passed, and flashes of lightning lit up the peaks and valleys. We sheltered around a small fire and shared a bowl of broth prepared by the hut's inhabitants, a man and his four sons. Their women had fled to the Pakistani camps. We tore pieces of fresh bread with our right hands, dipped them in the broth, and drank sweet tea. The Afghans use their left hands to wipe their bottoms and their right to eat; that's why cutting off the right hand of a thief is such a severe punishment. Not only does he lose the hand but he also loses the ability to eat with his friends, for nobody would eat from a bowl used by the left hand of a man. He becomes an outcast. I was adapting quickly. In my notes on this meal, I wrote, "It is all very civilized."

The hut had whitewashed walls, and as the men leaned forward to dip their bread or stand up, the fire threw their shadows—billowing clothes, hooked noses, rifles—across the walls in a play of light and dark like a shadow theater. The other rooms were covered with colored rugs and lit by little gas lamps. We slept on a floor soft with hay and rugs, a dozen of us covering every inch as the rain beat on the wood-and-mud roof. Guns were piled in a corner, and the four sons took turns guarding us.

The next morning we were joined by more refugees from near Naray, and the news they brought was bad. Columns of Soviet tanks and troops were reaching the area, readying for yet another assault on Naray and the surrounding villages. Most of the fighters had left, but some groups hiding in mountains nearby were preparing to harass the Soviets. They had no hope of winning a direct confrontation, but they could worry and wound the soldiers. My group was torn. They wanted to hurry on to Naray, but clearly they had no stomach for a real war with the Soviets. Their weaponry was good only for a stealthy night ambush, or for robbing foolish journalists. The decision to go on or return to Pakistan was delayed by torrential rain, which forced us to spend the early morning in the hut.

I was grateful for the rest, and also for the opportunity to talk quietly with Abdul Sadr. I tape-recorded our conversation to use for some radio reports. "We are losing control of our country," Abdul said. "But we will never lose control of our lives. With these weapons we cannot defeat the Soviet army, but they cannot defeat our minds. We will never stop fighting, never, never. Time is on our side. They will be sorry they ever came to my country. We would rather die in Jihad than live against Allah."

Abdul's words and the sentiment they conveyed were not unique. Every Islamic militant, in Iran, Afghanistan, and Gaza, has said the same thing. What was different was the dramatic backdrop to Abdul's passion. It was dawn, and the sun was rising over the Hindu Kush. The brilliant stars were fading and the moon retreating as day broke. Mountain peaks were bathed in orange, and shadows crept down the hillside. The only sounds came from the birds and the crackling fire. The rain had stopped, and the air smelled of wet pine. God seems present at these times and in these places, closer to the soul than amid the cacophony we have constructed to accompany our Western lives.

In these fierce hills, less is more. The refrain "There is no God but God" rarely touches as it does here. In Abdul I felt it and understood it in a way I never had before or have again. The Soviets offered equality in life and material goods, in theory at least, and the Americans offer equal opportunity to accumulate assets such as man had never imagined; but who needs it when God is so close? Did I agree with how these mountain Muslims punished crime or oppressed their women, their religious bigotry or their worship of martyrdom? No. Did I understand where they were coming from and where they hoped to go? Yes! As I sat beside Abdul, the career difficulties I suffered as an American network reporter with a British accent seemed irrelevant. Let them fire me, I thought; I'll buy some land in the Hindu Kush. Should be cheap.

Abdul continued: "Some people think if you brush against a Russian, you should cut off your clothing that touched his, because they do not believe in God." Yet one thing was even stronger than Islam, and that was the tribe. "We Pushtun live on both sides of the border, in Afghanistan and Pakistan. We come, we go, and no one can stop us. All Pushtun are fighters. We fight for each other. We have big families, and if anybody is killed, we will avenge them. There is no end in the fight with nonbelievers. It is my tribe and Allah. How can anybody defeat us? This war will never end until they run away."

It was military might against the power of the people, their faith in Allah, and I had seen it all before. Two years earlier, when I had first flown into Tehran to cover the Iranian revolution, I had been stunned by the vastness of the shah's army. The Air France jet descended toward the runway of Tehran's MehrAbad Airport, passing the military airfield. We flew past miles of armor: hundreds of jet fighters, hundreds of armored helicopters, hundreds of tanks and armored personnel carriers, acres of jeeps with machine guns mounted on the backs, military vehicles of a kind I had never seen, dozens of models, thousands of them, all lined up in endless rows, flashing by through the windows as the airliner dropped and flattened to land. It was a display of military might that could never be defeated, I felt. How could unarmed followers of the old graybeard Ayatollah Khomeini have a hope against one of the world's largest and best-equipped armies? It'll be a massacre, I thought, a genocide.

But then the next day I went into the streets to witness a demonstration calling for Khomeini's return from exile in Paris. Again, I was stunned. My TV crew and I couldn't walk. Bodies crammed against bodies; there was not an inch of pavement to spare. We took the elevator to the top of the InterContinental Hotel and went out onto the roof to survey the scene. Every street in every direction was packed with black-clad men and women, yelling, *"Marjd-el-Shah!"*—"Death to the shah."

The demonstrators said there were 2 million people in the streets. The next day there was another gigantic protest, and the police kept well away. As I struggled through the crowds, talking to students and doctors, fathers with little boys on their shoulders and old women with covered faces and big, peasant hands, it was clear to me: Even guns have their limits. The shah's secret police could kill twenty a day, or even fifty, without the world taking note. But nobody could support the shah if he massacred his own people. Khomeini would return, and the shah would either be killed or run away. The power of the people would win in the end.

Would this prove true in Afghanistan? As Abdul Sadr spoke, in his calm, strong way, about the power of tribe and Allah, it certainly seemed so. Torture and murder work by forcing the other side into submission. But against these radical Muslims, for whom the very word *Islam* means "submission"—submission to Allah—there is no way to win. They cannot submit again, to the gun, because they have already submitted to God, who promises salvation in Paradise. How can you break the spirit of a man whose spirit has been claimed by Allah?

As Abdul Sadr explained his faith and his heritage, I didn't feel quite so sorry for this bunch of underequipped mountain men going to what I considered a certain death. Instead, I began to feel sorry for myself. If the Mujahideen died fighting, they would go to Paradise. But where would I go? As I understood that fear was not part of their makeup, fear quickly entered my personal calculation. To hell with Lamprecht, I thought. To hell, too, with Paradise. I just want to go home in one piece.

After the rain stopped and the Mujahideen drank their delicious sweet tea, they decided to continue. They set off again at a blistering pace, with Abdul and me in hot pursuit. Naray was about a day's march away, and the Mujahideen were anxious to join the fray. They had no means of communication, apart from my small transistor radio, on which they listened to the BBC Pushtun-language broadcasts, but the news brought earlier by the refugees had galvanized them. Abdul and I barely kept up, and we didn't exchange a word again till close to midday, when they stopped to pray and rest in the shade of trees by a mountain stream. By now we had been under way for five days, climbing and walking ten hours a day, and I was exhausted.

The Mujahideen washed their hands and feet before prayer, but otherwise they were stale and sweaty and smelly, and so was I. I decided to wash in the stream. The stories of Afghan homosexuality and sodomy, especially toward prisoners, which I effectively was, were legendary, so I walked upstream a bit until I came upon a hollow in the rock face with a shallow pool surrounded by bushes. I stripped down to my underpants, glanced around, and ripped them off. Lying facedown in the icy water, I dunked my head several times, my skin tingling until my body temperature fell. The clear water enveloped me. Because my head was half underwater, I didn't notice anybody approaching. Then the water rippled and I saw two Mujahideen sitting on rocks nearby, talking and laughing. My pale body interested them. I sat up sharply, dressed, and took my leave.

So far, the film I had shot of the Mujahideen at war was pretty thin. There are only so many ways you can depict thirty-five guys marching, praying, and eating. Each time we had come close to Soviet helicopters, we had hidden under our cloaks or under trees. I couldn't film the choppers because it was sunny, and if I had pointed the lens toward them, their gunners would have seen the sun reflecting off it. I may as well have given our position away with a mirror. I filmed what I saw along the way, but that wasn't much. We had passed the skeletons of mules that had died in the winter, and we had seen wounded Mujahideen helping one another back to Pakistan. I had interviewed Abdul Sadr in English, but he was more of a guide than a real fighter.

In one valley we had come across a party of Mujahideen who had captured an old Soviet armored personnel carrier. They drove it around for me but couldn't put it into reverse, so last seen they were clanking off into the distance looking for a place wide enough to turn around in. Nice pictures, but to satisfy NBC, I needed a war, and quick. I didn't want to spend the next two months wandering around Afghanistan. Anyway, I had gotten the message. Without Stinger missiles and rocket-propelled grenades, these Holy Warriors, despite their faith in Allah, didn't have a prayer against the Soviets.

The next afternoon we arrived, at last, at a peak overlooking Naray, way down on the valley floor. We could make out fires and smoke, and traffic on the roads, which must have been Soviet vehicles, but we were still too far away to assess any damage. Now our challenge was to descend without being spotted. We found some flat ground in a wooded gulley and spent a chilly few hours hunkered down, waiting for the cover of darkness. Around midnight, we began the descent. A half-moon lit the way, and it was surprisingly easy going. I was getting used to the inclines, the loose rocks and treacherous ledges. We moved slowly among pine trees and down gullies, carefully staying in the shadows. The Mujahideen feared Soviet patrols, or even their collaborators in the Afghan army, as they put it.

Despite the drama and tension, I still didn't have much worthwhile footage. I couldn't film our descent because it was nighttime. We walked for a couple of hours and were about halfway down the mountain when to the left a sudden volley of machine-gun fire rang out, not so far away. Another burst followed, and then single cracks and flares that hung low in the sky and threw white light onto the ground. The moon shadows of trees disappeared in a flash and a glare, and patches of the mountain became clear as day. We hurled ourselves to the ground, although, luckily, we were still in the darkness. The action was a few hundred yards away. I began to tremble. I had the camera, but I didn't want any of the little red and green lights of the control panel to betray our position.

Suddenly there was a terrific blast, and another one, about half a mile away on our hillside. We didn't know what was going on. Nobody moved. We heard faint shouts in the distance. I couldn't hear if it was Russian or Afghan, but I could make out Abdul's wide eyes. He was terrified, and so was I. It was like a horror movie, where all the action echoes offscreen. The worst thing was that I didn't trust my companions. I was scared they would throw themselves at the enemy, seeking martyrdom and leaving me to find my own way to Paradise. But as I raised my head, there didn't seem much danger of that. The few Mujahideen who hadn't legged it were curled up into balls every bit as tight as mine. Their preferred posture when confronting Soviet Spetsnaz troops appeared to be the fetal position.

It all suddenly seemed ridiculous. There was no point putting my life in danger if I couldn't work, and I couldn't work because my life was in danger. What were these bearded bozos thinking? How could they take on the Soviets? My only hope was that their leader in Peshawar, Gulbuddin Hekmatyar, had adequately stressed that they were to guide me in and out again safely. This was not really a war party, I believed, but a group of refugees on a recce to their home, with a brief to kill any enemy they came across but not, I hoped, to engage a mighty Soviet armored column accompanied by a dozen armored M1-24 helicopters, let alone elite Soviet mountain troops lying in ambush along the guerrilla infiltration routes from Pakistan, such as the one we were traveling on.

The flares faded, and the mountain fell again into darkness. The already faint voices grew fainter. The action was moving away from us. But we didn't move for several hours. Maybe some of the Mujahideen had fallen asleep. Many of a war correspondent's assignments lead to the anguished query "What the hell am I doing here?" and this was another one of those. Earlier, Abdul Sadr had attempted to explain to me that his attitude toward death evolved from *kismet,* the Afghan notion that everything is destiny, or the will of Allah. *Makhtoub* in Egypt means the same, and in some forms of Christianity the concept is known as *predestination.* I was more familiar with the word *beschert,* which is Yiddish for "meant to be." I had plenty of time to ruminate on this concept as I froze on the slopes of the Hindu Kush. Personally, I preferred the more individualistic free choice of Western thought, and my choice right now was to get the hell away from Naray and head back to safety. *Makhtoub* for me at that moment was a stiff brandy from John Suchet's secret stash at the alcohol-free Peshawar InterContinental.

As my muscles stiffened in the cold, I remembered another moment when I had wished for a stiff brandy at another InterContinental, the NBC hotel in Tehran a year earlier. Then, too, I had almost pushed myself too far for a story about Islamic militants. The Iranian students holding the U.S. diplomats hostage had gotten it into their heads that among the foreign press besieging the gates of the embassy there was an American spy—me. The day before, they had spotted me atop a nearby building as my camera crew filmed inside the embassy. The students grabbed us, seized our tapes, and, apparently, by a complete fluke, my cameraman had zoomed into an opening that the students called "the secret door."

The next day, I returned with a different crew. Half a dozen armed students pulled me from the crowd of journalists and tried to bundle me into a car. At first I resisted, but I caved when one of the students hit me on the head with his gun. They drove me to the InterContinental, sandwiched on the backseat between unshaven men carrying Uzi machine guns under their green combat jackets. There they searched my room for spy apparatus. Up to that point, I hadn't been afraid, safe in the knowledge that they wouldn't find anything and glowing with the prospect of the world-beating story I would soon file. However, when their search came up empty, they didn't drive me straight to the embassy, and that's when I got scared. Where were we going? Did these goons really think I was a spy? I could be in deep trouble.

After about twenty minutes, we reached the embassy the back way, avoiding the press. My captors brought me to a room where they had kept the camera crew arrested with me and treated us rather well. Later I learned that NBC had appealed to the Iranian foreign minister, who in those early days of the siege still held some sway with the students. He was negotiating for our release. Although I was unaware of the efforts to free us, my spirits rose. I was confident again that we would soon be freed. After all, I really wasn't a spy. And now, I realized, I had a genuine scoop. I was the first reporter to get inside the occupied U.S. embassy. I didn't see any hostages, but I did talk to one of the student leaders, who assured me that no American hostages would be freed early. There had been rumors that the women and black males, diplomats and marines, would soon be freed. "Forget it," he said, "no way."

After nine hours, the students let us go, and I had my scoop—no early release. I informed the world, and NBC was over the moon with our exclusive story. I basked in the glory for one day, until the next day the students released the women and the black males.

You really can't trust anybody, I reflected back on the mountainside, as I watched the Mujahideen powwow briefly before dawn. Yet all of a sudden it appeared that they did share my concept of free will and destiny, after all, for they stood, stretched, and began the long trek back to the border.

Looking back on it, I see that our foray to Naray conformed to the message on a T-shirt that some judicious journalists had made during the civil war in Beirut: "We came, we saw, we legged it." Naray would have to wait. My comrades weren't afraid; they had just made a rational choice. The Soviets were far too powerful, and as much as the Mujahideen genuinely embraced martyrdom, it was pointless to throw away their lives.

Our trek home was every bit as fraught as the journey in. I heard on the BBC World Service radio broadcast that the Soviets had introduced a new tactic. Their helicopters were flying low over the mountain trails used by the Mujahideen from Pakistan, dropping antipersonnel land mines to maim and kill them. We soon saw the proof. The mines were small explosives disguised as cigarette packets, transistor radios, flashlights, and clips of banknotes. Others looked like stones or rocks; their aim was to blow off the hands or feet of the victims. The Soviet tactic was not to kill but to wound and maim so as to force guerrillas to carry the victims back to Pakistan. Some of the land mines were even disguised as toys to attract children. It was a fearsome tactic that wounded more children and old folks escaping from the fighting than guerrillas. Still partly traumatized by the minefield in Cyprus, when my soundman was killed and my friends wounded by land mines, I found myself in a funk. Yet there was no choice but to follow the Mujahideen, who believed in Allah enough to ignore the threat. They laughed and sang as I stared at the ground and picked my way painfully past each suspicious stone.

It took six days to reach the hills above Naray, and another five to go back. We heard the sounds of war, distant explosions, and low-flying planes, and saw the cost: terrified refugees, wounded Mujahideen, and the occasional captured Soviet vehicle. Yet we never came close enough to film any fighting. My guerrilla comrades avoided roads and even many of the dirt tracks, preferring to clamber up and down virgin hillside rather than risk being ambushed on the regular infiltration routes. That alone spoke volumes about the weakness of the Mujahideen and their need for modern weapons, but when I returned to the Hezbi Islami headquarters in Peshawar and made the mistake of speaking frankly about Mujahideen deficiencies, officials of the Islamic Party fell strangely silent. I had seen what they wanted me to see, but they were not pleased. My message offended their honor, and honor, I had come to understand, was the pivot around which all else—family, tribe, nationalism, Islam—revolved. Islam was the rallying cry of resistance, but honor was the source.

The next year, I witnessed the birth of Hizbullah, the radical Shiite response to Israel's occupation of South Lebanon in 1982. Five years later, in 1987, I was also present when Sheikh Ahmed Yassin founded Hamas, which was an Islamic response to Israel's suppression of the first Intifada. Hamas remains an incendiary mix of Palestinian nationalism and Islamic fundamentalism united by the demand for an Islamic state in all of Palestine. As I got to know Hamas and Hizbullah, I recognized them as versions of the earlier Afghan liberation movements. Each of these groups told its followers: Time is on our side. Each grounded its ideology of nationalism and fundamentalism on that potent mix of family, tribe, and honor. Whenever I spoke to Hamas or Hizbullah members, they reminded me of Abdul Sadr. But to me, his fervor was distorted by their methods—suicide bombs, kidnappings, and, in the case of al-Qaeda, beheadings. These were Rip van Winkle warriors, I thought, assassins from the Dark Ages awoken in modern times. They would no longer go quietly into the night.

. . .

Gulbuddin Hekmatyar was not in Peshawar when I returned from Afghanistan, and I never saw him again. Instead, a much lower functionary, Mangal Hussain, an unctious man in his late twenties, received me. He spoke excellent English and used it to try to browbeat me into admitting that the Mujahideen were invincible warriors who terrified the Soviet infidels. I explained that I had seen no evidence of this, and I outlined what disappointing pictures I had been able to film, which together would hardly make three minutes of television. I understood, however, that Mangal Hussain was leading me somewhere, and we soon arrived. Did I want to buy some film? He had film of the Mujahideen fighting the Soviet troops, and, if I handed over enough money, he would give it exclusively to me. He wanted me to take nine undeveloped Super-8 film cassettes, which he promised showed dramatic pictures of the Mujahideen burning Soviet tanks and killing Soviet soldiers, use them as part of my stories, and then return them so that Mujahideen emissaries could take them to the Persian Gulf to help raise funds. Oh, and that would be $2,500, payable part now, part after I had used the film.

I was delighted. Hussain had saved me; his pictures would add the tension and conflict that mine lacked. I could return home a hero after all with Afghan combat footage that had rarely been seen. Yet it was not to be. When NBC developed the film in London, the pictures turned out to be much tamer than advertised. To make matters worse, some of the emulsion had rubbed off, rendering about a third of my film useless. I had had a tiring, dangerous adventure, the hardest of my life, and could show little for it. My budding career as an NBC reporter took a blow, but much worse was to come.

Bill Small demanded loyalty, but he didn't show it to a reporter with a British accent. My work in Afghanistan and other dumps counted for little with him. Jerry Lamprecht was able to put off the bullet, but slowly Small pushed me off the air. After Afghanistan, my reporting assignments became few and far between, and I returned to producing. When the boot finally fell, it wasn't so bad. Small sidelined me to Frankfurt as the temporary bureau chief. I was wary of the word *temporary* but agreed anyway. My friends thought that the posting was the kiss of death, that a permanent bureau chief would be found and I would be fired. But I always looked for the silver lining. I spoke German, and even once worked as a German translator. Now I would have the opportunity to perfect my language skills and become more familiar with German culture.

I understood, however, that this was the end of my brief and not-quite-glorious career as an American network correspondent. I thought I had done well. I had taken a big risk and a drop in status and salary when I left the BBC to become an agency cameraman. But in a few short years I had joined NBC and moved from cameraman to producer, a rare but not unheard-of promotion. Then I became a reporter, which for a former network cameraman was almost unique. And I was the first American network reporter with a British accent. Maybe, I thought, I had risen too far, too fast. Like Icarus, I had flown too close to the sun. Burned by Bill and Becky, I believed.

But then, before I even moved into my new house in Frankfurt, my luck turned yet again. In March 1982, Bill Small was out of NBC News and was replaced by one of the great pioneers of television journalism, Reuven Frank, who began his second incarnation as leader of the news division. I had never met Frank, or the man he appointed as his number-two, Tom Pettit, who had been a longtime NBC correspondent in Washington. But my first-ever phone conversation with Tom changed my life. I was sitting at my desk in the Frankfurt bureau, wondering how to get Hagar to leave Paris, which she adored, and join me in Frankfurt, which she hated, when the phone rang.

"Hello, Martin. This is Tom Pettit."

"Oh. Hello, Tom."

"Martin, Reuven and I want you to be the NBC correspondent in Israel. Do you want the job?"

"Yes." Yes! Yes!

"Okay, we'll deal with salary and stuff another time. You got the job. When can you start?"

"This afternoon. But what about my accent?"

"Don't worry about that," Tom said. "We're the ones with the accent."

Five

The Home Front

Pettit's phone call made not only my career but my marriage.

Hagar was now pregnant. A few months earlier, we had exchanged brief vows in a scruffy courtroom in the American Virgin Islands—far from the trauma of a family wedding. The witnesses in a criminal trial did extra duty as the witnesses to our marriage. But back home, Hagar was desperately delaying her arrival in Frankfurt, preferring life in Paris. Who wouldn't? Then Pettit's call came through, and we began to dream and prepare for an idyllic family life in the Holy Land. Since the Israeli-Egypt Accord in 1979, Israel had been pretty calm. True, it had been just as calm when I began my previous assignment, one week before the 1973 Arab-Israeli war. I was bad news wherever I went. Four days after I went to Cyprus, the Turks invaded. We joked that, if I were coming to Israel, war would certainly follow. Sure enough, three days after Tom Pettit handed me the coveted correspondent's job, Israel invaded Lebanon to destroy Yasir Arafat's PLO. Pettit called again, a slight edge to his voice: "Get there, now!"

This time I couldn't, for I was sick. A strong, dry cough shook my body and wouldn't go away. I swallowed with difficulty, and then the coughing started again. German doctors couldn't explain it. After a week of fruitless tests, I flew to London to see a specialist. He peered down my throat but found nothing. Then he asked, "Have you experienced any changes in your life recently?"

"Well, my girlfriend got pregnant, we married, I've got a new job, and I'm moving to a new country."

"That'll explain it." He laughed. "You need to reduce your stress levels."

Since there was nothing physically wrong with me, I decided to head straight to war. Two days later, I was on the outskirts of the city of Tyre in South Lebanon, hiding behind an Israeli tank as the gunner fired furiously at Palestinian militiamen. Mortars exploded all around, and wounded men screamed for help. Then I realized that my coughing had stopped. I had found a way to reduce my stress.

Crammed against the side of the tank with me was my new driver, the larger-than-life Amikam Cohen, an ebullient thug who follows his belly into a room, grinning hugely, his arms spread wide as if waiting for applause: "Marteen, I love you like my brother!" Never has the term *driver* so mismatched the man. He was soon in the doghouse, yet again, for throwing NBC's former top anchorman, John Chancellor, out of his car, yelling at Chancellor, "In New York you may be the beeeg shot, but here you are nobody!"

Chancellor's furious response was "I'll make sure they fire you!"

Chancellor had made the mistake of telling Amikam that he wanted to leave Beirut and drive to Israel as quickly as possible. So, instead of following the route through the Shuf Mountains, which took three hours longer but would avoid the bombing, shelling, and sniping of the war along the coast, Amikam took Chancellor at his word. He drove straight down Sniper Alley by the airport, taking a shortcut across the tarmac, slaloming at high speed around the deep shell holes to befuddle the gunmen. Chancellor flew around the backseat, while his producer, sitting in the front passenger seat, buried his head below the dashboard, screaming at Amikam to slow down. By the time they emerged at the safer end of Sniper Alley, everybody in the car was screaming at everybody else. Amikam jerked to a halt, flung open Chancellor's door, and told him to shut up or walk home.

Because Amikam was invaluable, he kept his job. He loved to tell the story, adding a colorful detail here, a dramatic twist there, until, like most of his stories, it bore only the barest resemblance to the facts: " 'Choncellor,' I said, 'Fock you!' "

Over the years, Amikam became my occasional cameraman, soundman, producer, and, some would say, boss. He kept me safe and got me to the story. A soldier's "No!" to Amikam meant "Find another way." We bypassed army roadblocks in the dead of night, shutting off our lights and racing through plowed fields and olive groves and along sandy beaches. Nothing and nobody stopped Amikam. If stone-throwing Palestinians blocked our way, Amikam put his foot on the gas and raced forward, scattering them, giving my thigh a stinging whack, yelling, *"Alti dag, Marteen, ata itee!"*—"Don't worry, Martin, you're with me!" Under his seat, he kept his Smith & Wesson Bodyguard, a .38 caliber, nine-millimeter revolver. He also kept a heavy wooden club, "just in case I run out of bullets." I pretended not to know.

Covering Israel with Amikam began for me as just another war story. But slowly, things changed. Maybe it was the birth of my first son, Guy, in 1982, or of my second son, Daniel, five years later, or my third, Jonathan, the year after that. Maybe it was the location of this war—at home, close to my own life and family. Whatever the case, I began to think differently about the events I covered. I began to look closely and try to understand what I was witnessing, rather than rush from assignment to assignment. Previously, I had looked to my work as a source of adventure and excitement, treasuring the feeling of being there first and traveling by the seat of my pants. Now, I started to develop—dare I say it—emotional responses. In Israel, for the first time in my career, it was the people who interested me, not merely the action.

Although this evolution in my perception occurred gradually, one violent incident served as a catalyst, altering the way I saw and reported on the world.

The NBC cameraman Rafi Kornfeld, who had been severely wounded in the 1973 war, was filming a minor demonstration on a street corner in the Nablus casbah. It was a routine clash during the first Palestinian Intifada. Palestinians were at one end of a street throwing stones and rocks, the Israeli soldiers fifty yards away firing with rubber bullets and tear gas. Whenever the soldiers charged, the boys fled. When the Israelis pulled back, the boys returned. It went on like this all day.

Rafi got there midafternoon, just as the young Israeli commander lost his cool. The soldier flagged down a passing Mercedes, hauled out the young Palestinian driver, and forced him to stand on the car's hood. "Tell them to stop," the Israeli soldier yelled. His victim refused. But seeing the Palestinian being threatened by an armed soldier, the boys stopped for a moment, confused, not wanting to hit the Palestinian with their stones. Then they started again, and a hail of stones scattered around the car and the soldiers. "Tell them to stop," the soldier screamed, his face contorted in rage, and this time he raised his wooden club and cracked the Palestinian on the head.

Seeing this, the boys stopped and melted away. The street went quiet. The soldier released the Palestinian, who quickly drove away. Passing Rafi, he flashed a V sign at the camera and yelled, "PLO, PLO!" A minute later the Palestinian boys returned, throwing more stones, and the Israeli soldiers rushed after them, firing tear gas.

It was a powerful scene caught on tape, and I wrote a short story for the *Nightly News* describing the drama's pointlessness. It was now several months into the first Intifada. We had broadcast dozens of stories like this, though maybe not quite so good. But after the show, at two o'clock in the morning Israel time, in the edit room at our office in Herzliya Studios, I asked the editor to play and replay the original tape. It was, I thought, a great television story. It had it all, in the simplest of terms: conflict, violence, pathos. Good guy and bad guy. Arab and Jew. Neat symbols—sticks and stones.

I asked the editor to show over and over again the point where the soldier hit the Palestinian on the head. Each time, I winced as the club hit bone. The popping sound made you feel it. But despite the soldier's fury, I realized, it wasn't much of a blow. More like a tap. Almost a regretful tap, not much more than the sound of a door knocker. The Palestinian didn't jerk his head back in pain, nor did he stumble from the force of the blow. Under the circumstances, the soldier seemed almost apologetic in his use of force. When he finally allowed the Palestinian to leave, the soldier offered him a hand to climb down from the hood.

As I looked again at the frozen moment of the soldier clubbing the man, I wondered: Who was this young soldier, with his helmet pitched boyishly over his eyes? In his screwed-up eyes, I now sensed as much fear as fury. And who was the Palestinian? He seemed quite calm. Did this often happen to him? Was he terrified, or was this normal? Why did the soldier do it? What did the Palestinian feel? Is there a difference, morally, between a light tap on the head and an almighty blow?

I quickly answered this last question—sure, there's a big difference, if you're the Arab getting hit. But other questions popped up. Were this Arab and Jew enemies? Did they hate each other, or was this to them more like being mugged on the street—an unfortunate encounter, further proof that you lived in a tough neighborhood? And their parents: Where did they live? What did they think about what their children were up to? After all this, could they ever make peace?

Driving home through the peaceful avenues of Herzliya Pituach, less than thirty miles away from the mayhem of Nablus, I decided to find the Arab and the Jew, the soldier and his victim, and ask them.

For three months, we couldn't spare the resources. We were swamped by the storm of the uprising. With daily violence still leading the news, *Nightly News* didn't care what an Arab and a Jew thought about each other. Finally I sold the story to the more reflective, and longer, weekend morning news.

Now our challenge was to find the two men. We gave a Polaroid picture of the Palestinian victim to Awad, a Palestinian tipper, to show around in Nablus. It was hard at first, because nobody trusted Awad. They thought he must be a collaborator, working for the Israeli secret service.

After three days, Awad wanted to give up stomping the streets, but he agreed to continue when we increased his daily rate. Some people recognized the face in the Polaroid but didn't know the man. Others said he lived in a distant village, maybe. Finally, Awad flashed his photo in the office of a local Arab newspaper and hit pay dirt. The advertising manager recognized him. The victim's name was Fouad Younis, the son of a bus driver. He lived on Balata Street, opposite the Mercedes garage.

We had far less difficulty locating the soldier. Another researcher showed his photo to the first Israeli soldier he came across in Nablus. "That's Ran Schwartz," the soldier said. "But you won't be able to talk to him. He's finished. Some Arabs pushed a concrete block off a roof. Smashed his head in."

That night I called Schwartz's home in Upper Nazareth, heart thumping, fearing for my story. "How is Ran?" I asked his mother.

She told me that her son, a twenty-one-year-old paratroop sergeant, was back on his feet but that he suffered from lack of balance, poor hearing, bad headaches, depression, nervousness, and partial memory loss. She invited me to tea the next day at the family's home. It was a pleasant afternoon, with a cool breeze and shadows lengthening as the sun sank. Their garden sloped off toward an endless, peaceful view of Emek Israel, the Israel Valley, where, his mother told me, Jews had drained the swamp and turned it into the best agricultural land. Her husband, Chaim, chimed in: "It's the land of Israel!"

Ran had difficulty remembering details, but he had no problem describing the concrete block that hit him on the head. "It was huge," he told me. "We'd been there all day with rocks bouncing off the walls. But I got hit because of the cook. He's always in the camp, but this time he brought our food to the casbah. It was his big chance. He thought he was some kind of Rambo, and he decided he was going to go up the alley and teach the Arabs a lesson. I ran after him and stopped him. Then we got trapped, rocks, metal pipes, everything. I pushed the cook against the wall to wait, by a shop, and then it happened. This huge concrete block landed on my head, split my helmet." Ran showed the size of the block with his hands.

They were strong and clean, like the rest of him. He was sitting on the sofa in his parents' tidy little house.

The next day in Nablus, in a noisy, small flat above an auto-repair shop on Balata Street, the main road into Balata refugee camp, I told Fouad what had happened to Ran. He wasn't happy, as I thought he might be, but rather confused. "He didn't deserve it," Fouad said. "Or maybe he did. What do I know about him? All I know is what he did to me. I didn't deserve that. I was just driving by. But that's what it's like to live here, under occupation."

Then Fouad, sitting on the sofa in his parents' house, as if mirroring Ran, suddenly leaned forward, pulled up the sleeves of his shirt, and pushed out his wrists. "Look," he said, "here!"

Thin red lines, weals, were etched into his skin where white plastic handcuffs, like luggage tabs with sharp edges, had been pulled too tight. "Another time I was minding my own business and they picked me up. This big, fat soldier put my hands behind my back, tied the plastic around my hands, put his boot in my back, and pushed as hard as he could until the skin started to bleed. I hadn't done anything. You ask me what I feel about this soldier Ran? What should I feel? They are my enemy."

As Fouad, who was about twenty-three years old, showed me his scarred wrists, I noticed a wedding ring. "You're married?" I asked.

"Yes," he said, beaming. "I married last week. A pity, you could have come to the wedding." He told me that his uncle had brought his cousin back from Kuwait, and they'd married without having met before. As Fouad talked, he rubbed his ring and slid it on and off his finger, as if trying to get used to the feel. He looked fit and strong, with well-defined cheeks and jawbones. He had a black mustache and a lock of black hair that fell over his dark eyes. I congratulated him. He smiled. "Just married," he said again and shrugged proudly. He never introduced me to his wife.

Later, Ran visited me at my home. We sat in the garden, and the sun gleamed off the long, silky chestnut hair of Miri, his gorgeous kibbutznik girlfriend. She had dreamy green eyes and tanned skin. I had trouble concentrating on Ran. They were living together in Tel Aviv and planned to marry. They were as traditional as Fouad and his wife, only in their own society's context. Miri listened intently, stroking Ran's hand, as he remembered what happened that day:

"For hours they were yelling on that street corner, you know the kind of thing, 'Maniac, I fucked your mother,' 'Your sister's a whore,' the usual stuff. It's tiring, you can't shoot, you can't go into the casbah without an officer or the army will screw you. Your cameraman turned up at the last minute. We'd been there all day. I was angry, really angry.

"Sure, maybe I should have let them go on. Who cares anyway? Our job was just to keep them in the casbah, to stop them from reaching the main road. But I just wanted to end it. I was the unit commander. So I stopped the car and took the guy.

"I asked him to help us to stop the kids from throwing stones. He wouldn't, so I hit him, not hard, and then he did it. He shouted at them to stop. Ten minutes later it was all over. So it didn't look nice, but it worked. I didn't feel sorry for him. I didn't hit him hard, and I had no choice. I know already that you have to show superiority or they'll ignore you. How long can you take them throwing stones at you? Everyone has a limit."

Miri was still stroking his hand. He rested a minute and sipped some fresh orange juice. He said, "I've got a headache just thinking about it. What a shithole." He chewed some nuts thoughtfully and grimaced, as if recalling a bad moment. Or maybe his wound hurt. In any case, Ran carried on, unprompted:

"The kids, they burn tires, throw stones, and run away. We know where they run to and chase them into their homes, and all the Fatmas start screaming, saying the kids aren't there. Then we see all these kids under the blankets.

"The Fatmas start shouting, 'Don't touch them, they're sick! They're sweating!' Sure they're sweating! They've been running! So we look at their hands under the blankets, and they're all black and smelly from tires and oil, so we take them. Or they'll be in the shower with their clothes on and the water running and they think we won't come in. Usually they come quietly, but we have to push the mothers out of the way. That isn't always easy, they fight back."

On another visit to their home in Upper Nazareth, Ran's mother, Rivka, an attractive woman with curly brown hair, shook her head sadly, telling me:

"When I listen to my son, I think, That's not my son. Being in Nablus changed Rannie. I saw the television pictures your cameraman took. Rannie was terrified. I've never seen him shout like that. He was always so quiet, gentle. He volunteered for the Red Cross. Then he volunteered to be a paratrooper. But he didn't want to fight women and children. It all came so suddenly.

"I remember when I saw the news on TV, the riots in Nablus. I was taking a course on relationships between Arabs and Jews, how to live better together, and we all saw the news together. It was embarrassing for all of us. I thought, Oh, I do hope Rannie isn't there. Then he called and says, 'Don't worry, Mummy, it's tough, but I'm okay, I'm calling from a shop.' Then he left the shop and was hit by the rock." Tears filled her eyes, and she looked away.

Back in Nablus, Fouad's mother, Monnah Sabbah, looked every bit the woman who had raised ten children. Her noble face had hooded eyes and deep wrinkles. She seemed exhausted and rested her chin on her elbow across the kitchen table. She didn't want to talk. "What is there to say?" she asked. "Look out the window. It happens all the time. We don't want them here, so of course our boys throw stones. The soldiers should go. What are they doing here?"

Fouad suddenly leaned forward and gripped my knee. He fixed his eyes on mine and said: "Is this humiliating? What do you think? I had just got home from my marriage ceremony. I had been married just a few hours. And in the street the *shabab*, the boys, were burning tires, just outside our house, so the soldiers came in here, and they forced me and my father to go outside and clean the street. In my wedding clothes! My wife saw this. I was humiliated before my wife. We had been married only a few hours and I had just brought her home. Can you understand what this means? I am not master in my home. The Israeli is master in my home. This is occupation!" He had tears in his eyes.

Monnah added, "Nobody cares about us, especially not the Arabs. Our youth have lost hope, and now they wish that through violence there will be a solution." At that moment, a boy, about eight years old, dashed in excitedly to report the latest news. A coup in Cairo! Mubarak has been killed! The room erupted in yells of joy. They smiled at one another, said, "inshallah"—"If God wills it, we will be saved yet." There was an excited babble in Arabic, and my translator joined in, all smiles and nods and winks. "Good," they said, "he was an American puppet." When I confirmed with a phone call to NBC that the rumor was false, there was a moment's regret. From this they recovered with remarkable ease, as if they were used to disappointments. "One day," they said to one another. "Inshallah."

Each time I tried to bring the conversation back to Ran hitting Fouad, they rejected the notion that something unusual had happened. "So what?" Fouad asked. "This is quite normal. There is only one way forward now—armed struggle. We don't see it as terrorism but as legitimate resistance. That's what we want now. And I'll tell you something. You want to know what I was doing there when I drove by the soldiers? Was I there by chance? No! I knew there was a protest and that we were being attacked. So I drove my car there to take the wounded to the hospital, to see if I could help. I always do that. Or I give a ride to a journalist. I am part of the struggle, part of my people's fight. Of course I am. Why shouldn't I be? The Jews are my enemies."

"You see, you see!" Ran shouted, leaning forward and pointing, when I had showed him Rafi's film of his confrontation with Fouad.

As Fouad drove away, he had shouted at the camera, "PLO, PLO!"

"You see," Ran shouted, "PLO, PLO! He *is* the enemy!"

I asked Ran and Fouad if they would care to meet. Neither liked the idea, but each arrived at the same conclusion: Why not? Ran warned he would not shake hands. We arranged a meeting on neutral ground, in the parking lot of the Afula Hospital, where Ran had gone for treatment for his wounds. But when Fouad saw Ran arrive in his uniform, carrying his rifle, he refused to meet him, quickly got back into his taxi, and drove away.

Neither young man, it seemed to me, really wanted to fight, yet neither were they ready to stop fighting. They were simply following their leaders, acting out the roles thrust upon them, unable to cast aside the slogans and the symbols.

Their story reflected the greater truth of the Israeli-Palestinian conflict. Despite the heated talk of borders, Jerusalem, refugees, and land, I was coming to understand that this conflict was not between Arabs and Jews or Israelis and Palestinians. Rather, it was between those who were willing to compromise for peace and those who weren't.

In recent years, polls have routinely shown that, if a real peace agreement were on the table, ready to be signed, a clear majority of Israelis and Palestinians would take it, almost regardless of the details. Dozens of times I have heard Israelis and Palestinians, over a coffee or when working together, slap each other on the shoulder and say, "If it was up to you and me, we'd make peace in five minutes!" But the absence of peace, or even talks about peace, allows the extremists to set the rules and sacrifice other people's children.

That was the end of my story on Ran and Fouad, but it wasn't the end of theirs. An Israeli TV channel saw the NBC report and invited the two young enemies to their studio. On national television, Ran and Fouad finally talked to each other about that first confrontation, their lives, and their hopes. The two men subsequently stayed in touch and visited each other's homes. After Ran left the army, Fouad took him for a drive around Nablus. The first Intifada had ended, the soldiers had left, and the Palestinian boys had nobody to throw stones at anymore. The highlight of their drive was visiting the street corner where the Jew had hit the Arab, before the two men had become friends.

Why did I care so much about these two young men? At the time, I thought I was just giving some good background to the news. The truth,

I now realize, was much more profound: Delving into their stories made me think more deeply about my own family's story. Most of my parents' families were gassed or shot or died of fatal diseases in concentration camps. My parents rarely talked about it, and I rarely asked. It was just too painful to deal with. To this day, I have yet to see a film about the Holocaust, not even *Schindler's List* or *Sophie's Choice*. But Ran and Fouad gave me access to the Holocaust in a way that I could tolerate. The deeper I dug into their stories, the more I compared their experiences with the few stories my own parents had told me about their lives in Austria before the Holocaust.

Fouad hit a nerve when he described how he and his father had been forced to clean the street after youths set fires. We had filmed this sort of thing several times: old men and women lugging concrete blocks, pushing smoldering tires with broom handles, collecting broken glass and piling it by the roadside, as Israeli soldiers looked on. Fouad's humiliation before his new bride made it even worse. It reminded me of one of my mother's few childhood stories about life under the Nazis in Vienna. Her own mother had been humiliated when Nazis rounded up Jews like cattle and forced them to scrub the streets with toothbrushes. Austrian neighbors had crowded around, laughing and jeering. Later my mother had hurried to a Nazi office to claim her sobbing mother and bring her home. "*Aber das war ganz üblich,*" my mother told me in her dry way, empty of emotion— "It was quite normal."

The stories of Palestinian men dragged from their homes handcuffed at night reminded me of an even worse moment in my mother's life, when the Nazis came to drag away her stepfather, Onkel Max. My mother had mentioned that catastrophe in her life, but only in passing, with no detail or emotion. "It so happened that I had to leave home in rather a hurry" was the typically understated way she had introduced it. Now, inspired by the stories of Ran and Fouad, I wanted to know more. On my next visit to London, I sat my mother down in the living room, set a small video camera on a tripod, dimmed the lights, and asked her the questions we had always avoided.

After fifty years living in London, my mother, Edith, still spoke with a thick Austrian accent. She told me that, at seven o'clock one morning in late 1938, a unit of brown-shirted SA, the Nazi storm troopers, banged on the door of the Feibelmann household in Hietzing, a wealthy, leafy Vienna suburb. Luckily, a short time earlier the Nazi commander of Vienna had ordered that arrests, even of Jews, could be carried out only with a warrant. "I heard the commotion and came out of my room," my mother said into the camera. "I demanded to see the warrant to arrest Onkel Max. They said, 'We don't need that, we'll take him anyway.' So I said, 'If you don't leave immediately, I'll call the police!' Not that they would have done anything."

A tug-of-war developed, culminating when my mother slapped the officer's face and slammed the door, saving Onkel Max. The Nazis shouted that they would be back.

They returned the next day with all the official papers necessary to arrest—my mother. But she was already two hundred miles away in Czechoslovakia. As soon as the door slammed on the Nazis, my mother's parents had understood that they had to save their daughter. They hurried to her room, where my mother quickly packed a bag with her diaries, photos, letters, an ornament, the drawing of a cat that hung over her bed, and one golden locket with a photo inside of her parents. Her parents took her straight to the rail station and put her on the next train to Prague. Because she had a German passport from her real father, which did not have *J* for *Jew* stamped on it, she was allowed to cross the border to safety. My mother was eighteen years old. She was eighty when I asked how it felt to leave her parents, whom she would never see again. "Now that is a question you don't have to ask," she replied. Sixty-two years later, and she still couldn't talk about it.

Her parents and almost all their relatives were put to death in the concentration camps. Their home and property were stolen. The same happened to my father's family. More than fifty people were killed from our little clan. The home where I grew up in London was a dark place where the Holocaust was rarely mentioned but never absent. It seemed that almost every day my father lit a *Jahrzeitlicht,* a memorial candle, for someone.

My family's sad and helpless past left me with an enduring hatred for bullies, matched by sympathy for their victims. This is why, as a displaced Jew, and one with an Israeli wife, I naturally feel a deep sympathy for Israel and its fight for survival. Yet it is the greatest contradiction that, in the context of the Arab-Israeli conflict, it is often the Jews who are the bullies. So while I have every sympathy and understanding for Israel's plight, I feel the same for the plight of the Palestinians. My family's experience has helped me to understand this conflict by putting the competing claims into some interpretive frame. After all, like many Palestinians, I am the son of refugees. But unlike the Palestinians, I was not raised to hate, or to demand restitution of every final inch of earth.

The address of my mother's house in Hietzing where she threw out the Nazis is Gehlengasse 4. Every couple of years when we were little boys, my mother would visit Vienna and take my brother and me to see her childhood home. I would grip the wrought-iron gate, which was much taller than I, and peer through the bars at the big old house and the massive trees surrounding it. One hot day a little rainbow sparkled through the sprinklers; it must have looked the same in those summers long ago, when all my mother's young Jewish friends met in her huge garden because they weren't safe in the parks and Jews weren't allowed in the local swimming pool. On our last visit, my mother rang the bell, explained who she was, and asked one of the families living in her house to let her in to look around. She pointed to her bedroom, which looked onto the street. The new owner refused and shut the door. We stood outside, looking in. I was embarrassed and gripped my mother's hand. She turned, spat on the ground, and we left, never to return.

Like many Palestinians, my mother was a refugee who could never forget. And like the children of those Palestinians, I was the son of bitter refugees. My family lost more, much more, than any Palestinian ever did. But my mother and father did not bring me up to hate the Austrians and the Germans. They did not tell me, peering through the gate of Gehlengasse 4, that this is rightfully mine. They didn't hand me a rusty old key and say, "Martin, this is the key to your real home. Everything else is temporary.

Never rest, always fight, until you throw out the people who live in your home."

I have heard many Palestinian mothers pass this message on to their own children. Mothers like Umm Muhammad in Gaza, who told me, "I am proud my son is a suicide bomber, a martyr, and I would send all my children to die the same way, until we kill the Jews and make them leave our land." Or Mariam Farhat, who posed happily in front of a poster of three of her sons, all killed while fighting Israel. She was proudest of her eldest son, Mohammed, who had cut through a fence and surprised Jewish boys studying the Talmud, murdering five of them before guards gunned him down. The section of fence with the hole cut by her dead son is stuck to the wall of her house, like a treasured museum piece.

As I visited Palestinian mothers like these, who praised their martyr sons and promised to fight for their robbed land for eternity, part of me sympathized with their losses and their tragic lives, while another part felt repulsed. Many millions of people for centuries all over the world have lost their homes and rebuilt their lives elsewhere. Why not you? I would think, as they cried to the camera. My mother did.

It had taken me fifteen years of chronicling the tragedies of strangers before I finally began to face up to the suffering in my own family.

In Israel during the first Intifada, my professional and personal lives began to merge, for the first time in my career. It wasn't merely a question of reliving the Holocaust but also the grind of covering a conflict that, day after day, took place at home. I was reporting on my own people, not strangers in distant lands. My wife's relatives were soldiers, and my own sons soon could be. I was too close to the story. An Israeli song called "Shooting and Crying" describes the dilemma of a sensitive soldier. It could also apply to a television crew filming war at home.

One evening stands out for me when I remember the emotional toll of covering a war at home. In February 1997, two Sikorsky helicopters collided while hovering near the Lebanese border. I got the call and raced to the office at 10:30. As I drove, I found myself thinking about the parents of the soldiers involved. One thing that unites all Israelis is the knowledge that, at age eighteen, their sons and daughters will join the army and probably go to war. Then the long nights will begin, when the parents will fear every sound. Is that a knock on the door? Who can that be at this hour? Every Israeli parent lives in dread of that tentative knock or the short ring of the bell. Every Israeli parent fears the sight of the rabbi and the doctor—the Israel Defense Forces notification team—and the news they bring. So as I drove, I wondered who would hear that awful knock this evening. And I understood that, if I stayed long enough in Israel with my three sons, one of those knocks could be on my door.

When I arrived at the office, there was no time to spare. With two and a half hours to go until airtime, the *Nightly News* still hadn't decided if they wanted a story on the crash. There were certainly enough strong pictures. The local agency cameramen had arrived at the scene within minutes. Soon video began streaming in from Reuters and AP, as well as from the Israeli TV channels—dead bodies, blood, wounded soldiers screaming, explosions, rescue workers running, ambulances with sirens blaring, flares in the night sky, helicopter parts riddled with holes and stained with blood, soldiers smashing the windows of burning homes where the flaming choppers had crashed, looking for survivors, shattered trees with scorched clothing flapping in the branches, wild-eyed officers calling to their men, crying women and dazed children looking on at the carnage.

As the correspondent, my job was to decide what scenes to include, arrange them in sequence, sift the information, and write the story. Yet it still wasn't clear if NBC even wanted a report. In addition, the news kept changing. At first we heard there were ten dead and some wounded. Then it became fifteen dead, then twenty-five, and the death toll climbed higher and higher like a basketball score.

It was another example of McClurke's law of relative news judgment, the pecking order of death. No thanks, said NBC at ten dead. At twenty the acting foreign editor, Ed Deitch, decided that they would take voice-over only—about fifteen seconds of pictures with Tom Brokaw giving the bare facts. As we brought in fresh pictures, the number of dead soldiers kept edging up until it reached fifty. Fifty young men dead, and still NBC didn't want to do a story.

"We must!" I told Deitch. "This is huge, the highest death toll ever from an accident, and great pictures."

"I agree," Deitch said, "but the big man says we have too much American news tonight." Still VO only. Then, with seventy dead and still counting, Deitch called back: "Okay, we'll take a piece. But keep it short; we're expecting the OJ civil verdict. A minute twenty, give us back a few seconds if you can."

With information flooding in over the wires, as well as from radio and TV and our freelance reporter in the north, with video appearing every ten minutes by taxi and by microwave, and with our office understaffed as usual, we rushed a report onto the air within an hour. One minute twelve seconds. We even gave *Nightly* back eight seconds.

At two thirty in the morning, after the story broadcast, I drove home through empty streets, drained by the effort and the tragedy's enormity, knowing that in little Israel everybody would know somebody touched by so many deaths. I wondered if any lives close to us would be shattered. I slept briefly and poorly, and at 7:00 checked in on the computer. There was a long message from Ed Deitch. "We were very disappointed with your report," it read, like a message from Mars.

We wanted more color, more drama. Why didn't you tell us who died, what their mission was, the history of the unit, and the effect on their morale? You didn't give us any anecdotes, you didn't pull the story together, and you just gave us the dry facts. You did such a brilliant report on Hebron last week, we were really there, we felt the place, and you pulled the audience into the story with your intricate weave of characters and emotions and brilliant writing. Why didn't you do that last night?

In a minute twenty?

Later I spoke with Deitch. "You didn't begin with the best pictures," he told me. "You should have begun with the dramatic images of the explosions and the flares, but instead you began with boring, repetitive shots of dead bodies. Why? And the sound bite of the young guy with the blond hair explaining why he couldn't help the wounded, we couldn't understand him, his English was lousy, so we cut him out. Couldn't you find someone with better English? You didn't do a good job."

He was probably right, I thought. It would have been better to start with the explosions and the flares, even though chronologically they happened later. Rule number one: Begin with the best pictures. But I hadn't been thinking straight. For once, my personal life had trod on my day job. I had been thinking of my three sons.

Talking to Deitch, I felt torn between doing the best job for NBC and worrying about my family. I knew the network couldn't care less. They'd just say, "He's too close to the story, move him somewhere else." But for the first time in my life I was living somewhere with meaning for me, reporting on a story that I cared deeply about. Before I came to Israel this second time, I had been on the road for ten years. I had wanted to settle down and raise my family. It would be hard to go somewhere new that I didn't care about, to report on a story that didn't interest me, doing a job I didn't want to do. Of course, I thought, it's harder to see your son don a uniform and board a helicopter with a rifle and hand grenades, and then go to sleep fearing the knock on the door.

The next morning, Hagar and I breakfasted at our neighborhood café in Herzliya Pituach. She smiled and touched my hand. "You have tears in your eyes." I glanced quickly around the crowded café and wiped my eyes with the back of my hand, hoping nobody would notice. I had worked through half the night on what for me was an emotional story but for NBC was just another marginal one, and I was tired.

On a practical level, covering a war at home poses a unique set of challenges. Your home becomes the front line. Any correspondent would be distracted knowing his spouse and children were in immediate danger. Never did such dilemmas hit home for me more viscerally than during the first Gulf War.

In late 1990, Saddam Hussein had promised to respond to any American invasion with an immediate attack on Israel using chemical or biological weapons. He threatened to "burn half of Israel." So to keep our minds on the story, the day before America invaded Iraq to liberate Kuwait in January 1991, NBC generously shipped all the families of the network's staff in Israel to luxury hotels in the Red Sea resort of Eilat, well out of harm's way. This freed up the staff to cover the war. Saddam had threatened nonconventional war, and NBC News entertained the notion that I would become the first correspondent ever to report while under chemical attack.

Since the rumored nerve gas, mustard gas, and sundry other potential threats in Saddam's biochemical arsenal could kill and maim within minutes, we had all been issued ABC kits. We were to face the dizzying threats of atomic, biological, and chemical warfare armed with yellow sailorlike plastic coats with hoods that covered our faces, yellow plastic pants that folded into big rubber boots, plastic gloves, and, finally, gas masks. When the sirens sounded a Scud missile attack warning and all Israel hastened to bomb shelters or sealed rooms, my crew and I were to jump into the crew car, chase the bangs, and defy incineration.

The prospect of facing chemical or biological war unnerved almost everyone and led to one of the numerous fiascoes of my career. In my defense, I would submit that I qualified my words carefully when, on live television, I informed the world, erroneously, that Tel Aviv was under chemical attack. Israel radio reported it, too, as did numerous other broadcasters.

I was broadcasting live from the NBC studio in Herzliya, which had been transformed by civil defense experts into a large sealed room. Heavy plastic drapes, taped windows, and seals over the air conditioners and other vents would allegedly prevent gas from seeping in. As a final precaution, we were told to wear gas masks and even full chemical war suits whenever an alarm sounded. The only person who took this seriously was the tape editor, David Short, who wore a full ABC kit at all times. When he edited the tape, his thick gloves made it impossible to hit a single key, so each time he tried to make an edit he would hit three buttons at once, sending the edit machine into meltdown. Whenever David played a tape with the sound of a siren, everyone would drop to the floor. As our studio was the only sealed room, the sounding of an alarm brought the entire Herzliya staff, about fifty people, into my room, sitting and lying by the walls and chatting behind the camera as I tried to answer Tom Brokaw's questions live.

When the first reports announced that gas and chemical warheads were hitting Israel, Tom ordered me, on air, to don my gas mask. At first I didn't want to, as we were in a supposedly sealed room, but my producer, Hanani Rapoport, cannily pushing the instant reflex button, informed me that the ABC reporter, Dean Reynolds, was right now putting on his mask and commenting that he hoped his mother wasn't watching. So it wasn't fear of gas war that prompted me to don my gas mask but competition with Dean.

As I struggled with the mask, which Hanani finally brought over my head, pulling the rubber straps hard, I said to Brokaw, "Tom, this gas mask may come in useful after all. We've just been told that one of the warheads that fell in central Tel Aviv has a chemical warhead. That's from our man who's listening to police frequencies. . . . This is no time for heroics. . . . In this thing it's like being in an aquarium. . . . We don't know if it's a chemical or not, it's happening now, gas war, at least one gas warhead, at least one conventional, we know that."

But we didn't. As I struggled to breathe in the unfamiliar clammy black rubber mask with the bulging mouthpiece and the bug-eyed plastic goggles, I continued to give live reports for hours, sounding as if I were speaking from the bottom of a well. America sat transfixed while the television networks and cable channels broadcast the launch of Desert Storm in Iraq, Kuwait, and Saudi Arabia, at 3:00 A.M. Iraq time, January 17, 1991. But a key drama that first night centered on the first-ever nonconventional attack on Israel, which, as it turned out, never happened. It was a critical mistake, shared by Israeli military intelligence. Warplanes were within seconds of taking off to exact severe revenge on Iraq.

Because I couldn't use the telephone with my gas mask on, and I wore it much of the time, my main communication was via the computer. NBC has a top-of-the-screen instant-messaging system, which became my main source of information during those dramatic hours. The retrieved messages from the network in New York and my colleagues in Tel Aviv provide an insight into the fever pitch of live television in wartime. The first message, from one of NBC's smartest newsmen, Marc Kusnetz, who spent years as Tom Brokaw's producer, hit fifty-three minutes before the launching of Desert Storm.

KUSNETZ   *Thu Jan 17 19:07:14 1991*
get ready to go live

JEWCZYN   *Thu Jan 17 19:07:20 1991*
are you hearing air raid sirens?

KUSNETZ   *Thu Jan 17 19:08:04 1991*
i listening to u. can u talk to me . . . tell me what u know.

POLSTER   *Thu Jan 17 19:13:34 1991*
get that damn mask on, martin!

SFREID   *Thu Jan 17 19:18:07 1991*
TALKING TO MULLA NOW WHO SEZ IT'S NOT
CHEMICAL WEAPONS !!

Yossi Mulla was one of the NBC cameramen roaming the streets under Scud attack. He was phoning in reports to our young desk editor, Stephanie Freid, who did an incredible job under stress to keep me honest with the flood of information. Her news desk was on the next floor, directly above the studio from which I was broadcasting.

SFREID   *Thu Jan 17 19:18:28 1991*
IT WAS A MISSILE IN SOUTH TELAVIV. THERE
ARE OTHERS ON THE

SFREID   *Thu Jan 17 19:18:33 1991*
WAY AND LANDING

SFREID   *Thu Jan 17 19:19:05 1991*

AT LEAST ONE OR TWO MISSILES HAVE LANDED
BY NOW IN

SFREID   *Thu Jan 17 19:19:07 1991*

TELAVIV

SFREID   *Thu Jan 17 19:23:47 1991*

RADIO SAYING FOR PEOPLE TO PUT ON MASKS

SFREID   *Thu Jan 17 19:24:17 1991*

BEN BASSAT SEZ IT WAS NEAR WOLFSON HOSPTIAL

SFREID   *Thu Jan 17 19:24:49 1991*

BEN-BASSAT HAVING HARD TIME GETTING
REPORTS DUE TO FONE LINES

SFREID   *Thu Jan 17 19:25:08 1991*

BEING TIED UP—WE'LL GET UPDATES FROM HIM

SFREID   *Thu Jan 17 19:27:45 1991*

MULLA ON PHONE SEZ MORE BOMBS NEAR HIM IN
RAMAT CHEN

KUSNETZ   *Thu Jan 17 19:31:09 1991*

cant get thru on phone. circuits busy.
have someone try to

KUSNETZ   *Thu Jan 17 19:31:29 1991*

call me at 7395. we lose bird at ten before hour. need to

KUSNETZ   *Thu Jan 17 19:31:35 1991*

establish phone contact

SFREID   *Thu Jan 17 19:32:29 1991*

RADIO TELLING PEOLE TO PUT ON MASKS, HOW
TO GET READY, ETC.

SFREID   *Thu Jan 17 19:32:34 1991*

NOTHING OFFICIAL YET HAS COME UP

SFREID   *Thu Jan 17 19:35:17 1991*

BEN BASSAT SAYING IT'S CHEMICAL WEAPONS,
IN TELAVIV. ONE

SFREID   *Thu Jan 17 19:35:28 1991*
           MISSILE FELL 10 MINUTES AGO, AMBULANCES
           ON WAY . . .
SFREID   *Thu Jan 17 19:38:59 1991*
           HECHT REPORTING 3 MISSILES IN NORTH
           FELL—NEAR TSFAT, AND IN
SFREID   *Thu Jan 17 19:39:06 1991*
           HAIFA—UNKNOWN IF IT'S CHEMICAL
SFREID   *Thu Jan 17 19:40:34 1991*
           ISRAELI RADIO REPORTS OF MISSILE ATTACK
           ALL TO WEAR MASKS
SFREID   *Thu Jan 17 19:40:47 1991*
           AND ENTER SEALED ROOMS.
SFREID   *Thu Jan 17 19:41:58 1991*
           BENBASSAT SEZ ANOTHER NEAR PARDESSSIYA
           WHICH IS IN THE SHARON
SFREID   *Thu Jan 17 19:41:59 1991*
           AREA

Chaim Dekel is another cameraman who was chasing the Scuds. Between broadcasts, I was taking some phone calls, but I never knew when the camera would suddenly return to me.

SFREID   *Thu Jan 17 19:46:41 1991*
           PICK IT UP—DEKEL HAS SEEN STUFF
SFREID   *Thu Jan 17 19:46:59 1991*
           HE'S THERE IN TELAVIV SEZ HE SEES PEOPLE
           AFFECTED BY
SFREID   *Thu Jan 17 19:47:03 1991*
           CHEMICALS IN STREET
SFREID   *Thu Jan 17 19:47:53 1991*
           DEKEL SEZ ONE BUILDING HAS BEEN DESTROYED

SFREID   *Thu Jan 17 19:50:38 1991*
          RADIO CONTINUES TO REPORT SAME
          INSTRUCTIONS OVER AND OVER
SFREID   *Thu Jan 17 19:50:50 1991*
          AGAIN—FOR PEOPLE TO GET INSIDE ROOMS
          AND DON MASKS
SFREID   *Thu Jan 17 20:00:49 1991*
          RADIO GIVES NO INFORMATION YET = ONLY
          SAYING THAT THERE WAS
SFREID   *Thu Jan 17 20:01:04 1991*
          A MISSILE ATTACK AND TO WEAR MASKS—THEY
          THEN GO STRATIGHT
SFREID   *Thu Jan 17 20:01:14 1991*
          TO ANOTHER SUBJECT. MULLA HAS PIX OF SIRENS
          GOING OFF AND
SFREID   *Thu Jan 17 20:01:23 1991*
          THAT'S IT—HE SEZ THAT PER SCANNER, THERE
          ARE DEFINITELY
SFREID   *Thu Jan 17 20:01:35 1991*
          WOUNDED BUT FROM CHEMICAL OR WHATEVER
          UNSURE. CAN'T FIND
SFREID   *Thu Jan 17 20:01:36 1991*
          DEKEL

Dekel had sensibly stopped looking for the Scud impacts and was hiding in a bomb shelter.

SFREID   *Thu Jan 17 20:02:52 1991*
          BEN BASSAT SEZ THAT ONE OF THE MISSILES THAT
          ORIGNIALLY FELL
SFREID   *Thu Jan 17 20:03:04 1991*
          IS NEAR JAFFA—NOT KNOWN IF IT'S CHEMICAL
          OR NOT. . . .

SFREID	*Thu Jan 17 20:07:03 1991*
	BEN-BASSSAT SEZ THAT NERVE GAS HAS BEEN
	DETECTED IN GIVATAHIM
SFREID	*Thu Jan 17 20:09:56 1991*
	GILA REPORTS HIT IN NOF YAM
SFREID	*Thu Jan 17 20:17:31 1991*
	BOTH CREWS ARE INSIDE CITIZENS' HOMES
	IN TELAVIV
SFREID	*Thu Jan 17 20:25:02 1991*
	MULLA SAYING THAT IN HERZLIYA AREA THERE
	ARE REPORTS OF NERVE
SFREID	*Thu Jan 17 20:25:03 1991*
	GAS HITS
MROSENWA	*Thu Jan 17 20:33:56 1991*
	anything on israeli retaliation???
TUNIK	*Thu Jan 17 20:46:24 1991*
	shiffer just said he would be very careful about
	saying
TUNIK	*Thu Jan 17 20:46:40 1991*
	war declaration, he has noone to check with now
	and thinks
TUNIK	*Thu Jan 17 20:46:47 1991*
	Washington knows the best.
BROKAW	*Thu Jan 17 20:59:48 1991*
	some of us think you're better in a gas mask.
BROKAW	*Thu Jan 17 21:00:08 1991*
	that's a joke, martin. ho, ho. in fact, you've never
	been better
BROKAW	*Thu Jan 17 21:00:24 1991*
	absolutely brilliant. back to you in a moment
TUNIK	*Thu Jan 17 21:02:41 1991*
	per radio senior official in the pentagon
	cleared israel

TUNIK   *Thu Jan 17 21:02:53 1991*
for it self defence right.

KUSNETZ   *Thu Jan 17 21:27:34 1991*
did u inject yourself?

KUSNETZ   *Thu Jan 17 21:28:23 1991*
sorry, but be serious for one minute . . . pls. reassure
me—u

KUSNETZ   *Thu Jan 17 21:28:34 1991*
did get that indirect message that back of leg may
be wrong

KUSNETZ   *Thu Jan 17 21:28:41 1991*
after all?

I had just demonstrated how to use our anti-nerve-gas injections by showing where to jab it in the leg. The NBC switchboard in New York lit up as dozens of anxious viewers called to tell me urgently that I was doing it wrong.

ALLAN   *Thu Jan 17 21:33:02 1991*
YO FLETCH. . . . YOU ALL OK? HAGAR AND THE KIDS??

ALLAN   *Thu Jan 17 21:33:23 1991*
YOU LOOKED CUTE IN YOUR MASK BUT IT WAS
CROOKED AND HID

ALLAN   *Thu Jan 17 21:33:35 1991*
ONE HALF OF AN EYE . . . MADE YOU LOOK KINDA
RAKISH. . . .

ALLAN   *Thu Jan 17 21:35:01 1991*
I'D HAVE RECOGNISED YOU ANYWHERE!

KUSNETZ   *Thu Jan 17 21:42:44 1991*
feeling here unanimous: u look better wearing
the mask.

FRANCIS   *Fri Jan 18 00:22:22 1991*
You are some kinda COOOOOOL. An incredible
performance . . .

FRANCIS   *Fri Jan 18 00:22:40 1991*
           especially with your family there.
PRINCE   *Fri Jan 18 11:28:55 1991*
           My wife said you really looked sexy in that gas
           mask last
PRINCE   *Fri Jan 18 11:29:09 1991*
           night. She's asked me to buy one. Sez it would
           improve our
PRINCE   *Fri Jan 18 11:29:17 1991*
           sex life.

Months later, still smarting from my false report, I tracked down the source of the mistaken nerve and chemical stories. Our own reporters had been sending me the wrong information, probably based on panic, but I wanted to know why officials had gotten it wrong, too. Finally I spoke to someone familiar with the policemen involved. The role of the first police on the scene of the first Scud attacks was to seal the area and protect the experts whose job it was to check if the Scuds carried chemical or conventional warheads. A pungent gray smoke rose from the debris of one of the first Scuds to hit, caused by the liquid that separates the fuel from the oxygen in the missile body. It caught fire on impact.

The first group of police saw the smoke. One of the officers became unsteady and then vomited into his gas mask—two symptoms of nerve gas. Seeing this, his colleagues panicked and bundled him into their patrol car. Arms and legs trapped in doors and hats flying, they hightailed it to the nearest hospital, radioing for help, calling out, "Nerve gas, nerve gas!" Journalists monitoring police frequencies heard the panicked transmissions. When the breathless policemen stormed into the hospital, sirens wailing and blue lights flashing, nurses didn't take any chances and rushed them straight into fumigation showers. So in answer to inquiries from the press and official bodies, the hospital spokesmen confirmed they had treated policemen for chemicals and nerve gas. Only later did the press and government officials realize that treating officers for nerve gas did not mean they actually had been affected by nerve gas, but that it was just a protective measure.

After two weeks of Scud war, and with the threat of gas attack fading, Hagar and the children returned home from Eilat. Although the sirens sounded regularly and missiles were still falling, they had had enough of hotel life in the south. Even war becomes routine, and we figured the worst of the Scud attacks were over. We were right, but we were soon to discover that danger comes in different forms. I would have a chance to achieve temporary hero status in the eyes of my children. It was a bizarre moment when I possibly saved my family's life.

When the siren sounded at night, Hagar and I routinely carried the three sleeping boys to the bomb shelter, put a gas mask on Guy, the eldest, and manhandled the two youngest, four-year-old Daniel and three-year-old Jonathan, into big plastic hoods with breathing apparatus. After closing the heavy bombproof door, I would leave to chase Scuds and report live from the studio. Normally I didn't check on my family, because I was too busy and assumed I'd hear if there was a problem. I always knew where the Scuds fell, and they rarely fell close to my home.

One evening, for no particular reason, I called home after a siren announced the all clear. I had never done that before. There was no answer. I did a live broadcast and then called again. Again no answer. I knew no Scud had fallen near home, but still, why wouldn't they answer the phone? It was 9:00 P.M., too early for them all to be asleep. Then, half an hour before my next live broadcast, I decided to call home again. Ten P.M. Still no answer. As I sat at my desk and looked at the clock, I felt a strange pull, an instinct telling me that I should go home quickly. I had twenty-five minutes before my next live shot. Ten minutes to drive home, ten minutes back again, five minutes to spare. It was a big risk, but something was pulling me.

I ran to my car, raced through the still-deserted streets, and opened the door with a sinking feeling. Silence. Then I heard a faint knocking, and even fainter words, "Help, help!" I rushed to the bomb shelter, pushed the heavy metal lever up to unlock the door, and found my family. They couldn't open the door. They had been stuck inside for five hours.

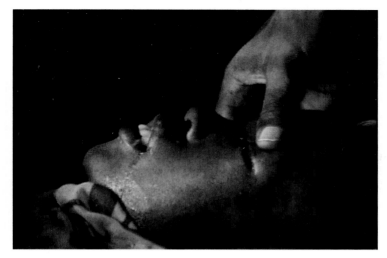

Fida Ibrahim's
moment of death
from starvation.
(*NBC News*)

MARTIN FLETCHER
NBC NEWS

MARTIN FLETCHER
PRIZREN, KOSOVO

LEFT: Ramallah, after Israeli bomb attack. (*NBC News*) RIGHT: With German troops in action for the first time since World War II, Kosovo. (*NBC News*)

Yehona Aliu with the
British army doll.

Golan Heights 1973. *(Sally Soames)*

(NBC News)

Once upon a time in Rhodesia 1976. (Michael Sullivan)

Martin, Jeff, and Dubi and friends, Rwanda 1994. (Mike Mosher)

With Neil Dav[...]
Horse and Houn[...]
Rhodesia-style.
(Peter Jordan)

My friend Paul Roque
treading on a land
mine. Cyprus 1974.
(Martin Fletcher, Visnews)

Journalists treated
against rabies.
Rhodesia 1976.

Rwandan refugees 1994. *(ML Flynn)*

BBC soundman Ted Stoddart lies dead after treading on a land mine. Wounded correspondent Simon Dring helped away by Turkish officer. *(Martin Fletcher, Visnews)*

Martin and family on their way to synagogue for Martin's bar mitzvah.

ABOVE: First press credential. Happy days. *(Martin Fletcher)*

RIGHT: Golan 1973. *(Sally Soames)*

Rocket hits, Gaza 2006.
(NBC News)

Israeli artillery firing,
Lebanon border 2006.
(NBC News)

Hizbullah rocket hits
Haifa, Israel 2006.
(NBC News)

Hagar's wedding dress on boat to ceremony, St. Thomas. *(Martin Fletcher)*

Tony Wasserman holding lens shattered by a bullet as he filmed. Narrow escape.
(Kowie Hamman)

Family: Hagar, Guy, Daniel, Jonathan.
(Martin Fletcher)

Martin with
Afghan guides,
1980.

Palestinian
Intifada 1988.
(NBC News)

Palestinian
Intifada 1988.
(NBC News)

LEFT: Ramallah boy with slingshot. *(NBC News)* RIGHT: In NBC sealed room/studio, January 1991. *(Hanani Rapoport)*

Afghanistan 1980, Pushtun tribal garb.

Israel 2005
(Rami Zarnegar)

LEFT: Ramallah bullets whizzing. *(NBC News)* RIGHT: Suicide bomb, Jerusalem. *(NBC News)*

Al-Aksa Martyrs' Brigades,
Lawahez translates.
(Jeff Riggins)

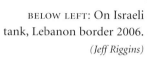

RIGHT: Traveling
companions,
Afghanistan 1980.

BELOW LEFT: On Israeli
tank, Lebanon border 2006.
(Jeff Riggins)

BELOW RIGHT: With Nasser
Abu Aziz, Al-Aksa Martyrs'
Brigades, Nablus.
(Jeff Riggins)

Age eleven, looking for trouble. *(Edith Fletcher)*

WASHINGTON JOURNALISM REVIEW   MARCH 1991 $2.95

WINNERS OF THE SEVENTH
THE
Best
IN THE BUSINESS
ANNUAL EDITORS' POLL

WJR

REPORTING
a new kind of
WAR

The Pro-War Press
Reporters Non Grata
TV: CNN's World
Newspapers: Clarity
Radio: Fast Food

Ready for gas war. *(Martin Fletcher,* Washington
Journalism Review*)*

Kigali, Rwanda, living accommodation. *(Jeff Riggins)*

Released eight hours later. (*Martin Fletcher, New York Post*)

LEFT: Mating ostrich takes exception to biblical quotes about dumb ostriches, Israel. (*NBC News*)
RIGHT: Yehona Aliu, lost child in Macedonia. (*NBC News*)

Al-Aksa Martyrs' Brigades safe house. *(NBC News)*

Fida Ibrahim's last chance to live. *(NBC News)*

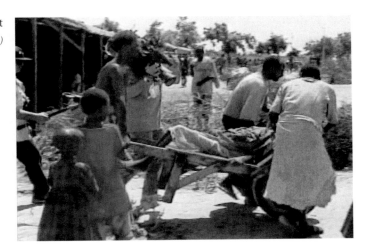

In Macedonia.
(NBC News)

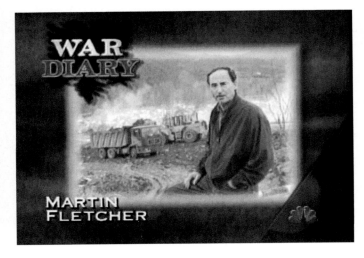

U.S. troops patrol Mogadishu. *(NBC News)*

With American troops in Mogadishu port. *(NBC News)*

Somalia—in good hands at last. But he died. *(NBC News)*

Hagar and her sister had pulled the door lever, hanging on to it with both their body weights, but it wouldn't budge. Finally they gave up and just yelled for help, hoping that for once I would come home early. Their mistake was simple, but it could have been fatal. They had been pulling the lever down, locking the door more firmly, instead of pushing it up, an example of what panic can do. And the old metal window cover was also stuck—rusted into place.

It's simple arithmetic. A person breathes one cubic liter of air an hour. I knew this from the briefings before the war. Five people in the bomb shelter. Five cubic liters an hour. The shelter was small, about forty cubic liters. Eight hours of air. By 3:30 A.M., the time I usually returned home, they would have been half an hour past zero oxygen and on their last breaths, if not dead. As I rushed back to the office, I felt a glow of manly pride. An inexplicable sixth sense had allowed me to rescue my family. My luck was holding, even on the home front.

This near miss became something of a wake-up call for me. "What happens on the road stays on the road" had always been the slogan, the passport to good times and high living in five-star hotels across the world. But it wasn't true. What happened on the road didn't stay on the road. Every single foreign correspondent I knew was divorced. I did not want to fall into that trap. Much as I loved my work, I valued my family above all else. After the first Gulf War, I began to mend my errant ways, slowing down my partying lifestyle when traveling and returning home from foreign trips as quickly as possible.

I had by this time lived in Israel close to a decade. During the late 1980s and early 1990s, in addition to almost daily forays into the West Bank and Gaza to cover Palestinian protests against Israel's occupation, I had covered the fall of the Berlin Wall, the immediate aftermaths of the Tiananmen Square massacre in Beijing and war in Panama, the Vietnamese withdrawal from Cambodia, the release of Nelson Mandela from prison in South Africa, and drought in Ethiopia. I had made a dozen more shorter trips, to Cairo, Amman, Baghdad, London, New York, Paris, and other pleasant and not so pleasant places. It was a dizzying time, and I took enormous pride in my job title: Foreign Correspondent.

Now, though, my goals were different. The challenge became to stay married while becoming the best reporter possible. I had grown, from a reporter covering places and events to a reporter covering people. A truism of Irv Margolies, the London bureau chief who'd hired me for NBC, hit home. He had told me, "People don't care about buildings or planes or guns. People care about people." For the first time in my life, I found myself deeply involved in the personal tragedies around me, and also within.

Six

Famine and the Warlord

As I found myself increasingly touched by the people I was covering, I became more sensitive to the lines we had to cross to report the news. These ethical questions never loomed so starkly for me as in Somalia during the early 1990s. Doing the right thing there was never in the cards. During a series of visits to cover war and famine in this failed country on the Horn of Africa, morality ranked a distant third to getting the story and staying safe. We were trying to help the hungry, and I liked to think we were doing some good. But if virtue is shaken in a storm, in Somalia we sailed mighty close to the wind.

How close can you place your camera to a dying person's face? The closer the camera, the better the picture, the more profoundly the victim's plight is conveyed, the more the audience may want to help save other victims. But there is also human dignity to consider. Would you want a camera in your face as you leave this life?

The need to exploit victims in order to save them or others is a contradiction that lurks at the heart of disaster journalism. As if that wasn't bad enough, journalists must also decide to what extent they should cozy up to the perpetrators. In many disaster zones, where power lies with the strong, your safety depends on the goodwill of bad guys with guns. So how much do you compromise integrity in order to stay alive and get the story? Do you scuttle the story altogether because it's too dangerous? Is no news better than tainted news?

No network rule book can predict or adjudicate the moral quandaries that war reporters encounter during the day-to-day slog. It's just you in harm's way, trying to do the right thing.

After three years of drought, famine, anarchy, and civil war that pitted fifteen competing clans and military factions against one another, Somalia in November 1992 was the baddest place on the planet. There was no government, no army, no police force, no judiciary, no telephone system, no post office, no electric grid, no running water, no international customs or immigration, not even jails. All authority had reverted to the traditional clans and subclans, and to clan leaders, who fought for power, money, and food.

Their weapons were the forty thousand guns abandoned by the defeated army of the ousted dictator Siad Barre. They included tens of thousands of the world's favorite automatic weapon, the Kalashnikov AK47, as well as heavy machine guns, field artillery, antiaircraft guns, and even air-to-air missiles mounted on rusty pickup trucks. Little wonder that in a mere three months of interfactional fighting early that year, 14,000 Somalis were reported killed and 27,000 injured in Mogadishu alone, and Mogadishu is a small place, with fewer than a million people. The battles were fought street to street, house to house, hut to hut. Many of the deaths were random, people cut down by stray bullets, rockets, and shells. The Somalis called the artillery rounds that smashed through the streets "to whom it may concern" shells because of their wild targeting.

It was a bad place with bad people, and the baddest warlord of them all was a smooth-skinned, sharp-faced, balding ex-general named Mohammed Farrah Aidid. A year later, in October 1993, his drugged-up fighters would kill eighteen U.S. Army Rangers and Delta Force commandos and humiliate the Americans into abandoning their military mission to Somalia. Aidid's specialties were protection, looting, and killing, but that only made him part of the crowd. All the factions did the same. Aidid just did it best. His biggest problem was that they had already bled the country dry and there was nobody left to extort.

Enter the international aid agencies, which came to help the starving. Within six months, with UN help, they brought in 28,000 metric tons of food aid. Of this, some estimate about half was stolen. Every stage of the aid operation yielded profits for the warlords.

It worked like this: The warlord's people unloaded the aid deliveries from the ships on behalf of the aid agencies, who paid them. Then more of their people loaded the food aid onto their vehicles, which were guarded by their people against bandits who were also their people. At the first stage, the warlords negotiated a 10 percent cut, and at every later stage they took more cuts, officially and unofficially. For most aid officials, it was simply the price of doing business in Somalia. Better, they reckoned, to get some food through to the starving than no food at all. But their compliance also fed the continuing anarchy, which in turn imposed more suffering on the hungry people.

General Aidid of southern Mogadishu split control of the key port installations, through which most aid entered the country, with his archrival Mohammed Ali Mahdi of northern Mogadishu, a former motel tycoon. Their men would often fight long and vicious gun battles that closed the port down until a cease-fire could be arranged to enable both sides to continue ripping off the international charities.

Aidid, a former Somali chief of staff and ambassador to India, usually won because he was the most ruthless, had the most men with the most guns, and above all, with his daily air shipment from neighboring Kenya, had the most khat, a root drug that kept his teenage gunmen chewing and spaced out for most of the day. That meant they didn't mind dying.

All this is to say that when my NBC producer in Tel Aviv, Hanani Rapoport, proposed that we travel to Somalia to report on the starvation, which was belatedly beginning to grab the world's attention, and when the *Nightly News* foreign editor in New York, M. L. Flynn, jumped on the idea, my first reaction was "Are you nuts?"

Apart from a handful of agency guys and freelancers based in nearby Nairobi, few international reporters had gone to Somalia, and nobody from the American television networks. Despite the horrific famine and the deadly civil war, the story was still not a blip on the network's radar. Somalia was way off the beaten track and insanely dangerous. Phones didn't work. No airlines flew in. It was too far to charter a boat, too dangerous to drive from Kenya or Ethiopia, and there were no hotels to stay in or cars to rent. If we went there, we'd be helpless and vulnerable. As a talented and prescient NBC producer, Phil Griffin, put it later when we went there with Tom Brokaw, we would be visiting a place where everyone had a gun but no money, and we would have lots of money but no guns.

"Are you serious?" I asked Hanani.

There was no upside apart from one small detail. It was a great story. The more I researched the Somali situation that afternoon, the more I saw that it was a remarkable story. Civil war had made a cyclical famine a thousand times worse. While the militias fought, Somalis were starving to death; the militias made it worse again by stealing food aid. I had had no idea how bad it was. Few people did. We needed to tell that story. Besides, it was Africa, and I loved the challenge of telling great stories under tough conditions. But I also wanted to stay safe.

"This guy, Aidid," I said to Hanani, lifting my head from the press clippings spread across my desk in the bureau. "He's the key. We need security. We can't just pitch up and hope for the best. Let's get in with him. Tell him the world's pissed off with him and his bandits and that we want to come and see what the truth is. He used to be ambassador to India. He can't be all bad. Can he? His guys can look after us."

That may sound cynical and exploitative, but I had learned that, if you're dealing with a rogue, rogue rules apply. The NBC rule book doesn't have a section on how to behave with warlords.

"Good idea," said Hanani, who'd once served in Israeli army intelligence. "Let's see what we can do."

"Otherwise, I'm not going," I said.

It still amazes me, but it took Hanani precisely twenty minutes. "Okay, Aidid is expecting us." It also amazes me on what slim guarantees we traveled to that hellhole. Hanani had contacted Aidid's man in Nairobi, who liked the idea and said, Sure, come on over to Nairobi, we'll fly you in and you can stay with General Aidid. We'll give you whatever you like.

So on the basis of a single phone call to an unknown Somali on the east coast of Africa, there began a series of the most bizarre reporting trips of my career, during which a truly appalling, unscrupulous, power-hungry warlord entertained us in his home, fed us with looted foreign aid prepared by an excellent Italian-trained chef, and assigned his chief deputy to visit us over breakfast to plan our forays into Somalia's stricken regions, all in order to pull the wool over the world's eyes and claim that he was misunderstood. Our challenge was to stay honest while staying alive. It didn't help when his deputy heard me recording a piece to camera calling his so-called police force a private army of thugs.

We began our first journey into Somalia in November 1992 by politely declining the offer from Aidid's Nairobi contact, a kindly old fellow who wouldn't stop talking, to fly in with the daily drug run to Mogadishu. The plane was a small, twin-engined Cessna whose seats had been removed to make way for dozens of bales of khat, which we'd be sitting on. It wasn't the question of comfort but rather our guess that drug running might not tally with the stringent business practices of NBC's new owners at General Electric, even if it would save us the price of an air ticket.

Our foreign editor, John Stack, whose budget we were spending like water, agreed with our assessment of GE's business practices, although he seemed a little less convinced when we told him the price of chartering our own small plane from Nairobi to Mogadishu. Along with the danger premium to the pilot, we would be spending a cool $10,000. We hadn't even set off for Somalia, and we had to wait for more money.

Nothing I had read or heard in our brief research prepared me for anything that followed, although that didn't prevent Hanani and me from reassuring our teammates on that first trip, the cameraman Yossi Greenberg and the soundman Dubi Duvshani, that all was taken care of. What are you worrying about? Not a problem. All set up. Piece of cake. Safe as houses.

Yossi and Dubi packed light for our adventure. Sixteen aluminum cases of cameras, lights, sound gear, food, medicines, satellite phone, as well as tents, sleeping bags, and sundry other purchases of designer outdoor apparel courtesy of NBC News, none of which we needed. The one thing we most needed, a spare battery for the satellite phone, we forgot.

As our heavily laden Cessna swooped low into Mogadishu airport from the Indian Ocean, bored dogs trotted over to check out the noise while a UN jeep, driven by members of a tiny and ineffective Pakistani peacekeeping unit, passed obliviously across our approach path. The pilot pulled up sharply, did a low turn back out to sea, and buzzed the strip to check for obstacles. Between dogs, Pakistanis, and children, he spotted a brief window of opportunity, pushed the stick down, and bumped to a halt.

Awaiting us were immigration and customs control, in the person of a skinny fellow swimming in oversize clothes, sitting under an umbrella on the runway. As he stamped our passports, his only question was "How much cash do you have?" which I understood to mean "Should we rob you now or later?" Fortunately, at that moment our airport limos pulled up. We did a double take: *Mad Max*.

It was the cavalry. Two smashed-up Toyota pickup trucks, .50 caliber machine guns welded onto the back, with *Mad Max* movie rejects grinning and chewing khat, wearing shades and flip-flops. There were three boys on each truck, all bearing AK47s. One had two ammunition belts crisscrossed over his narrow chest, hanging down loosely like an extra-large jacket. As the gunships jerked to a halt, a box of hand grenades slid and clattered into the back of one cab. These were the famous "technicals," so named because charity workers, unable to acknowledge gunmen and protection in their official expense sheets, called their bodyguards and gunships "technical assistance."

The oldest boy looked maybe sixteen. They were all shiny with sweat and had yellow-green teeth from the constant mashing of khat. One had dirty white bandages seeping blood wrapped around his shoulder to cover a bullet wound. We shook hands, introduced ourselves, loaded the gear, and climbed into the technicals. I said words to the effect of "Take me to your leader." That would be my host, the supreme warlord Mohammed Farrah Aidid, a leader of the Habr Gidir subgroup of the Hawiye clan, leader of the Somali National Alliance, and, as he insisted on calling himself, the president of Somalia.

As the technicals bumped and rattled over Mogadishu's rain-filled potholes and ditches, severely endangering our delicate electronic camera gear, we fell silent at the extent of the civil war's damage. Even Beirut had had nothing on this. Every building left standing, and in the center of town there weren't many, was pocked with bullet holes, and most had smashed roofs hanging off at crazy angles. Telephone and electric poles stood broken and bare of cables. Shot-up cars and trucks lay rusting and abandoned by the road, picked clean of wheels, windows, fenders, anything that could be stolen and sold. The streets were filled with rubbish and debris.

Huts along the main roads served as shops. They had a few bananas or leaves for sale but otherwise stood empty, apart from boys lounging outside with guns. They all stared at us as we drove slowly by. Younger ones ran alongside, laughing and peering, banging with their fists on the doors, and trying to snatch our sunglasses. They crowded so close that their bodies shut out the light. We wondered if we were making a humongous mistake.

Twice on our journey gunfire broke out. Our boy-guards whipped their machine guns around to the source of the shooting while our driver trod on the gas, hurling us against the hard metal.

Passing a soccer stadium and a narrow market, we turned in to a dusty dirt road lined with high walls. We pulled up in front of a tall metal gate that swung open to reveal a leafy villa and domestic servants waiting at the main entrance. We were astonished at the contrast. Eager hands unloaded our vehicles and carried all the heavy cases through a huge split-level, open-plan ground floor to our bedrooms upstairs. A maid in jeans and a very revealing blouse threw open the windows and gestured to the leafy subtropical gardens. Another servant arrived with slices of bananas and other fruits and glasses of sweet tea.

Within minutes a commotion erupted as more technicals drove into the yard. Out stepped a hard-bodied, middle-aged man accompanied by yet more gunmen.

"I am Osman Hassan Ali Ato," he announced, "and I welcome you to Somalia in the name of our president. I am responsible for your stay here. You will be safe with me." His English was excellent, emphatic, and colloquial; he exuded confidence and command. He was Aidid's chief adviser and moneyman. I found out later that he made his first fortune in oil fields. When the civil war broke out, Somalis say, he added extensively to his wealth by stealing all the copper wiring and telephone cables from the poles we had seen on the drive in. They say he stole the region's entire telephone system, switchboards and all, as well as factory equipment, doorframes, window frames, anything that could be ripped from its moorings. They say he then shipped it all off in loot convoys to the minor Gulf States in a lucrative used-goods trade.

Osman bought and sold guns to anyone able to buy, including to his own rival, Ali Mahdi, of northern Mogadishu. When Aidid asked him about it, he is said to have answered that it was just a way of getting Mahdi's cash, because any time they wanted they could steal the guns back again. It wasn't that Mogadishu played by its own rules. There weren't any. It was pure anarchy.

We had arrived in a violent world of mayhem and murder, armed only with cameras and press cards, all on the basis of Hanani's one telephone call.

The next morning, over a breakfast of rolls, fruit, and tea, we told our new friend Osman what we wanted to film. It was a laundry list of scoops. Let's go to Baidoa to see the worst of the famine. Then let's interview Aidid. Then we'll check out what you're doing to rebuild the country (ha-ha, sop-sop). We also want to go north to talk to the other main warlord, Ali

Mahdi (grimace from Osman). Oh, and thank you so much for helping us. We will convey your point of view to the world. We are the largest television network in America, you know.

I felt unclean. Playing along with evil people, gaining their trust, eating their stolen food, has a price. Like many of the killers I have met, Osman was a perfectly pleasant, straightforward, smart man, but he reminded me of a snake charmer. Unfortunately, I was the snake, pretending to be charmed, hoping to use him for our own ends. It was just part of the challenge, reporting while staying on the right side of morality. But as I have discovered many times over the years, morality in anarchy is hard to define and impossible to achieve. There's always a trade-off. If aid workers paid off the warlords, we, too, surrendered some of our virtue to get the job done and stay safe. I was fine with that.

Osman's strong preference was to start off by showing us Aidid's reconstruction of Mogadishu, which the president was selflessly financing out of his own pocket. This should be interesting, I thought, but we played along. Not that we had any choice. Anyway, as the TV station had long since been looted and destroyed, and we couldn't broadcast any reports until we had returned to Israel, it didn't matter in what order we shot them.

Osman's first stop: the new jail. I wondered what anyone could possibly have done that was so much worse than anyone else as to land behind bars. We arrived at the jail next to the port presumably just a little earlier than expected, because we glimpsed a dozen Somali men and women hastily slipping into the cells as the doors clanged shut behind them. As we walked by the locked doors, two prisoners called out for help, saying in faltering voices that they hadn't seen daylight in years. I was impressed by their proper English. Then we continued to the central police station, where an officer was interviewing a suspect while other Somalis fought for space at the door and windows to observe this unusual diligence. We filmed everything, and I asked questions about the crime rate. I was relieved to hear that President Aidid's emergency program to stamp out crime had been so successful that there really were no statistics worth mentioning anymore, or even available.

From there we were taken to the police barracks to witness a parade of new recruits marching up and down in ragged shorts and flip-flops, carrying pieces of wood in place of weapons. It seemed the only men in Somalia not to have guns were the police. That was where I did my piece to camera and noted that, in this state of anarchy, there was a very thin line between the formation of a so-called national police force and that of a private army of thugs. I have to say, it took considerable courage to force myself to say this under the scrutiny of our admirable and murderous host, but there was a limit to how much I was prepared to kiss ass to get a scoop. Apparently it was sufficient, though, to stay on the right side of Osman, because our next visit was to the man himself, our protector, the president, who had apparently eliminated crime from Somalia, General Mohammed Farrah Aidid.

Aidid was our neighbor, living in the villa next to ours. His office was the villa opposite, next to a giant junkyard where his men assembled and maintained the technicals. Trucks and weapons were married into *Mad Max* fighting machines. There were piles of machine guns, cases of bullets, spare parts, and packing cases, some of them with the clasped-hands logo of U.S. humanitarian aid. Each compound had a high wall around it with guards outside, sitting in burned-out cars or under beach umbrellas to escape the sun and the dust from the dirt road. The whole street was Aidid's stronghold and later became the focus of the Delta Force hunt for him.

Osman guided us to the villa where Aidid worked. We climbed the outside staircase to a small side room, where we took off our shoes, set up the camera and lights, and waited while Osman went off to find Aidid. We sat on cushions on the floor, which was covered with thick, colorful rugs. What a mundane scene, I thought. I was excited to meet the warlord but also full of contempt. How inapt the word is, I thought—*warlord,* a powerful and romantic concept, mustachioed horsemen galloping along the Russian steppes or Chinese giants with long curls wielding huge curved scimitars, leading violent hordes on an orgy of destruction. Death, rape, and looting. *Bullying*, the word I most abhor. Still, Aidid was our ticket to the story. Our benefactor and protector.

The door opened, Osman entered with some more aides, and then, after a pause, in came The Man, slowly and cautiously, glancing from us to his people and back to us. Aidid wore dark trousers and a plain white shirt open at the neck. When he sat down, he barely smiled, and when he did, it was with quick and nervous movements. His piercing, cold eyes hardly moved. As he glanced at each of us with short movements of the head, he reminded me of a wary poisonous snake, and I was very glad he was on our side. "Welcome to Somalia," he said.

I decided to begin the interview right away, as clearly small talk was not an option. I thanked him for his hospitality and fine food, checked that the camera was rolling, and asked, "Why doesn't more food reach the starving people who need it?"

Aidid answered carefully, in only slightly mangled English, "We are able to assure the security of the food to reach their destination."

"So why don't you?"

"We are doing it, we are doing it," he replied.

"So who is robbing it?" I asked.

"Nobody is robbing except the bandits." Pronounced "bandeetees."

"And who are the bandits?" I asked.

"We do not know," Aidid said. "Otherwise we would stop them."

"People say it's your people," I continued. This isn't going well, I thought, he's getting pretty nervous with me.

"This is not true. Who says that? Tell me who." Aidid leaned forward, his icy eyes boring into me, his jaw twitching.

Now here was an interesting journalistic dilemma. How far do you push a mass killer when the only law in town is his gun, you are entirely dependent on him for your safety, and anyway you've already got your story? It's okay being Mike Wallace and doing the "Mike Wallace is here!" number when you're protected by the First Amendment and in case of trouble there's a police station down the road. "Martin Fletcher is here!"

didn't cut it for me in the jungle where Mad Max ruled and I was talking to him. Anyway, Wallace earned about thirty times what I did, and the best part of his life was over. I wasn't about to push this particular warlord one inch further. Maybe later, on the way out of town.

I had been down this road before, when NBC paid large amounts of money to a freelance producer to help me become the first foreign correspondent to go into Cambodia with the Khmer Rouge. The goal was to interview Son Sen, Pol Pot's army chief, who was responsible for organizing the annihilation of up to 2 million of his own countrymen. My freelance crew and I had walked into the country at an unguarded section of the Thai border and rendezvoused with a column of Khmer Rouge fighters. They'd driven us thirty miles into Cambodia to a secret Khmer encampment. I became Son Sen's guest, or prisoner, depending on how you looked at this surreal moment. I was sitting at a long narrow table in a jungle clearing, eating his cold French fries, drinking warm, sweet, fizzy orange juice with insects crawling in the mouth of the bottle. He sat opposite me, perspiring, in an olive green shirt with gold buttons, wearing horn-rimmed glasses and, at first, a friendly, wide smile. Khmer Rouge fighters surrounded us, and I was trying to grill him about the killing fields. After a few setup questions, I gulped and dove in.

"So, Son Sen, why, given how many Cambodians the Khmer Rouge killed, do you expect the people to want you back in a new government?"

The follow-up question was "Some U.S. politicians want you tried as one of the great murderers of the twentieth century . . ."

I was just getting going, but I was also noticing a certain *froideur* setting in around the eyes of this mass killer. I veered away from the quicksand of the next question on my list, which began, "One writer said anything bad you write about Pol Pot will be true." Son Sen offered quick, short smiles, more like nervous tics. His eyes flashed to the side to meet those of his officers. Still, I felt I hadn't come all this way to be the first to find this man and not ask him the obvious questions. But when he simply kept denying the genocide, claiming that scientists had proven that all those broken skulls were at least a decade too old for the Khmer Rouge to have been responsible, and when I had run out of follow-up questions, and when the old Khmer Rouge slogan "To keep you is no benefit, to destroy you is no loss" came to mind, I chickened out. After all, he was my only ticket out, and if he didn't like what was on that tape, well, it would be unfortunate, but accidents do happen, especially deep in the Cambodian jungle.

Strangely, the only person who seemed angrier than Son Sen was the American producer who'd set up the whole trip. For him, this was supposed to be a confidence-building interview on the way to the real scoop, the number one leader, Pol Pot. He said I'd been too tough with Son Sen and had blown his plans. He even wrote a letter of complaint to NBC saying Fletcher had been too hard with his questions. I thought I'd gone too easy. Maybe he was right, because he never got his Pol Pot interview. I felt we had left with our honor intact.

In another twist, a pretty Asian woman dressed in a red and black silk cocktail dress and high heels sat nearby and gazed lovingly at Son Sen through most of the interview, as if we were on the set of an American campaign commercial, not deep in the Cambodian jungle. But all good things come to an end, and a few years later Son Sen fell out with Pol Pot. It was Son Sen's turn to get a bullet in the head.

Having backtracked somewhat and remained in Aidid's favor, I had several long conversations off camera with the president, and it became clear that this was a very sharp man who meant every word he said, and what he said was prophetic. He swore that nobody else would lead Somalia, and that, if the UN or the USA tried to impose order by force, "we will fight, we will fight for our liberty." He always insisted that he wanted the UN to come and help fight the famine, and he wanted the United States to mediate between the factions, but their interests diverged over the question of why. Aidid and his men saw the international aid organizations as deep pockets from which to steal. The more charities and nations were involved in saving Somalia, the more money there was to be made. And if they installed him as president, all the better. But as soon as Aidid understood that any U.S. intervention would place him on the same level as the other warlords with pretensions to political power, he was no longer willing to play ball. His tactics reminded me of a traditional Somali credo: "Myself against my family, my family against other families of my clan, my clan against all other clans, and all the Somalis against the rest of the world." It was an ethos of violent confrontation that helped explain why every male had to have a weapon, be it a sword or a gun. So when Aidid warned that if the Americans did not recognize him as supreme leader, or at least first among equals, he'd kick them out, I believed him.

Having gathered enough material for half a dozen stories, and with no satellite in Somalia to send them to New York, we had to leave the country to file our reports. That was our excuse anyway. But then, sitting on our gear at the airport, waiting for the charter to arrive from Nairobi, we were startled by the radio news. The United Nations would send a large force of multinational troops to Somalia to back up the Pakistanis, who hardly dared leave the airport. The goal was to protect the food aid and fight the famine. American troops would lead the military effort.

"Incredible," we said. "We're in the right place at the right time." Instead of taking a night or two to visit old haunts on the wrong side of town in Nairobi, we hurried back to Tel Aviv to begin a series of reports that put NBC way ahead on the biggest story of the year. Everyone wanted to know about the most powerful warlord, Aidid, and we had the answers. We had been supping with the devil. The brunt of our reporting was: Do not underestimate the power of the bully in his own backyard. We quoted the Pakistani commander, General Imtiaz Shaheen, who had told another reporter, when sending American troops to take control of the militias had still been a hypothetical: "Bash up the Blackies? That's no answer. There's a complete lack of civil infrastructure here. No hospital, telephone, water, police. Bring in the marines? Wrong!"

Even though we had been his houseguests, we had clearly demonstrated Aidid's complicity in the humanitarian crisis; more than once I found myself hoping fervently that he and Osman had no way to watch NBC News. But most of our reporting focused on the awful extent of the famine. This, too, was not without its painful moral dilemmas.

On subsequent trips, we concentrated much of our humanitarian coverage on a single refugee camp, a feeding station in the south of Mogadishu, not far from Aidid's home. This small camp, one of many in the capital, held three thousand starving Somalis who had trekked to Mogadishu and found shelter here. They were dying at the rate of a dozen a day. We visited daily just to say hello, to get to know the refugees and the volunteers, and sometimes to shoot part of our reports. We drank tea with the nurses, chatted with the armed guards, and even, to celebrate the arrival of the American troops, danced with refugees as others clapped and laughed. I preferred to get to know one place well rather than many places just a little. That way my reports could go deeper. Also, focusing on this feeding station allowed us to stay safe in these anarchic and insanely dangerous streets.

If we had to do a story on an aid worker, or food distribution, or gunmen stealing food from the starving, or the role of women, we didn't search all over Somalia, we just climbed into our technical and, with our half a dozen bodyguards armed with pistols and Kalashnikovs, headed for Camp Smola Smola, our Hebrew nickname for the feeding station. *Smola Smola* means "left, left." We found the camp by following my theory of disaster coverage: You don't have to drive a hundred miles or think for hours. Just get in the car, turn left, left again, and more likely than not you'll find the story. In a country where death was everywhere, Smola Smola became our own ecosystem of suffering, our laboratory of starvation. By returning day after day, we began to understand it and be accepted by the desperate Somalis. They started to trust us and help us because they accepted that we wanted to help them and not just exploit them. It was the same with the international aid workers. They volunteered months and sometimes years of their lives to help the hungry Africans and were often scornful of and even hostile to journalists who dropped by for an hour or two. They knew we wanted to help them, so they helped us.

Dawn at Smola Smola was the moment of truth. The weakest died overnight. The rest emerged hesitantly from beneath blankets on the ground or from huts of leaves and branches to find a place to relieve themselves or, if they were lucky, to light a fire and brew tea from whatever leaves they could find. Their dark shapes silhouetted against the early sky resembled a charcoal drawing in grays and blacks. The only sounds were of coughing and spitting and sick babies crying. When it rained, water washed underneath the huts and turned the earth to mud. Shoulders were hunched against the cold. When the sun rose and warmed the body, the skin itched from the heat and mosquitoes that might carry malaria. The place smelled of disease and feces and woodsmoke. Everyone was dirty and hungry and miserable.

But it got worse. While parents fed their children with what little there was, one child was often neglected in the back of the tent, so certain to die that there was no point feeding him or her. Why take food from a child who may live to feed a child who will certainly die? It's triage of the most painful kind, performed by the parents.

We, too, had choices to make. During the fall of 1992, the American military had just arrived to stop the fighting and starvation. The U.S. networks sent their biggest stars to cover the latest American foreign involvement, but viewers also needed to understand the true human costs of what was going on. One evening in Mogadishu, Tom Brokaw said to me, "I want you to do a story on what it's like to die of starvation. We'll give you three minutes." For us that was feature length.

"What it's like to die of starvation?" a producer asked. "How do we do that—interview a doctor?"

"Not quite," I answered. "Tom could do that in New York. I have an idea. We're going to film someone dying."

As I uttered those words, I couldn't imagine anything more callous. But I also couldn't imagine a stronger way to connect to the audience, to say, This is what it's all about; this murderous civil war and famine aren't just a mind-numbing welter of statistics, numbers of victims and tonnage of food aid, dollars of tax money and soldiers on the ground. They are people dying.

A moral dilemma that has always fascinated me is the imperative that directs good people to do bad things for a good reason. This, I thought, is one of those moments. In television journalism, there are many of them.

Before dawn the next day, my crew and I set out for Camp Smola Smola. When we got there, we looked for Annette Callaghan. Annette was an Irish nun who had volunteered for three months' aid duty and was now in her seventh month. "The convent can wait," she said. In the course of our daily visits, she had become a friend, and when I had explained the assignment the night before, she'd been enthusiastic and told me not to feel bad. "We're all doing our job," she said, "and we all help in our own ways."

Every day at dawn Annette trod purposely from hut to hut, pulled back the plastic, and peered inside. Every so often she called for help and Somali assistants hauled out the dying bag of skin and bones abandoned way inside. That's how we found ourselves filming the last day in the life of Fida Ibrahim. Fida had walked for three weeks from a village near Baidoa, 120 miles away, where refugees were starving to death at the rate of more than one hundred a day. She had no hope there, and Mogadishu was her last chance. She had survived for four days, but now black flies buzzed around her bulging brown eyes, and her thin lips drew tight against her yellowing teeth as she cried. Her long bony fingers dug weakly at the worms under her dry and wrinkled skin, but she didn't have the strength, and her skinny arm dropped suddenly and dangled over the side of the broken wooden barrow Annette used to carry away the dying.

"This is your girl," Annette said as she helped carry Fida. "She won't last long."

"Follow them all the way," I muttered into the ear of Yossi Mulla, my cameraman, as helpers bumped Fida Ibrahim along the rough track in the broken wheelbarrow.

Yossi was crouching crablike by Fida's side, his wide-angle close to her face, so the world would see in close-up her pain, fear, and humiliation. Other refugees watched in silence as the little procession stumbled in the dirt and wove through the mass of tiny round huts made of dry leaves, twigs, and plastic sheeting. We emerged into a clearing and then passed into a small dark room off the makeshift clinic.

Fida whined and gasped in pain as the aid workers lowered her carefully onto a blanket on the bare concrete floor and inserted an IV drip into her vein. Every bone stuck out. She looked like a box of matches.

"All we can do is add a bit of dignity to her dying," Annette said gently, spooning drops of water into Fida's lolling mouth.

"How long will it take?" I asked, as Yossi quietly set up the tripod and the camera. And I thought, Dignity? The last thing she'll ever see is a lens stuck in her face like a pig's snout. I felt like telling Yossi to give it up, but we had a job to do. My very own *Nightly News* snuff movie.

"Maybe forty-eight hours," Annette said.

Yossi turned to me in alarm. "Two days? You want me to film her for two days?"

"As long as it takes, Yossi, till she dies on camera. That's our story."

Fida's arm jerked, and her filthy, torn dress flopped to the side, revealing a young breast. Quickly, the Irish nun pulled up the rag and cradled Fida's head, while the girl moaned shrilly. "The tuberculosis is pressing on her internal organs," Annette told me in her Irish brogue as Amikam Cohen, the soundman, held out a microphone. "And she's got malaria and scabies. We got her too late."

So there we were, waiting for Fida to die of starvation. Fida's father, Mohammed, squatted by her side, her aunt sat behind her head, and Yossi kneeled by his camera mounted on a tripod, focused on Fida. Annette fed her drops of water from a plastic spoon. It was a horrible thing to witness. But Annette said, "Where there's life, there's hope." She meant hope for Fida, but that was fading fast.

Every so often, Yossi emerged from the grim vigil to film the hope on display outside. Hundreds of little children, all naked and scratching furiously, many crying, were being washed down with water from a tanker that was guarded by bored-looking Somalis with AK47s and rocket-propelled grenades. "A wash, treatment, clean clothes, that's all it takes to beat scabies," said Annette matter-of-factly as we filmed the children showering and being scrubbed with foamy soap. "It should be so simple to save them."

Then we went back inside to see how Fida was doing. Mohammed was holding her body. It looked like a black pietà, but Fida was still breathing, and her milky eyes were open and blank.

And so we waited at the deathbed. We filmed Fida's bony chest rising and falling, slowly, sometimes with a rasp from her throat. A close-up of the resigned face of her father. Her aunt's hands stroking Fida's hair. Fida's blank eyes. We were voyeurs of death. It was hard. I knew we were abusing poor Fida, but I felt this was a scene the world should see and understand. If the viewer felt sick, good.

We filmed for another half an hour, then went outside again to follow the children to the feeding tent. We were in a hurry in case we missed the climax of the story—Fida's moment of death. If it sounds coldhearted and horrendous, it was. All the scrubbed little children were sitting in rows with their heads up and mouths open, like infant starlings in the nest, as volunteers spooned multivitamin syrup onto their tongues. On the packets was written, "For healthy growth and vitality."

Then we hurried back inside, and Yossi locked his camera onto the tripod again. Aid officials walked by, hardly pausing to look at Fida, whose chest was barely moving now as white spittle drooled down her chin. The workers fetched drugs, made tea, talked on the walkie-talkie, went about their business.

It took not two days but barely four hours. There was no sound or sudden movement. Just a realization that the gentle rise and fall of Fida's chest was no longer happening and the whites of her eyes seemed to film over. The last thing she may have heard was Amikam cursing the heat as he wiped his brow. As Fida's eyes fluttered a final time, she may have registered the merciless stare of a television zoom lens and Yossi squinting through it barely five feet away. Yossi zoomed into a close-up of Fida's face just as Annette's hand appeared in the frame to close the lids of Fida's eyes for the last time. It was an incredible shot. Her father gave no reaction. His shoulders just sagged even more, and he hunched his arms around his knees and looked at his feet. Maybe he had no tears left. He had already buried his wife and four other children, some in Baidoa and one here only two days earlier. With Fida gone, he had three children left.

Volunteers carried Fida's shrunken body across the road to the cemetery, a crowded field with mounds of freshly dug earth. There was a brief, austere Muslim service, and then Fida Ibrahim, looking like an infant wrapped in a white sheet, was lowered into the ground and covered with earth. Onlookers watched grimly, forming dark silhouettes against the blue sky, another charcoal drawing of stick figures. Children ran and played with slingshots.

Then Mohammed walked slowly back to his hut, where he squatted by an upturned plastic bucket and silently ate a lunch of rice and beans provided by a Somali aid worker. Through a translator, I inquired what he would do next. It was a stupid question, but not as bad as the usual standby, "How do you feel?"

He chewed slowly and swallowed a couple of times before turning to me and answering with a dead face and simple African eloquence: "I just want to go home. Grow crops, raise cattle, find a new wife, and sit under the tree." But this was Somalia, the land where Mad Max came to life, and the worst was yet to come.

Despite our reporting on Aidid, America did seriously underestimate the strongman. The following June, confusion broke out about a legitimate mission by the Pakistani UN force to check Aidid's weapons. Aidid's militiamen thought the UN had come to shut down their radio station, which was at the same site, and a gun battle quickly broke out. At that time there was no such thing as civil discourse among Somalis. If you didn't agree with someone, you shot him. When the surprised Pakistanis tried to retreat, they ran into another Somali reality. There is no such thing as an orderly retreat. Every Somali man had a gun or a rocket launcher, and in southern Mogadishu they all supported Aidid. When they heard the shooting, men and women poured into the streets from all directions, pinning down the lightly armed Pakistani force with thousands of bullets and rockets. Half an hour later, the overwhelmed UN convoy was destroyed. Twenty-four Pakistani soldiers lay dead and fifty wounded.

Within a day of the massacre, Aidid was an outlaw with $25,000 on his head, and the U.S. Army's Delta Force and the Seventy-fifth Ranger Regiment were put on the case. Find General Aidid.

Shortly afterward the phone rang in our little Tel Aviv office. Aidid is the most wanted man in the world, M. L. Flynn from *Nightly News* advised. Go back to Mogadishu. Find the general and interview him before the Americans arrest him, and especially before ABC and CBS do it.

We left within hours for Nairobi, hooked up with a UN aid flight, and landed in Mogadishu the next morning, exhausted. It was our fourth visit in nine months, but this time there was a critical difference. Aidid wasn't there to look after us. He was in hiding, and we couldn't get hold of Osman or any of Aidid's people. And so we suffered the indignity of having to check into the Sahafi, a hotel that had reopened to profit from the world's press. It wouldn't have rated one star anywhere else. The rooms were tiny and boiling, food was scarce, and water was rationed. Somalis looking for work or hawking jewelry and souvenirs clogged up the entrance, and the noisy, busy street in front sent oil fumes and smoke wafting into the little courtyard. At night, the private generator was noisy and ineffective, so the dark corridors were crammed with journalists writing by flashlight while trying to escape the humidity of their bedrooms. In short, it was exactly the same as a dozen other press hotels in the world's war zones, only we'd gotten so accustomed to being in the well-stuffed pocket of the warlord that it came as a shock. The hotel was packed with journalists who shared one goal—find Aidid.

Hanani Rapoport and I knew there was no way to find Aidid unless Aidid wanted us to find him. But, knowing him quite well by now, I was sure that, under such pressure, he would yet again be aching to tell the world how misunderstood he was. So first we had to get the word to the general that we were back in town.

Southern Mogadishu is tiny, barely a square mile, about twenty blocks in every direction. U.S. Marines were manning military roadblocks and running patrols all over town, even at the entrance to Aidid's street. The whole area was surrounded by UN troops from a dozen countries. Still, it was a simple matter to walk around the familiar market area near Aidid's home until we found someone we knew. Being the only unarmed white guys wandering the crowded and noisy narrow streets, especially without guards, wasn't exactly advisable, but we felt we knew the area and the people well enough by now to keep out of trouble, and anyhow, it was the only way to find Aidid.

Sure enough, we soon spotted one of his gunmen lounging against a stall selling a few mangy vegetables. He was wearing the uniform of plastic sandals, cutoff jeans, and an open shirt, and he peered through his cool aviator shades at the whities as we approached. I could see him give a start of recognition, and a wide, friendly smile spread over his face. It was Jama. He was a nice guy apart from the fact that he was usually high on khat. He had horrible green and yellow teeth from chewing it for hours every day of his life since the age of six. On an earlier trip, he'd asked us to bring him some Ray-Ban sunglasses, and here he was, still wearing them. We'd kept our word. So now it paid off. Jama said he didn't know where Aidid was hiding, but he could get us to Osman.

The house next to Aidid's had been flattened by bombs. Aidid's own home had gaping holes in the walls and the roof, and all his gunmen had melted away. His street looked abandoned and eerie, so we waited inside the empty compound where they once put together the technicals.

Within an hour Osman turned up, wary but friendly and as hospitable as ever. He insisted we accompany him to his house, which he visited for an hour or two a day, and we drank tea and talked. He was calm— although he knew he would soon become a target, too. He agreed right away that we needed to get Aidid's view out into the public arena. Osman immediately started cursing the UN, saying they were the true criminals, not Aidid, who was just defending his people's integrity and land. By now I knew them all so well that I could have written the script for them. "The Pakistanis killed fifty of our people. Nobody talks about that, do they?" He jabbed his finger at me. "They're bloody colonialists! Right, right?" Hanani and I agreed. Just take us to your leader, we said, and in time for *Nightly News* tonight.

"Go back to the hotel," Osman said, "and wait. Someone will come to get you. Be ready, day and night. Don't tell anyone."

So Hanani and I waited in one of our smelly little rooms with Kyle Eppler, a versatile cameraman who worked as a one-man band and also did his own editing. He is rather an idiosyncratic person with a nervous laugh that usually came at the wrong time, as if he were laughing at his own thoughts, or maybe more to the point, laughing at us. Hanani and I were getting carried away at the thought of our imminent scoop. Our glee was directed not only at whipping ABC and CBS but at stomping all over our NBC colleagues in Mogadishu, who would be well and truly upset at our success.

As the hours dragged by, it became clearer that we were running out of time to make *Nightly News* tonight and that this could take days. Our mood flagged as we sprawled over the beds, swapping tired jokes and trying to keep our eyes open in the muggy heat. We wouldn't let Kyle leave the room, in case we had to take off in a hurry. He was just beginning to rebel when a Somali hotel worker knocked and told us someone was waiting for us at the gate.

I rushed downstairs to find a young man standing nervously on the street. But there was one small problem. I had never seen him before, and he looked like the last person I would trust. It was dark. I could barely see his eyes, which he kept turned away, and his shoulders were hunched, as if he didn't want to be recognized.

"Let's go," he said.

"Where?" I asked, trying to decide whether to trust him.

"I don't know. I just have to drop you off somewhere."

"What do you think?" Hanani asked me when I told him I didn't feel great about this guy. He could have been anyone, and there were plenty of crooks and killers around looking for easy pickings.

Kyle was ready to go, but as team leader I had to decide whether this was worth the risk. It was eight o'clock at night; some houses had private generators, but otherwise there was no electricity in town. In the streets, the only light came from the half-moon, which sent spooky shadows. There was a curfew, and the streets were highly dangerous. The only people out were nervous, light-triggered UN troops and Somali boys doped out on root drugs. A couple of nights earlier, almost directly outside the hotel, UN troops had blasted a civilian car, killing everyone inside, just because they broke the curfew, and the troops were on edge. The wrecked car stood as a reminder. Nighttime was the wrong time in Mogadishu.

"Okay, I say let's go," I said finally. "Anyway, this isn't going to happen during the day, is it?"

Hanani answered, "If it's okay with you, it's okay with me."

Kyle was already at the door, wondering what the fuss was all about.

We sauntered downstairs carrying the bare minimum: a camera, tripod, two small lights, and spare cassettes and batteries, trying not to look as if we were going out on a shoot. Press hotels are notorious. The moment one crew spots another leaving with a camera, they'll follow just in case you're on to something, and pretty soon the entire hotel of hacks will be trailing you to breakfast on the corner.

Now we were crammed into a small car and driving slowly down dark, narrow side streets to avoid roadblocks. We were entering deeper and deeper into the deadly labyrinth of southern Mogadishu, where, if things turned sour, there was no hope of rescue. The driver broke the silence to ask in English, "Aren't you afraid to be driving here with someone you don't know?"

Good question, I thought. I could have answered, "Aren't you afraid to be driving in a car with *three* people you don't know?" But the answer was obvious. What did he have to worry about? He probably packed a gun. We had a camera. He knew where he was going. We didn't. He had friends nearby to help him. Our friends were in New York. Was I afraid? Not really. By now we were committed, so fear didn't help. We had made the call, and judged it safe enough. But by any rational measure, we were nuts to put our lives into the hands of a stranger in a place like Mogadishu. It was another example of journalists committing themselves totally beyond reason just to get a good story; finding Aidid would kill the competition.

I judged the risk to be slight, but what the hell did I know? It was a Daniel Pearl moment, and there have been plenty of them. Would I do that today? Not a chance. Too many journalists have died in Iraq in recent years to be so cavalier about the risks.

Today, NBC would want to be part of the decision; they'd assign tough ex–British army bodyguards who would make risk assessments and say things like "We must reduce our TED"—"time exposed to danger." Once al-Qaeda operatives in Jordan offered me the chance to interview Abu Musab al-Zarkawi, their leader in Iraq with a $25 million price on his head. They wanted me to fly to Baghdad, then entrust myself to al-Qaeda terrorists on the ground. I politely declined.

Mogadishu was slightly more innocent in those days, though just as deadly. We came to a halt at, of all places, the hospital. When we got out of the car, the driver slammed his door and drove off fast. We stood lost for a moment, until another man took over and led us to the basement, where we waited a few minutes until yet another man came. He took us to a back door, and we climbed into another car. Another short drive, another car swap, another short drive, and we were in the courtyard of a rather fancy villa. The gate clanged shut behind us.

We had arrived. As we carried the gear up the outside steps to the first floor, I said to Hanani that there was no time to set up the lights. We would just do the interview with one sun gun attached to the top of the camera. "Let's get this over with," I said. "We've got to get on air tonight." It was a ridiculous moment. This was the most wanted man on the planet, an intelligent warlord with a lot to say to a world that would be fascinated to hear it, and all I could think of was "Okay, two questions, then let's get the hell back to make the show tonight." I was exultant. I kept winking at Hanani, and he grinned back. He was thinking the same thing: We did it!

But had we? Where the hell was Aidid? We sat and we fidgeted and they kept offering us tea and we kept declining, somehow hoping that would hurry things along. Was he even coming? I looked at my watch: 9:30 P.M. *Nightly News* aired at 1:30 A.M. Somali time. Time was running out to make the news tonight.

Then the door swung open. Osman walked in smiling. He held the door, and following him strode the man on top of the world's most-wanted list, the food-aid robber and Pakistani killer, the self-proclaimed president of Somalia, General Mohammed Farrah Aidid.

Kyle filmed as we smiled and shook hands. It was a strange feeling, he inquiring about my health and I asking him how he was. "Nice," he said in a rather quiet, tired voice, but he was beaming. He wore a well-pressed blue striped shirt and purple tie. As usual he spoke as if he was in denial. He could not understand why the UN saw him as a criminal and thought the world must support him. "I'm defending my land," he kept insisting, "my country. How can they decide?" he asked. "Just like that they decide to arrest a person who has not committed any crime?"

"It's simple," I said. "The UN sees you as the man whose men killed the twenty-four Pakistani peacekeepers, and for that reason they want to arrest you."

"This is untrue, absolutely." Aidid kept denying he'd had anything to do with the massacre and declared that the UN had issued the arrest warrant after getting false information from his enemies.

"Would you surrender?"

"For what reason I have to surrender? I am not guilty," Aidid said. "The people who are guilty, who have killed, who have destroyed Somali property, these people are guilty, and these people should be subjected to arrest, not me."

"What will happen if the UN tries to arrest you?" I asked.

"I believe my people will defend me," Aidid said.

Osman interjected loudly: "There will be a bloodbath."

Thank you and good night, I thought. Time to run.

Anybody seeing this interview and aware of the fanatic tribal support Aidid enjoyed on his home turf, as well as his own record as a cunning and tough fighter, could have predicted what would happen when Delta Force and the Rangers finally moved against him. Aidid's people did defend him, and it was a bloodbath. The Americans lost eighteen of their most elite fighters, and the Somalis lost as many as a thousand. Nobody ever did catch Aidid, or for that matter interview him again in hiding. He emerged from the shadows just that one time to deliver his warning and was swallowed up again, to reappear in public only after the Americans fled Somalia in disarray.

But equally predictable was the way of Aidid's demise. General Aidid and his chief backer, Osman Hassan Ali Ato, like the Khmer Rouge leaders, and like most bands of thieves, eventually fell out over control of their clan. After the Americans pulled out of Somalia, there was a quick return to anarchy. Osman started his own militia, which fought a number of gun battles with Aidid's fighters until one day Aidid was shot. His death at age fifty-nine is still a mystery, though. Some claim that he was felled by a stray bullet, others that he was shot twice, in the liver and neck, and that he died on the operating table. There are rumors that American Special Forces were involved, but then there always are. Aidid's own radio station claimed that he died of a heart attack "while performing his national duties."

One strange twist is for real: Aidid was succeeded as warlord by one of his sons, Hussein Mohammed Aidid, an ex–U.S. Marine who grew up in California and served his country for two weeks in Somalia as a translator.

While the press focus had switched to the troubled American role in Somalia and the hunt for the fugitive Aidid, the fight against famine, which had killed 350,000 people, was notching up successes. One nurse in a feeding center in Afgoi, near Baidoa, told me that, six months after the aid began getting through, there had been a dramatic reversal. In her feeding center, where they once had forty deaths a day, they were down to five a week. I had my own anecdotal evidence. The first time I'd come to Somalia to cover the famine, the children had followed us everywhere, begging for food. Today all they wanted was my pen.

On my last trip to Somalia, I thought a good story would be to check up on Mohammed, Fida Ibrahim's father, and see if he'd found a new wife, as he'd wished. Maybe his three remaining children would be looking after him back in his old village and he'd be feeding his cattle and planting new crops. I loved the image of him realizing his dream by sitting peacefully under a tree at last, and I hoped it was true. It would be a good way to put a face on the success of the international mission against starvation.

To find him, we went back to Camp Smola Smola, close to Aidid's area. But we had another reason, too. Our cameraman, Yossi Mulla, was on his own aid mission. He had told his ten-year-old daughter, Dana, about all the hungry children, and that all they had to eat was protein biscuits and various food supplements and, if they were lucky, rice. Dana, a lovely, sensitive girl, immediately got to work raising vast quantities of something she felt the starving Somali kids needed far more than boring old rice. She got all her school friends to give up some of their pocket money, and they bought buckets of candy for Daddy to deliver.

So while I was out looking for Mohammed, or somebody who knew what had become of him, Yossi, with the help of the aid workers, tried to line up hundreds of kids to hand out Dana's candy. He had bags of the stuff hanging from his shoulders, and pandemonium quickly ensued, but it was a happy, laughing chaos. The aid workers quickly stood back to enjoy the sight of the happy children and an even happier Yossi, a big, burly former Israeli paratrooper, who was doling out candy with one hand and snapping photos with the other. With her presents Dana included a note in English to the Somali children. It read: "For You With Love From Israel, Dana," and she'd drawn a little flower at the bottom of the page.

However, the Hollywood script ends there. Since we'd filmed the death of Fida, another of Mohammed's daughters had died in the camp. He had finally left the Mogadishu feeding station to walk back to his home village, taking his two surviving children with him. The refugee camp had not been his salvation after all. Maybe he figured, if they were all going to die, they might as well die at home. Although the aid workers remembered him because of our film, nobody knew the name of his village or how to find it. The trail faded out.

There aren't enough happy endings in real life, and certainly not in that miserable land of war and famine. Years later I read this Somali poem, and again I wondered whether Mohammed ever found his quiet place under the tree:

Three things one does not recover from—
Oppression that knows the backing of brute force,
Poverty that brings the destitution of one's home,
And being deprived of children.

Oppression, poverty, the death of children: These could also be the connecting threads of my career, all framed by war and mayhem. What a job, I thought. I could also do with a quiet place under a tree sometimes. But for me, taking a break from the sadness of Somalia in 1992–93 meant covering the Israeli-Palestinian crisis at home, and side trips to even worse wars, in Croatia and Bosnia, including the siege of Sarajevo. It was wearing. The closer I came to each conflict, the more painful they became for me to witness. The adrenaline rush of covering the news and staying safe could protect me only so far. I had begun to understand that danger isn't only physical. More than the body can hurt.

It was about this time that I first read a quotation from an unidentified French existentialist writer: "You cannot stop this world from being a place that tortures children, but you can stop some children from being tortured." This exhortation to do whatever little you can to make the world a better place guided me from then on. I could never forget Fida Ibrahim and the horror of her dying with our camera in her face. I think that story is the worst thing I ever did. But did it stop some other children from dying of starvation? I hope so.

Seven

The River of Death

First they came for the socialists and I didn't speak out—I wasn't a socialist.
Then they came for the trade unionists and I didn't speak out—I wasn't a trade unionist.
Then they came for the Jews and I didn't speak out—I wasn't a Jew.
Then they came for me—and there was nobody left to speak for me.

—Lutheran pastor Martin Niemoeller,
Nazi concentration camp survivor

In 1993, United Nations peacekeepers were dispatched to oversee a grudging peace settlement in a minor war between the mostly Tutsi Rwandan Patriotic Front and the mostly Hutu Rwandan government. Soon, however, warnings began to pile up of a Hutu "final solution" to the Tutsi problem. The government had bought 6 million machetes from Dubai for a population of 8 million people. Hutu radio stations repeatedly called on listeners to prepare for a slaughter of the "cockroaches." Officers from the UN reported that, in training, Hutu militias had increased their slaughter rate to a thousand Tutsis in twenty minutes. They even reported that Hutus planned to kill Belgian UN officers to make them abandon their mission.

Then, on April 6, 1994, two African presidents were killed in a mysterious plane crash. The men had unfamiliar names: Juvenal Habyarimana of Rwanda and Cyprien Ntaryamira of Burundi. A day later, eyewitnesses said the female Rwandan prime minister was gang-raped and shot in the head. When ten Belgian UN soldiers were killed by the Hutus, the entire garrison fled to Europe. With no one to stop them, and using mostly machetes and clubs, Hutu mobs killed eight hundred thousand defenseless Tutsis in one hundred days, making the efficient Nazi killing machine seem plodding.

There is no shortage of blame for the Rwandan tragedy. Certainly UN leaders ignored warnings from their own peacekeepers, and Secretary-General Kofi Annan even denied getting them. But the seeds were sown much earlier. Before Belgium won control of Rwanda from Germany during the First World War, real differences between Tutsis and Hutus hadn't existed. These people had lived quietly on the same land as one community, speaking the same language and sharing the same culture. Locally, the terms *Hutu* and *Tutsi* had referred to class rather than tribal identities. Anyone who owned more than ten cows had been considered a Tutsi; anyone with fewer than ten, a Hutu.

In 1916, in classic colonial style, the Belgians decided that they needed an "officer" class to help them control the land. They chose the minority Tutsis because, the Belgians claimed, this group was taller and had lighter skin and thinner lips. In other words, the Belgians thought the Tutsis were more like them, so clearly they must be smarter. From then on, Tutsis were sent to good schools and given the best jobs. Jealousy arose among the Rwandans, and when the Europeans left, civil war broke out. Belgium set up the rivalry, then turned away when it got bloody.

The media, too, contributed to the Tutsis' fate. Treating the initial civil war as just another African dustup allowed us to neglect it. I can't help but wonder what might have happened had Rwanda's civil war been portrayed fully and accurately as another evil colonialist legacy, instead of merely a simplified Tutsi-versus-Hutu tribal conflict. Maybe Europe would have assumed its share of responsibility in time to save lives. Maybe UN troops would have stayed instead of abandoning the natives. Instead, we all but ignored it. One analyst* added up the stories from Rwanda during the four-

---

*Peter Uvin is the Henry J. Leir Professor of International Studies and director of the Institute for Human Security at Tufts University. He recently published *Aiding Violence: The Development Enterprise in Rwanda*. An op-ed by him appeared in *The Providence Journal-Bulletin* on March 11, 1999 (p. 87).

year conflict leading up to the genocide and found that two-thirds were about saving the gorillas. When the press finally moved to cover the story, it was largely because so many of us found ourselves already on the continent, covering South Africa's first truly democratic elections.

First word of the genocide wafted gently into our Johannesburg newsroom like a breeze off the Rwandan hills. It was classic Africa: Stories begin with a rumor upriver—something's building in the bush. Usually there's an aid agency statement, followed by a report from UN troops and then a short news service bulletin. Information builds like a drumbeat. There's fighting in the villages, children are fleeing. Refugees reach the towns with horror stories. The first reaction to the horror stories beginning to emerge from Rwanda was no more than the classic "It's nothing to worry about." Just another tribal punch-up. What do you expect? African civil wars rarely attracted much attention, unless, as in the Shaba invasion of Zaire, whites were involved. As for those names, they were almost comic: Hutu versus Tutsi. Who? What's the difference? Even I, who had lived in Africa for four years, knew little about Rwanda, a landlocked country the size of Maryland in the continent's east-central area.

Events showed later that, if the world had intervened forcefully, the Hutus could have been stopped in their tracks. Hundreds of thousands of lives could have been saved. Yet we journalists got it wrong, which leads me to a painful and complicated question: What share of the blame did I personally bear? In Somalia I had faced serious dilemmas about how to shape my own coverage: whether to film a dying girl, how deep to put myself in the pocket of the warlord. In Rwanda, by contrast, I had little freedom to maneuver. This was genocide, and all I could do was look on from safety across the border. Yet this is small comfort. Like everyone else, I turned my back on Rwanda, getting there late, then returning to the comfort of my family life in Israel and coming back only when it was all over. As a son of Holocaust survivors, burdened by the world's failure to save my family, I should have done more, done something, done anything. To this day I regard Rwanda as the world's failure, a hard lesson on the limits of the world's conscience, and my own.

. . .

Tom Brokaw fingered the world's apathy in his studio introduction to my first NBC report from Rwanda, on May 4, 1994, almost a month after the bloodbath began. In Bosnia, Tom pointed out, NATO had intervened as two hundred thousand people died in two years. But in Rwanda two hundred thousand died in four weeks, and the world turned away. Why? He continued: "It is Rwanda, tucked away in the middle of black Africa. No strategic importance to us, no natural resources to speak of. So why should we care? Well, think about that as you watch this. Fair warning. It is a horror story of epic proportions. Martin Fletcher made his way to the Rwanda border with Tanzania . . ."

I had been in South Africa, part of a large NBC News team covering the historic voting that marked the end of apartheid and the election of Nelson Mandela as the nation's first black president. The story was just beginning to wind down when I saw an AP story datelined Ngara in Tanzania. The headline read: "Rebels Close Border after 250,000 Refugees Flee to Tanzania." The story went on: "Fleeing weeks of ethnic slaughter in Rwanda . . . the meandering river of humanity was sure to overwhelm international relief agencies . . . the border was closed Saturday by Rwandan rebels, stranding tens of thousands of other Rwandans seeking to escape the slaughter."*

This was the first formal report I'd seen of mass killing in Rwanda. With so many people fleeing over a small bridge, I thought, the story was huge. We had to be there. That news flash was read in the same instant by editors the world over, and I knew the rush was on. Who would get there first? Unfortunately for me, NBC assigned Brian Williams, a top reporter and already anointed anchor, to the story, and I felt crushed. But my luck turned. Brian had to return to the States for a court appearance, and I got the call. Could I get up there as soon as possible to do a magazine piece for NBC's *Now* program? You bet! Because NBC was in full foreign mode

---

*Reid G. Miller, "Rebels Close Border after 250,000 Refugees Flee to Tanzania," April 30, 1994.

covering the elections, we had a great team in place. I was blessed with two of the network's top producers, *Nightly News*'s M. L. Flynn and Mike Mosher from the Burbank bureau. With two camera crews, including our man in Africa, the legendary Tony Wasserman; Maurice Roper, an excellent freelance cameraman; and Vicky Butler, an American fixer with extensive knowledge of aid matters, I couldn't go wrong.

Then the phone rang again. By the way, we want this story on the air in three days. What? I'm in South Africa, I pointed out. The story is in the jungle two thousand miles away. We'd have to get there, film the story, return, then write and edit it. About a week's work. And that assumed a smooth trip, which didn't exist in Africa. But *Now* was a weekly show, and if we missed the program, the story wouldn't air at all. And on the other end of the phone was Jeff Zucker, *Now* magazine's executive producer, who thirteen years later would become president and chief executive of NBC Universal. Jeff was NBC's wunderkind; no was not an option.

Our journey was a forty-eight-hour stab into the heart of Africa. It took a scheduled flight to Nairobi, a single-engine charter flight to Mwanza in Tanzania, another small charter to a dirt landing strip near the border, six hours in two jeeps, a hand-winched river ferry, and another jeep ride to reach one of the eeriest, most horrific sights I have ever seen, on the bridge over the Rusumo Falls along the Kagera River, which marks the border between Rwanda and Tanzania. Two days earlier, the little bridge, wide enough for one car, had seen what the UNHCR called "the largest and fastest refugee exodus in modern times." Two hundred and fifty thousand people had squeezed across in one day, some prodding goats, cattle, and oxen, some wheeling bicycles, but most carrying nothing.

We drove our jeeps along muddy trails through lush green hills and thick bush, past children with machetes and men with spears, until we arrived around midday at an open field of scrub and head-high elephant grass that stretched to the horizon, with scraggy bushes and a single large tree in the distance. I looked on in amazement. It was as if you had taken several football stadiums of people and dumped them outside town. Way outside. A quarter of a million people stood or lay aimlessly on the ground as dark clouds gathered overhead. Some had constructed cover from sticks and grass. Most had no shelter or food. The only water available came from a nearby animal watering hole, where dirty scum was already collecting on the surface. Smoke from the campfires stung the eyes, and the air carried the piercing, choking smell of feces and sweat. These were the refugees who had crossed the bridge in the twenty-four hours that it was open, a small window of opportunity between the fleeing Rwandan army abandoning the border post and the Tutsi rebels closing it. Aid agencies were already overwhelmed, and tens of thousands more refugees were said to be waiting inside Rwanda, desperate to escape.

We decided to spend the night with the refugees and leave the next morning. It seemed an awfully short stay after such a long journey, but we had a deadline to meet and competition to beat. Some journalists had beaten us to the camp, including, to our discomfort, Ron Allen, then of ABC News, a formidable competitor. However, he seemed equally put out by our arrival, turning on his heel and disappearing among the crush. It was easy enough to cover the story: The tableau of suffering spread out before us was appalling. But I had other ideas. I wanted to keep driving. I had the original AP story in my hand, and what gripped me the most were two sentences in the seventeenth paragraph. It seemed to me that AP had buried the lead: "Bradley Guerrant, a World Food Program field officer, said bodies were floating down the Akagera River, which marks the border, at the rate of one every fifty yards. 'They are fully clothed women, children, men,' he said."

Every man and his dog will reach the camp, I thought, and they'll stay here, like ABC. I want to be the first to reach the river. So after a brief discussion, we agreed to split up. M.L. would stay in the camp with Tony and begin to film the refugees. Mike, Maurice, Matt the soundman, and I would head west, toward Rwanda. I already had the killer phrase for those bodies swept downriver: "The River of Death." I know it sounds hackneyed, cavalier, and callous. But covering the news contains a basic dichotomy: extreme sympathy for the victims coupled with the extreme thrill of the chase. In our ability to enjoy our jobs, reporters may be compared to the heart surgeons who work while listening to music and discussing football. Or to firemen who, on the way to a deadly blaze, joke about girls. Weird as my occupation is, it comes with certain demands, and one of them is to write the script.

We had no idea where the river was, so we just kept driving west, through the bush and the trees that closed in on the road. It took an hour to cover the ten miles, and words can't describe the sight that greeted us. Until then, there had been almost no pictures of the Hutu genocide against the Tutsis. In the first days, almost four weeks earlier, fleeing journalists had managed to snatch a few pictures of piles of bodies, but the BBC, for instance, refused to broadcast them because they were too gory.* Not surprisingly, nobody had filmed any scenes of killing. It was much too dangerous for journalists to enter the country. The Hutus had killed white soldiers, so they'd have no hesitation about killing white reporters. A couple of reporters continued bravely to file for radio and print from their homes in the capital, Kigali, but nobody was foolish enough to wander around with a big television camera. So reports were emerging, but with no visual proof. Now here it was, before our eyes.

It was a long, drifting journey for the victims, macheted in the neck, arms and heads hacked off, faces crushed by clubs, bodies burned, some lucky ones merely shot or drowned. What we couldn't see was the terror they had suffered. We learned about it later: mass government-sanctioned rape, the killing of the girls, husbands forced to kill wives, children herded into schoolrooms and set ablaze, neighbors beheading neighbors, the remains then tossed into the Nyabarongo River, which carried its gruesome jetsam into the Kagera River and over the Rusumo Falls beneath our feet. All this in the name of some fanciful ethnic distinction.

In better times, honeymooners may snap pictures of each other here. It is a beautiful small waterfall where the river narrows before entering the

---

*Tom Giles, "Media Failure over Rwanda Genocide." BBC news online (http://news.bbc.co.uk/2/hi/programmes/panorama/3599423.stm).

gorge. Thick trees and bushes line the banks, while big dark rocks divide the waters. Upriver, the current gathers clods of grass and fallen branches, but these were now clumped together with corpses and body parts. They glided gently in the stream, like dead fish. The sun flashed off them as they began to toss and turn in the surging water; then the human wreckage gathered speed as it reached the precipice and plummeted over in cascades of water. The waters met halfway down, churning their awful contents, which smashed into the river ten yards below. Stiffened, whitened bodies, many naked with bloated genitals, washed against one another in quiet eddies at the foot of the falls.

As I leaned on the yellow railings of the bridge, looking over the falls, I began my report by ad-libbing to the camera:

> This has to be the most grotesque contradiction I've ever seen. Look at that waterfall, all the power and strength and beauty of Africa, and yet you look closer and you see, what's that, going over the waterfall, and you realize, it's a body. This waterfall also hides all the evil and ugliness and violence of Africa. Bodies are falling over this waterfall at the rate of 30 an hour—4,500 bodies a week. Both tribes in Rwanda, the Hutus and the Tutsis, slaughtering each other for the last month and dumping the bodies into this river— the river of death.

The bodies, which drifted all the way to Lake Victoria, 120 miles from Kigali, polluting the river as they went, were just a tiny fraction of the victims. Yet in the horror of the moment, I made a mistake that typified the stereotypes of Western reporting. "Both tribes in Rwanda, the Hutus and the Tutsis, slaughtering each other for the last month . . ." It was what I expected, derived from the common Western perception that, after all, that's what they do to each other in Africa. I still did not realize how one-sided the genocide was. And by assuming, in my ignorance, that it was a mutual destruction, just more African bloodletting, I made it easier for viewers to turn away. I presented the killing in purely tribal terms. I didn't yet know enough of the history of the Hutus and the Tutsis to present the story as it really was: yet another wicked legacy of Europe's wildly successful colonial policy of divide and rule.

But it gets worse. In my hurry to cover the story and get back to Johannesburg on deadline, I didn't realize that most of the 250,000 refugees in the camp were not Tutsis fleeing the genocide but Hutus fleeing Tutsi revenge. After the killing started, the Tutsi Rwandan Patriotic Front, based in neighboring Uganda, had swept across the border to stop the slaughter of its people. The Hutu-dominated government army, so effective at raping and murdering civilians, quickly fled and encouraged a mass exodus of Hutus in front of the advancing RPF. Most of the people whom we were filming in the camp, then, and whom the aid organizations were helping, were the Hutu killers and their families, while Tutsis were still being annihilated by other Hutus inside Rwanda. Those Tutsis who did manage to reach the camp were now surrounded by their Hutu tormentors. It was as if Jewish survivors of the Holocaust were housed next to the very Nazi guards who had operated the gas chambers.

Wandering through the dense crowds, we came across one remarkable woman, a thirty-year-old Tutsi called Alpeeza, a name I can render only phonetically. She was lucky. She had walked for a month with her husband and their four children, and all were still alive. They even had a pot, a pan, and a blanket. Like many Africans in tragic moments, she spoke in short, clear phrases, each of which contained a world of tragedy and pain that can hardly be imagined.

Standing among her friends, I asked her, piercingly, "What happened to you?"

She answered, "We could sleep on the road with no food, with no water, people died on the road because of hunger. I saw those who were shot on the border, just as they were about to cross the border. They shot them, just like that."

"You saw that?"

"Yes, I just crossed the border, then they put those behind me in a line and then they shoot them."

"And what did they do with the bodies?"

"They throw them in the river."

When I asked Alpeeza's friends to raise their hands if they had lost a family member, I couldn't count, there were too many hands up. Many Tutsis had lost a hundred or more relatives from their extended families. Only a few were able to escape through the woods and the bush.

"Do they want the war to end now or do they want revenge first?" I asked.

Alpeeza translated, and a low murmur rose from their throats. Then, in her strong, dignified voice, clearly enunciating each word so that I could understand her accent, Alpeeza pointed the way to what is today the most hopeful development from the Rwandan genocide: the desire of both Hutus and Tutsis to put the slaughter behind them and to live together in peace. "They want the war to stop so that they can go back," she said. Today, broadcasters in Kigali are told not to say "Tutsi" or "Hutu," only "Rwandans."

We passed that night in a tent among the refugees, waking before dawn to film their early morning rituals: the search for somewhere to relieve themselves, the search for dry twigs to make a fire, the search for water and food, the search for everything we take so much for granted. Many had simply slept in the open with no protection. An hour after daybreak, a truck arrived, driven by two men who carried bows and arrows for protection. Refugees got a pound of beans each to last four days. They fought over sacks of rice. Aid workers warned of the danger of malnutrition and epidemics of malaria and dysentery from the filthy water.

We couldn't do a satellite feed from the field, or transmit via the Internet, so before noon we began our mad dash back to Johannesburg, hoping to put together the reports before we missed the show. We made our deadline for the *Now* program and also provided reports for the *Today* show and the *Nightly News*.

The pictures of bodies crashing over the waterfall were indeed seen as the first real evidence of the mass slaughter; in fact, the show couldn't get enough of them. Initially we included just three shots, trying to stay as tastefully wide as possible so as not to shock the audience with crushed heads and slashed torsos. But Jeff Zucker kept insisting that we include more and more, until every picture Maurice Roper had taken of the victims in the river appeared on air. And Zucker was absolutely right. The world needed to see those relentless pictures: corpse after corpse petrified in grotesque poses, gulped down in the surge of water, then thrown up and floating gently downriver again. These corpses bore witness to man's savagery, and our failure to prevent it. It was a shocking, powerful report that won a News and Documentary Emmy for Outstanding Background/ Analysis—ironic, I thought later, given that I had failed to understand who was doing what to whom, and why.

From South Africa I returned home, and the appalling things I had seen in Rwanda quickly slipped my mind. The day I got back to Israel, we celebrated Hagar's fortieth birthday. A week later, my partner and I won the Israeli catamaran racing championships. I was proud of being a national champion for the first time in my life, never mind that I wasn't Israeli or that there were only six boats in the race. A week later, I traveled to London to spend time with my sick father. Then I covered another gigantic event in the sorry history of Palestine, the triumphant return of Yasir Arafat and the PLO to the West Bank and Gaza. It was a busy couple of months, marked by happiness, concern for my father, and hard work. What I didn't think about much was the carnage in Rwanda. Like everyone else, I knew about it but had other things to do. By the time the genocide ended, around July 6, when the RPF took control of the capital, at least eight hundred thousand Rwandans, mostly Tutsis, were dead.

Even when I returned to Rwanda, on July 25, I still didn't fully get it. If it was possible, the scenes that greeted me in Goma, a small town on Zaire's border with Rwanda, were even more horrific than those in the Kagera River. A million refugees had crammed into the Goma camps, with hundreds dying daily. Others had succumbed to fatigue, disease, and hunger. Their bodies, wrapped in rags and blankets, lined the roads for miles, little bundles of death, sometimes stacked in piles. Bulldozers scooped them up, threw them onto trucks, and buried them in mass graves. By now, though, the world had mobilized. The small airport on the outskirts of Goma was packed with humanitarian flights, military planes from Europe and America, and officials briefing the press on how much they were helping. Chiefs from the U.S. Army called the aid effort a race against time to save the sick and dying.

As at Ngara three months earlier, journalists initially confused the identity of these men, women, and children fleeing Rwanda. They were not Tutsi survivors, as one might expect, but the Hutu killers. As the Tutsi RPF continued their advance through Rwanda, the government army fell back, until eventually it dropped its weapons altogether and fled across the borders, persuading Hutu tribespeople to flee, too, by warning them of Tutsi revenge massacres. Soon, though, the real story became clear. The Hutu militias were still operating, hidden among Hutu civilian refugees and receiving humanitarian aid inside Zaire's refugee camps. And here was the world, which had stayed away when the Tutsis were massacred, finally rushing in to help the perpetrators, while the victims searched for their dead in Rwanda.

My team and I resolved to turn our backs on the Hutu suffering in Goma, which by now was saturated with media, and head into Rwanda, where no network journalists had gone, to find the Tutsi victims. But I had another reason for leaving Goma: I couldn't take it anymore. For the first time in my career, I had come up against a scene of human suffering that I couldn't stomach, couldn't film, couldn't witness.

It was early in the morning, and we were already out in our jeep, cruising around the camps, looking for a story. The sun was just rising as we drove along the deserted main road. On the grass shoulder lay the piles of bodies that had been dragged from the camps for collection and burial. Beyond the corpses, tents of a Red Cross medical station cast shadows over a wide field. It was still a gloomy gray, but pinkish light filtered through the curling smoke of wood fires. A mass of about a thousand refugees were packed against one another, some sitting with their arms curled around their knees, others lying on the ground and beginning to stir, so that their heads started to move and rise above the others. In the middle of it all was the Red Cross flag. Next to the flag, a nurse in a white uniform glanced down and picked her way through the sick people.

A man on a stretcher looked up at the nurse as if for help. Their eyes met, and she walked on. For some reason, the eerie, ghostlike quality of the nurse in white, locking eyes with the ragged dying man and moving on, unable to help, cut to my very core. I flashed back to an event that had happened years before, when I was covering the famine in Sudan. I had looked into the eyes of a man at the very instant he realized that his tiny son, in his arms, had died, and he began to wail. At that moment, I had understood viscerally the reality of death. Now, reliving this, my thoughts flitted to the Holocaust. I found myself imagining the helplessness and hopelessness of the victims, their sense of abandonment and the futility of resistance, their bewilderment at the apathy of the world outside, as well as the hatred and viciousness of the killers, their unwavering determination to hurt me and kill me and kill everyone like me.

All this may be a lot to hang on a quick glance out the jeep window at thirty miles per hour on a dim morning in Africa. And certainly this scene in Rwanda wasn't much worse than other things I'd encountered—the starvation in Somalia the previous year, for example. But now I felt such a haunting sensation of proximity to evil that I couldn't bear it any longer. As I looked away from the nurse, my cameraman, Brian Calvert, said words to the effect of "Hey, great stuff, let's stop and shoot." For the first time ever, I said, "No, I don't want to look, let's keep going."

We packed up two jeeps and crossed the border into Rwanda, heading deeper into that most overworked of African concepts, "the heart of darkness." It fit Kigali at the time. Until then we had only been on the borders. Now, three weeks after the RPF had conquered the capital, we were entering the killing fields. We passed ragged convoys of refugees stretching for miles along a road that wound through beautiful hills and farmland. It seemed almost as though the bright sky and lovely weather were mocking them. Orphans, or "unaccompanied children" as they were termed, were gathered up by aid workers with trucks and driven to one of dozens of orphanages back in Zaire. Many were not orphans at all but children who had lost their parents in the rush to escape. They were Hutus, still fleeing the rumors of massacres by rampaging, revenge-seeking Tutsis. But as we rounded the last hill and descended into Kigali, sixty miles from Goma, we found only a few lone Tutsi soldiers, some UN forces, and one mad dog in a former school, where we set up camp under a big tree.

We had difficulty finding a story, for Kigali was still a ghost town almost literally. When we went into the fields to relieve ourselves, we found dead bodies. We bought vegetables from occasional vendors and scrounged food from French soldiers. We set up a satellite phone and jerry-rigged a shower by the side of a house. We went out in search of people to interview. But nobody was there. The Hutus had fled, and the Tutsis were dead.

It was only ten years later, when I read about the opening of Rwanda's new genocide museum, built upon the tombs of 250,000 victims and featuring heartrending photographs of the 300,000 children who died, that I was able to comprehend how fully we had failed to prevent another holocaust. My friend Arik Bachar, an Israeli journalist, wrote about his visit to the museum and then went on to teach a university course about the common threads of the Nazi holocaust and the Rwandan genocide. Banners at the opening of the Rwandan museum echoed the Jewish lesson from Auschwitz: "Never Again." Arik wrote that, as he stood outside the Gisozi memorial on the hills above Kigali, two Germans tourists arrived on bicycles. There they stood, two Germans and a Jew outside the Rwandan holocaust museum. It could be the opening line of a sick joke. As they discussed their joint history, Arik told the Germans that his grandfather had died in Auschwitz. The Germans' response, speaking for their nation, was like a punch line: "We didn't know."

Maybe some German civilians living under the Nazis didn't, but we certainly didn't have that excuse about Rwanda. We knew. And did nothing. Why? That question, so pertinent for my own family's history, remains with me to this day. Why didn't we stop the killing of eight hundred thousand people? Couldn't we? Is Pastor Niemoeller's statement of self-interest—basically "I'm all right, Jack"—enough of an explanation?

It certainly goes a long way toward explaining the lack of governmental intervention. But government reaction, although most critical, is only part of the story. Some soul-searching by the media wouldn't hurt either. Do the media bear responsibility, too, for having dismissed the conflict until it was too late?

It has frequently been asked whether the Nazi holocaust could have been prevented if television cameras had been present to record the horror and inform the world. But that misses the point. The real question is not whether the world would have listened but whether cameramen would have filmed it. The answer, I think, is no. Nobody filmed the killing in Cambodia, even though there were plenty of television cameramen in the region. Why? Because it was—and is—easy to stop cameramen from filming; just threaten to kill them, and carry out your threat a few times to prove you mean it. That's what happened in Kosovo, which is why there was no television coverage of ethnic cleansing during the war there. I remember standing on a hill in Macedonia, looking across the border into Kosovo, seeing the smoke of burning homes rising in the distance and beating myself for letting the victims down by not daring to cross.

Television would not have prevented the Nazi Holocaust, because the Germans would not have been dumb enough to let anyone film it. And in the same way, apart from a couple of very short shots on the end of the zoom lens, nobody was able to show on television the mass killing in Rwanda. That failure contributed to the genocide.

There were other factors, too. History shows that the value of African blood does not weigh as heavily as European blood for the Western media. For example, the media afforded the Balkan wars heavy coverage for a decade, yet ignored Rwanda until it was too late. Was this because war in the former Yugoslavia threatened the security of its neighbors? Was it because conflicts in Africa are considered routine, while, fortunately, today in Europe they are rare?

It's tempting to think that the media downplayed Rwanda because getting the story was too dangerous. But you don't have to be there to cover the news. It was also too risky to enter Kosovo when the Serbs raped and murdered Kosovar Muslims, burned their homes, and forced them out of the country. So the media besieged the borders for weeks, reporting every twist and turn from the safety of Macedonia and Albania. However dangerous it is, if we want to, we can always find a way to report the news, even if it's just a live cross talk with a correspondent hundreds of miles away from the action.

Maybe it's too expensive to send teams to Africa for weeks at a time? That's certainly an important factor, but media pockets are deep enough when American troops are involved, as in Somalia. Earlier in this chapter, I alluded to the phenomenon of Africa fatigue, the newsman's weary response to yet another tribal dustup. Darfur is just the latest example. Sudan forbids coverage, so there are no television pictures of the killing, only of the burned villages and dislocated refugees that are its aftermath. It is only with the greatest reluctance that news organizations bow to guilt and occasionally pony up the money to send teams to neighboring Chad, from which they can approach the border.

In pondering the media's performance in Rwanda, one might wonder whether covering the story fully would have made any difference. The answer is a resounding yes. The final decision by NATO to intervene in Bosnia was sparked by public outrage at the graphic and shocking pictures taken by ABC News when their crew happened to be filming in the main Sarajevo marketplace as mortars exploded, killing sixty-eight people and wounding two hundred. Three days later, NATO warplanes destroyed four Serb aircraft, setting the stage for NATO intervention. That was on February 8, 1994, two months before the Hutus began killing eight hundred thousand Tutsis, out of sight of the television cameras.

In pointing to my profession's collective failure, I am hardly trying to evade my own responsibility. Sure, I showed up—twice. But each time, I left again and went back to business as usual. In fact, my own insensitivity in Kigali still makes me squirm. After a day or two looking for Tutsi survivors, we drove down a deserted wide street near the center of town, fishing for a story, and came across a lone man pushing up the shutters of an antiques store. We stopped to film and became his first customers. He had excellent items: old ivory carvings, wooden statues, tribal masks from West Africa, Ibo wood carvings, as well as copper and bronze jewelry and beautiful glass beads. Despite my passion for Africa, I had never bought many antiques because I found the wood carvings somber and depressing, and the jewelry too touristy. But this man's collection was of the highest quality, and clearly he needed the business. He would have happily sold the shop's entire contents cheaply, and we would have happily bought it, if we'd had the room to carry it.

As we registered some surprise at the modest amounts he was requesting, it slowly dawned on me why he was in such a rush to sell at these bargain prices. At first I had thought he must have decided to open his shop for a few hours and was in a hurry to sell what he could, make some money, and disappear back to safety. But then it occurred to me: He's breaking into the shop, and we're buying his loot.

A couple of days later, our little shelter under the tree had become a regular campsite as other journalists followed us into town from Goma. They all admired our purchases, and we sent them to the antiques store. I was delighted to see that the shop was open again, and the man had quadrupled his prices. It turned out that he was indeed the rightful owner of the store, one of the first Tutsis back in town, and business was already booming. I felt good for him.

But as I look at my Rwandan acquisitions now—the three masks, the amazing fetish carvings, and the ivory and horn sculptures—I shudder at how detached I must have been to think of bargaining for antiques in Kigali after all the horrific things I had witnessed. It brings me back to the most essential question: How could the world have stood by as so many were slaughtered, in so many places? Well, how could I have bought antiques that I thought had been looted from people whose bodies were still rotting in the fields? I was part of the problem, but then again, that is like saying I was part of the human race. As Pastor Niemoeller belatedly understood, few of us care enough about anybody else until it is too late.

Eight

"Kosovo, Oh, How I Love You"

f I didn't care enough in Rwanda, in Kosovo maybe I cared too much. The Balkan catastrophe began quietly enough. In June 1991, eleven years after the Yugoslav dictator Marshal Tito's death, the Slovenian and Croatian republics finally dared to declare independence from the Socialist Federal Republic of Yugoslavia. The Yugoslav army, controlled by ethnic Serbs, attacked tiny Slovenia the next day. It was a short conflict, unbloody and, for the press, rather pleasant. The Slovenian capital, Ljubljana, was a delightful town with pretty, crooked old houses in pastel colors lining both sides of the river Ljubljanica. It was the summer cherry harvest, and there were many little restaurants with shaded gardens offering music, good, cheap wine, and *zelena solat*—green salad topped with grated Parmesan cheese.

The Yugoslav federation let Slovenia off lightly, ending the war after ten days and about seventy dead, because it preferred to throw all its tanks at Croatia, which had a much larger Serb minority. The Croatian war was long and violent, as was the Bosnian war, which killed at least one hundred thousand people and included an almost four-year-long siege of the Bosnian capital, Sarajevo. I had the dubious privilege of witnessing all the conflicts. When the Bosnian war broke out, NBC assigned Arthur Kent, the famed Gulf War Scud stud, but he refused to go because he had been given late notice and didn't have a flak jacket, helmet, and other protective gear. In a bind, NBC asked me. Although I was aware of the lack of equipment in Bosnia, I didn't hesitate. I knew I could rustle the things up somewhere along the way. Anyhow, after the war in Slovenia, and several trips to the fighting in Croatia, I was keen to go. Vicious civil war in Yugoslavia had been feared since Marshal Tito's death. Now that it was happening, I wasn't going to let the lack of a flak jacket get in my way.

And there was something else. For me, these wars were personal. My family comes from villages and towns all over Central Europe and the Balkans. When I was growing up, my father would speak longingly of the Austro-Hungarian Empire. He would look in the mirror, stroke his mustache, and marvel at his resemblance to Emperor Franz Josef. And the Empress Marie Therese, he would say, such a wise woman! This was the region of my ancestors. I felt at home here. The very place names excited me. Fly to Vienna. Drive to Budapest. Train to Belgrade.

If my family history made me regard Yugoslavia's breakup as my story, it also made reporting there more challenging. After working in Israel, I had begun to feel closer to the people I covered, their stories, their suffering. My approach to reporting had changed: Earlier I had seen my job as a thrill ride, whereas now it was frequently an emotional experience. Here was I, the son of European refugees, seeing desperate refugees, tens of thousands of them, day after day and in the heart of Europe. And then there were the ironies of history to consider. For the most part the people who were now refugees, especially the Croats, were the very same people who had persecuted the Jews during World War II, while the bad guys, the Serbs, had actually helped my people.

The signing of the Dayton Accord brought uneasy peace to Croatia and Bosnia, yet the decade's bitterest Balkan conflict was just beginning. In 1996, when an ethnic Albanian group calling itself the Kosovo Liberation Army began attacking Serb civilians and security personnel, the Serbs responded brutally. The Yugoslavian army and Serbian police units began attacking KLA targets in Kosovo, executing civilians and in some cases wiping out entire families. In 1999, following reports of other Serbian massacres and the dislocation of hundreds of thousands of ethnic Albanians, NATO finally intervened with a bombing campaign against Yugoslavia. Although the Serbs initially stepped up ethnic cleansing in response to the bombing, NATO prevailed, and a few months later Yugoslavia agreed to a UN peace-keeping force in Kosovo. By this time, almost 1 million people, the vast majority of them Kosovar Albanians, had fled their homes.

Only about 10 percent of Kosovo's population was Serb, but the province meant more to Belgrade than just numbers. For Serbs, Kosovo was a kind of Holy Land, the cradle of Serb statehood and a shrine of religion and culture. Here, on the Field of Blackbirds in 1389, the Turks defeated the Orthodox Christian Serbs, ushering in five centuries of Ottoman domination. For me, too, Kosovo was special. Reporting from squalid refugee camps, where brutalized Muslims searched desperately for lost family members, I came closest to reliving my family's own tortured past. Indeed, Kosovo affected me more than any other conflict I have covered. Everything seemed to echo the past. My challenge there was to make sense of what I was seeing and to stay safe in a world that seemed to be repeating all its mistakes.

Each war generates its unforgettable symbols—the trenches of the First World War, the concentration camps of the Second, or POWs in Vietnam, or suicide bombers in Israel's conflict with the Palestinians. Muslim refugees symbolized the war in Kosovo. Serbs raped them, massacred them, and, finally, in an ugly euphemism that resonated around the world, ethnically cleansed them. Eight hundred thousand Muslims fled Kosovo in a vicious two months.

One of these was Yehona Aliu, a lost child whom we came across in a British army tent in Stankovic 1 refugee camp in Macedonia, a few miles from the Kosovo border. Yehona was five years old, with green eyes, a thin, pixie face, short chestnut hair, and an impish grin. A British army captain, Bob Soper, put her up in his tent, fed her, and swore he would find her parents. He called Yehona the "Face of Kosovo." He had taken a shine to this sweet face in the crowd.

And what a crowd it was. In an open field at Blace, just off the main road into Macedonia and down from the border post, sixty thousand Muslim refugees were crammed between the railway tracks and the road. Macedonian police built wire barriers to pen them in. Winter was drawing to a close, and the refugees huddled together and shivered in the wet and cold. Before the aid agencies arrived, the only food and water were brought by sympathetic local villagers who tossed bottles and bags into the crowd. The villagers were trying to help, but the scarcity led to pandemonium as men fought for the food while children fell and were crushed in the mud. Each day more trainloads of refugees arrived, and still others came by car or on foot. All were funneled into this seething human holding pen, and somewhere in there, as my NBC crew and I arrived to begin our work, were Yehona and her mother and brothers and sisters.

We journalists all had the same reaction. We were used to desperate refugee scenes in Africa and Asia, but in Europe? People who looked like us and wore clothes like ours and were accustomed to sleeping in warm rooms, having a fridge in the kitchen and a television in the living room, were suddenly reduced to living like famine-stricken Somalis or Ethiopians. In Africa, such tragedies fit into the seemingly endless cycle of drought, war, and famine. Here in Central Europe, they had seemed no longer possible.

The scenes we saw harked back to the Second World War. The Muslims had become the Jews, the Serbs the Nazis. Trainloads of Muslims were refused entry into Macedonia and forced to return to possible death in Kosovo, just like the Jews had been forced to return to Germany when no nation would take them in. Of course, the truth was a whole lot more complicated, but for me, these echoes of the Holocaust had a special ring because my own family had suffered in ways very similar to the scenes unfolding below me now in that cold, swampy field at Blace.

Like everybody else in the British army base, I lost my heart to Yehona. She was a tragic child who, hour after hour, drew pictures of her mummy and daddy and sang her own words to the tune of a famous Kosovo folk song her father had taught her. As Yehona sang, "Kosovo, oh, how I love you," she added her own refrain, "Oh, Daddy, where are you, why have you left me?" The Muslim woman who was holding her looked away and cried.

Later we learned that, when the Serbs burned houses in their village and began to kill Muslims, Yehona's father, Sherif, had spirited his family away and told his wife, Sadie, to escape to Macedonia through the mountains. He'd stayed behind to fight the Serbs and had not been heard of since. Like thousands of refugees, Sadie, her son, and her daughter Yehona, had taken to the woods and, moving in groups of ten and twenty, had evaded the Serbs. After two weeks of cold and hunger, they made it to Blace, where they huddled together with the masses of refugees hoping for a warm welcome. This they did not receive. Their lives had been saved, but their problems were just beginning.

In the teeming, squalid crush, Yehona had wanted to go to the toilet but had been too embarrassed to squat down in front of strangers. She wandered off, looking for a spot to be alone. When she tried to find her mother again, she couldn't. She was lost and frightened in a horde of desperate refugees. She had nowhere to go and nobody to care for her.

At night, the temperature fell to the low thirties. Yehona's only protection came from the clothes she wore. Nobody could spare a blanket. Around her, women gave birth, while others, sick, called for medicine. Pneumonia and dysentery began to spread, and there was talk of measles. Each night half a dozen people, especially the old and the young, died of exposure. Noon brought heavy rain that turned the earth to mud, and a cold wind froze it. Every moment brought more misery, more frustration, more people. One day, I watched as five trains arrived from Kosovo, each with eighteen coaches and about five thousand people. A woman told us, "The Serbs came with machine guns. I remember the film about the Nazis and the Jewish people and how they put them in the trains. It was exactly the same scene." Twenty people were forced into a carriage that seated eight. They stood all the way, crammed together just as the Jews had been in the Nazi transports.

Others who couldn't board the train from the capital, Pristina, found the tracks and followed them a hundred miles out of Kosovo. One small, dark man trudged along with his frail father lying across his shoulders, his paralyzed legs sticking straight out as if pointing the way. When they finally reached the border, the refugees passed through a corridor of women lining the railroad tracks. The women were frantically scanning the exhausted new arrivals for a familiar face, hoping to find a husband, father, or son. There was a chilling absence of men of fighting age. Everyone knew of the shootings and massacres. American officials spoke of one hundred thousand missing men. It was as if the new arrivals were running a gauntlet of love and hope, but in all the time I was there, I didn't see a single happy reunion.

After two weeks, the overwhelmed Macedonian government had had enough. The country had taken in 130,000 Muslim refugees from Kosovo, and, in addition to the anarchy and terrible publicity they were receiving in the world's press for their poor organization, they feared that the refugees would upset the already delicate balance of Muslims and Christians in the country, especially in the areas bordering Kosovo, which were already mostly Muslim and were threatening secession. So during yet another bone-chilling Balkan night, with no warning, 350 buses drove up to no-man's-land and forced all 35,000 remaining refugees to climb up the muddy grass shoulder to the road and into the buses. Those who could not walk were carried. Some were driven to hastily constructed NATO refugee camps nearby. Others were just taken back to the border with Kosovo and dumped. Still others were driven to Albania or flown to countries like Germany, Turkey, and Norway. Now even more families were split up.

The next morning, April 7, 1999, when we made our daily visit to Blace, we found an extraordinary sight. Where eighteen hours earlier there had been probably the biggest and filthiest refugee camp in modern European history, now there was just an empty field with abandoned huts and an occasional smoldering fire. In the early morning mist, we could make out occasional figures wandering dazed through the debris, and one of those left behind must have been five-year-old Yehona, alone, terrified, hungry, and freezing.

The British soldiers had found her, and by the time I met Yehona, a week later, she was scrubbed clean and well fed, hugging a big doll with long curly blond hair and fat pink cheeks. She wore a denim jacket that engulfed her tiny frame.

Children make great television stories. They look sweet and helpless and unthreatening in every way. They draw in the viewer's attention because everyone wants to help an innocent little boy or girl. A close-up of a child's smooth face with a little smile or tear and the tinkle of that melodious, high voice is captivating. The child's innocence is, for better or worse, what we call "the hook," the path into the story, a way to get the attention of people who ordinarily wouldn't give two hoots about Kosovo.

Clearly, little Yehona was a great story. But equally clearly, in her fragile state, it would do her no good to have a camera crew following her around all day asking silly questions that she couldn't answer. But we had to do it. In a simplistic television world, where a powerful story is often defined by the clarity of opposites—black versus white, right versus wrong, good guys versus bad guys—little children are the ultimate good guys. Moreover, if it is true, as Professor Susan Moeller wrote in a 1999 study,* that children are portrayed on television primarily in five ways—"as angels, as martyrs, as victims to be rescued, as torchbearers, and as literary crutches"—well, Yehona was all five rolled into one, with a pretty face.

At that time, in April 1999, NATO was still bombing the Serbs in Kosovo daily while building up forces to invade from Macedonia and Albania. Refugee camps held hundreds of thousands of Kosovar Muslims, and the world's focus was on war. In the midst of this mayhem, we decided to put a face on the chaos of Kosovo and, as Captain Soper said, that face was Yehona Aliu. While reporting from all corners of the conflict in Macedonia, Albania, and Kosovo, we kept in touch with Yehona and followed Soper's search for her parents.

---

*Susan Moeller, "Innocence Abroad: Images of Children in the American Media" (paper prepared for the Global Interdependence Initiative, 1999).

Out of his own small army salary, Captain Soper printed up a poster with a large black-and-white photograph of Yehona. He distributed this poster to as many Balkan refugee camps as he could, asking anyone who knew the girl to contact him on his private cell phone. Yehona's name was also on the top of the Red Cross's missing children list. But after a week, and no results from the poster campaign or from the Red Cross, it became clear that the British army could no longer care for her. Captain Soper took Yehona by the hand and walked her to an aid tent where the workers were more qualified to handle a lost little girl.

Throughout her ordeal, and even as she was taken from her new friends and put yet again into the hands of strangers, Yehona stayed lively and gay, if not happy. But this latest move was the worst. The aid workers took Yehona to a large tent full of lost old people who were coughing and spitting and staring blankly at nothing. For Yehona, the old folks' tent was a frightening place; it was the first time that she stopped smiling. She stared at the old people, and they stared back. She was quickly removed from there as the aid workers looked for somebody to care for her.

Finally Yehona ended up in tent D-258 in Stankovic 1 refugee camp near the Macedonian capital, Skopje. Fatimre Cecelia and her husband, Xhavit, had a tent all to themselves, and they took Yehona in. They dressed her in cute clothes donated by people from around the globe. Yehona slept in the corner, where her big blond doll sat against the canvas wall. "I love Yehona as if she was my own," Fatimre said. "We'd love to adopt her if she can't find her mother and father. Every night she speaks in her sleep. She says, 'Where is my mummy, where is my daddy?'" That made tears streak down Fatimre's cheeks, leaving black mascara smudges. She brushed them away. As we stopped filming and turned to leave, Fatimre pulled at my sleeve. "Please, wait a moment," she said. Then, as if to emphasize the enormity of the suffering around us, she dug into her pocket and pulled out a photograph. She held it out to me, crying again. "See, this is my little boy and girl. Have you seen them anywhere? I lost them three weeks ago."

. . .

There was no shortage of misery in the refugee camps of Macedonia, but the clock was ticking on the NATO invasion of Kosovo, and the fate of Yehona seemed to be overtaken by events. After my team and I took a brief rest at home, we were sent to Albania to prepare to go in with the invading German army. Strange, I thought, today the Germans have become the saviors. But instead of musing on my heritage, I was back in more familiar territory—covering a war.

The nine-hour drive from the Albanian capital, Tirana, to Kukes, on the border with Kosovo, passed through spectacular mountain scenery. This was marred somewhat by the steep, narrow, winding, potholed road with treacherous three-hundred-foot drops. In places, the road narrowed to a single-lane dirt track with no guardrails. Fatal accidents were marked by dozens of white crosses painted on the cliff face. It was the worst road I had ever seen or heard of. The driver of our red Volkswagen minibus rarely got above third gear.

Then there was the small matter of the bandits who preyed on travelers, especially foreign journalists flush with cash. One BBC television team hired a small truck and driver. Just as they were approaching the final leg of the journey into the country's wild and poor northeast, they ran into a group of armed men who stopped their vehicle at gunpoint and demanded money. The producer handed over his shoulder bag with envelopes of cash, and they were allowed to proceed unharmed. The team was shocked, but the producer chuckled and said, "Don't worry, I'm not dumb, that was just a token in case we got robbed. The real money is in my boot." The team laughed with relief, whereupon their Albanian driver stopped the car, put a gun to the producer's head, and stole the rest of the money. Then the driver forced everybody out and drove off with their gear. And he was one of the good guys.

We spent a week in Kukes awaiting the invasion. We had heard that Kosovo was a ruin, bombed by NATO, burned and looted by the Serbs, abandoned by the refugees, so we were expecting to find little in the way of sustenance. Our producer, Hanson Hosein, went off to the market to buy enough supplies to last us for at least a couple of weeks. Our haul included a generator, fuel, tents, sleeping bags, water containers, medicines, food, and anything else a freeloading television news team could add to the tab when spending the network's money unsupervised. Hanson was ably aided in this enterprise by our cameraman, Jeff Riggins; our soundman, Dubi Duvshani; and myself. We were old hands at these road trips into anarchy. Jeff and Dubi had been with me and other NBC colleagues in the field in Kigali, with no food or water, and surrounded by dead bodies. We all remember it fondly. Hanson was younger and fresher and maybe a bit shocked at our profligate ways, but I assured him that everything we bought now would make life bearable on the road in Kosovo, and I joked that anything we didn't actually use we could sell at a vast profit.

When our truck full of survival goodies rolled up in the ancient town of Prizren, our Kosovo base, we were surprised and delighted to find the town's main hotel open and well stocked. We didn't need anything we had bought; it was a complete waste of money. We agreed to donate our stuff to needy Kosovars along the way. But that same night, our Albanian drivers and translators sold the truck's entire contents and claimed they had been stolen. Then every night they drove the truck to Kukes, filled it with goods scarce in Kosovo—like fuel, cigarettes, alcohol, soap, toilet paper, cooking oil, and a host of vital foods—and sold it all at inflated prices in Prizren. When challenged about the morality of using the NBC truck for smuggling and ordered to cease and desist, they essentially laughed in my face and made it clear that either we could pay for the truck and their services, and thus they would take our money in a friendly way by earning it, or they would just take our money anyway and clear off the same day, taking the truck with them. As I said earlier, these were the good guys.

Our initial entrance into town had been exhilarating. The German army oversaw the southwestern sector of Kosovo, which included Prizren, the province's second largest town, and when the green light was given to the NATO invasion, it was like the start of a grand prix. The press gunned their cars and raced across the border from Albania to see the Germans take over the land that the Serbs had abandoned days earlier. Hanson, Jeff, Dubi, and I crossed with the pack, but, unlike the others, we didn't stop along the way to film the destruction. We just kept driving toward Prizren until we came across a column of German Leopard tanks. We overtook them one by one, passing the convoy so that Jeff could get the money shot, the German column liberating Prizren. What wonderful irony: The path the Germans took from Albania ran through the exact same mountain passes and valleys that the Nazis had taken half a century earlier when occupying Kosovo. But now the Germans were liberators, not occupiers. The bad guys had become the good guys.

What happened when we reached Prizren ahead of the convoy exceeded our wildest expectations, but not those of Second World War adventurer Ernest Hemingway, who gleefully claimed to have liberated Paris, or at least the bar of the Hotel Ritz. Now Paris, Prizren ain't, but we did feel that certain je ne sais quoi that Hemingway described when his jeep rolled into the City of Lights just a hairsbreadth ahead of the advancing American army, earning him a raucous Parisian welcome.

Ernest, I know what it felt like. I know the glory! I drove the first jeep into Prizren. I steered our white Toyota, followed by the second NBC jeep, our very own liberation convoy, ahead of the German Leopard tanks down Prizren's cobbled alleys. Jeff wanted to get into position to film the tanks arriving. Cheers rose, drowning out even the din of the tank's treaded tracks, as word of our arrival spread from the rooftops. Conquering heroes!

As we navigated narrow alleys into an ancient town square, dozens of beautiful girls in tight jeans and clinging clothes leapt onto our jeep, while hundreds of townspeople surged forward, pressing the girls onto us, as thousands more cheered from balconies and windows.

"NATO, NATO," the girls cried. "We love you, thank you, thank you." They threw flowers inside our jeep and blew kisses to me and my startled colleagues. Others looked shyly from a distance and smiled invitingly. A tall blonde caught my eye and winked. My heart raced.

Jeff Riggins, our tall, square-shouldered California cameraman, grinned hugely. He pointed and waved triumphantly to the men, high-fived the girls, and called upon me to stop, yelling, "Hey, lookit that ass!" Then, one wizened, toothless old man appeared by the windshield, tears streaming down his drawn cheeks. He tried to touch us with his wrinkled brown hand, like the leper reaching out to Christ, but Jeff shouted out, "Hey, git back, old man, make way for the blonde!"

Hanson, our swarthy young producer, blinked disbelievingly at the crush of adoring young girls and shouted, "Hey, I'm a Moslim, too!" and "Give me your phone number!"

"Sorry, Hanson," I pointed out, "the phones don't work."

That evening, after we sent our story via satellite to NBC, a kind Moslim family we had met earlier in the day served us dinner. They dressed up for their first guests in months and shared their best food, which consisted of scones, crepes, jam, and salad. The wine and vodka, at least, were plentiful. When talk turned to the German NATO troops that had rolled into town, we related how we had witnessed the German troops in their first action since World War II. That afternoon, as a thousand Kosovars were celebrating and dancing around the tanks right in front of our hotel, two Serbs inside a small white car had fired Kalashnikov assault rifles at the Germans. Everyone had raced for cover, and the Germans had shot back with everything they had. They'd killed both Serbs and poured so many bullets into the car that it rolled backward.

The family's patriarch, a slight man with a mottled face and drooping salt-and-pepper mustache, nodded in approval and said they all felt safe now. The German soldiers are excellent, he said, adding, "I should know, I used to be one." Then he snapped his arm up in a Nazi salute, shouted, "Heil!" and laughed merrily.

A younger man at the table said proudly, "Yes, my father was SS."

I smiled and nodded encouragement to my Israeli colleague, Dubi Duvshani, who grinned greenly and raised his glass in a mock salute. The Albanian Muslims, as well as the Croats for that matter, had been enthusiastic persecutors of the Jews under their Nazi patrons. This really was supping with the devil. Still, thanks to my reporter's mind-set, I felt more interested than angry. Hanson, the Muslim, kept trying to tell them tactfully that they had Israelis and Jews at the table, but our hosts were too far into their cups to worry. They continued to reminisce happily about the good old days. So Jeff told them about a strange order the German NATO soldiers had been given: no waving with the right arm. The German media advisers, it seemed, were worried that a photographer would freeze them in the moment of appearing to give a Heil Hitler salute. But my host didn't see the problem. "So what?" he shouted joyfully. He shot out his arm again—"Heil Hitler!"

In the excitement of the NATO advance into Kosovo, we had almost forgotten about little Yehona. But then Hanson got a call from a delighted Captain Soper reporting that his poster campaign had finally paid off. Yehona's uncle had called. He lived with his family in a small house in Skopje, only ten miles from Yehona's camp, and he was about to drive to Stankovic 1 to pick up his niece. Through a piece of quick coordination via the NBC assignment desk in Secaucus, New Jersey, we managed to have a cameraman there when Yehona rejoined her family.

We expected a dramatic, joyous reunion, but real life rarely follows the script. Yehona was very tired and shy and did not want to get in the car with her uncle. After all, her parents were still missing. It took the bribe of an ice cream to do the job. When she arrived at his home, late at night, she did not greet her cousins with the kind of happiness one would expect. After eating her ice cream, all she wanted to do was to go to sleep. Yehona was no longer a lost refugee, but she still did not know where her mother was, or whether her father was dead or alive.

We wanted to keep following Yehona's story, but we didn't have the manpower. All the NBC teams were sent into Kosovo. At this point, Hanson, Jeff, Dubi, and I were well into one of those road trips that you never forget. We were driving through Kosovo's hills and valleys, and every day was more dramatic than the one before. The Serbs had retreated into Serbia, leaving Kosovo in NATO's hands. The aid organizations wanted to delay the refugees' return until the land was cleared of land mines, and food supplies and first aid stations could be organized. But at the first sight of their oppressors' heels, the bravest of the refugees rushed back across the border from Macedonia and Albania, desperate to locate their missing loved ones, to find out what remained of their homes, and to begin to rebuild their lives. It was mostly men on the road; they had left their women and children in the refugee camps until it was safe to return. At least in the camps there was food and shelter, whereas nobody knew what awaited them at home.

As we followed the stream of refugees tramping down the main road from Albania into Kosovo, we noticed a solitary figure walking against the tide. He carried nothing with him but had a determined look as he dodged the oncoming refugees. It was about thirty miles to the Kosovo border. We asked him where he was going, and why. He was happy to take a breather and told us that his name was Esak and that for two months the Serbs had forced him to work as a slave laborer. They beat him routinely, but he said he could forgive the Serbs for that. He could never forgive them for making him miss the birth of his first child. His wife had fled to Albania with the rest of the family and given birth there, and all he wanted now was to find his wife and see his baby. He did not know if it was a boy or a girl, and that uncertainty was eating him up.

The Serbs had freed him a few days earlier as they began their retreat. Since then, he had been walking in search of his family. He told us not to walk in the fields because the Serbs had planted mines everywhere. He knew this because they had forced him to dig the holes. As we interviewed him, one of those bizarre made-for-TV moments happened—in the background a cow stepped on a land mine and exploded, limbs landing over a wide area. Dogs came and tore at the flesh. Jeff caught the cow exploding on tape, and we agreed it would be wise to stay clear of the fields.

We offered to drive Esak to Albania to help him find his baby. He almost cried in gratitude, and when he sat in the back of the jeep he lapsed into silence, too exhausted to talk. But his luck held. At the first camp we reached, among the thousands of milling refugees, Esak immediately found his father, and they fell into each other's arms. His father had good news. The birth had been successful, and he knew where Esak's family was staying. So we all jumped back into the jeep and drove another five miles down a bumpy path to a small village with just a few old stone houses standing amid orchards. It was a quiet, peaceful place, a world removed from the craziness Esak had survived. There, at the end of a grassy trail, by almond trees in fragrant white blossom, Esak was reunited with his wife and saw his baby for the first time. Again, real life did not follow the script. There was no hugging or crying, no great camera moment. They were all exhausted. They didn't even shake hands. Esak and his wife just looked at each other and smiled, and Esak took the baby into his arms. He hugged the girl and kissed her and then gave her back to his wife, but she was shaking so much that she could not hold the child.

Not all young mothers were so fortunate. In an Israeli emergency field hospital in one of the camps, we filmed what should have been the most wonderful moment in the life of a family, a child's birth. Doctors and nurses surrounded the mother, Samiray, and in a cacophony of Albanian shrieks, Hebrew encouragement, and English mutters, the infant plopped into the world. But when the nurse happily presented the newborn to her mother, Samiray did not want the baby. With an exhausted flick of her wrist, she gestured to take him and turned her head away. Later Samiray, sitting up painfully on a metal hospital cot, explained that she blamed the baby for all her troubles. She knew it made no sense, but to deliver a baby amid such squalor and misery and pain was a crime, she felt; she did not want to bring a baby into such an evil world. Her confusion was very painful to see and hear. Even the baby's father, who proudly carried his infant through the camp to his empty tent, asked what there was to celebrate. So many returning refugees discovered their loved ones' bodies, or heard about the discoveries of mass graves, or found their villages razed to the ground, that it was hard to disagree.

Then the cell phone rang. Captain Soper had located Yehona's mother in a refugee camp in Albania. He told us that, if we wanted to film the reunion, we should get there double quick.

What a shot to cap off Yehona's story! But there was no way we could get out of Kosovo. And NBC no longer had a crew in Albania. Moreover, with NATO forces spreading through Kosovo and with NBC News crews scattered across the region working around the clock, nobody gave a hoot whether Yehona met her mother or not—nobody, that is, apart from Hanson and me.

Yehona's story was a wonderful, heartwarming tale, but it was no more than another great story. Now we were knee-deep in history, and although every journalist gene in my body wanted to be there when Yehona found her mother, we could not leave Kosovo, even for a couple of days. So we missed the ending to the Yehona saga. The story had no climax; it was a terrible lost opportunity. Still, we were glad she had found her mother. We only wondered whether her father was dead or alive and whether she even had a home to go back to.

Those uncertainties were shared by hundreds of thousands of Kosovar refugees. As they made their way back to their towns and villages, like so many refugees from so many wars before them in this very same bloody part of Europe, we noticed it became harder and harder for our translator, Hamdi, to relate their grim stories. I assumed he was exhausted. We all were. We were leaving the hotel in Prizren at dawn, driving hundreds of miles in search of stories, returning at dusk, then writing and dispatching our reports close to midnight. This went on for weeks. No wonder Hamdi sometimes had tears in his eyes as we wandered through the ruins of his country.

Hamdi was a gentle soul in his mid-twenties, with brown hair swept back and a soft voice you had to strain to hear. He was tall and thin with a beaten look, stooping but trying to stand straight. Before we had arrived in Kukes, an NBC producer, Kevin Sites, had found Hamdi in a field, sheltering under an open wagon with thirty other people. Because Hamdi spoke excellent English, Kevin hired him on the spot, and then my team took him over because he came from the Prizren area, where we knew we would be based. In my enthusiasm to cover the story, it never occurred to me to ask Hamdi what had happened in his town.

One day our cameraman, Jeff, who combines a rakish exterior with a sensitive heart, did ask Hamdi what was wrong. He answered that, like all the refugees we were meeting, he, too, would like to go home to find the rest of his family and friends, to see who was alive or dead, to see if his house was still standing, to see what had happened to his dog, and whether he could still make a life there. That threw us. We had been laughing and joking for weeks while next to us he had been suffering. Our cynical jokes are a kind of protective shield against the sadness around us, but how smug and heartless we must appear to the victims who work with us because they have no money.

Hanson immediately proposed that we take Hamdi to his home. Hamdi rushed to his hotel room to gather his few clothes and the money he had earned, and for the first time in weeks he was excited and chatty in the jeep. He told us the name of his small town. Suva Reka—four syllables that roll off the tongue, but it was a name that came to symbolize the worst of Serb brutality. We did not know that yet, and even Hamdi joked and laughed on his way home. But the closer we got the more silent he became.

Suva Reka had a population of twenty thousand, of whom 90 percent were Albanian Muslims and 10 percent Serbs. It was a tight-knit community of farmers and small-business owners. Hamdi's family lived comfortably, in a nice small house with a big garden in front and fruit trees in the back. His relatives lived all around.

As soon as Hamdi walked down the lane leading to his house, he began to sob quietly. He pointed to a hedge and said, between gulps for air, that as he had left his home he had seen a dead body there, that there had been dead bodies everywhere. Then, as he approached his home and opened the gate, there was some good news. It became clear that his house had gotten off lightly. The wooden door was intact, and not even the window-panes were broken. But when Hamdi entered his bedroom and saw the smashed furniture and clothes thrown all around, he could not control himself and he continued to cry while he went from room to room. We went out the door and turned in to the back garden. There Hamdi found his dog. By now he was numbed. All he said was "Look at what they've done." Tied to a post, with a red collar around its neck, was the skeleton of a dog.

Two out of three houses were damaged or destroyed, and there were craters and tank tracks deep in the roads. There was no sign of Hamdi's family or friends. He was among the first to return.

Hamdi hugged an old man in a lane near his home, a neighbor who had managed to stay alive in his house throughout both the Serb rampage and the NATO bombing. He told Hamdi to take us to the shopping center in town, to go to the old pizza place, the Kalabria. "There has been an awful massacre there," he said.

It is a terrible thing to follow a broken person as he discovers just how little he has left in life, but Hamdi had become our guide to his own tragedy. We had just wanted to help him go home, but now Hamdi had become another story.

When we arrived at the pizza place, a couple of men were staring in through the smashed glass, poking at the debris with long sticks. They told Hamdi that the Serbs had herded about fifty Muslims, most of them from the same family, into the small room and slaughtered them by throwing in hand grenades and firing with Kalashnikov rifles. There were bullet holes and marks of grenade blasts and bloody smears on the walls where dying people tried to hold on as they fell.

The men thought they knew where the bodies had been taken. There was a Serb army training base about ten miles up the road toward Prizren, and everybody believed that this was where the victims were buried. But the Serbs had laid land mines and booby traps in many of the bases they had abandoned, so nobody had gone to look, not even the relatives of the missing.

Hamdi agreed to guide us there, but we faced the usual dilemma. How much should we risk ourselves for a television news report? We were the only one of all the NBC TV crews in the Balkans without an armored car to protect us from land mines. On the other hand, this was a great story.

We set off in the two jeeps and found locals willing to guide us to the abandoned Serb base. The gates were wide open. At the dirt path inside the base, we again consulted. How dangerous did it look? Were there mines buried along the path? Booby traps? What would a booby trap even look like? We had no way of knowing, but by now we were determined to find the bodies from the pizza massacre in Suva Reka. We left the car at the entrance in case there were antivehicle land mines along the road.

Jeff, Hanson, Dubi, Hamdi, and I continued past an avenue of trees and open training fields until, after ten minutes, we came across large mounds of freshly dug earth. We walked carefully over them and poked around, hoping there were no booby traps. If the NATO troops had gotten here first, we would not have been able to get within two hundred yards of the place. They would have roped off the area and sent in the bomb disposal squad. Apart from any considerations of danger, we were contaminating a crime scene. But we got there first, and what we found sent Hamdi deeper into depression. Lying on top of the earth were clumps of human hair, parts of smashed skulls, a jawbone with broken teeth, cash, a wedding ring, coats, shoes, and finally a watch, sticking invitingly out of the earth. One end of the strap was buried, but the watch face and the rest of the strap were exposed. The glass was cracked and the watch had stopped, but I could read the time and date. March 24, 4:30 P.M. Same time, same day as the pizza massacre.

I smiled grimly at Jeff.

"Yes," he agreed. We had worked together for so many years in so many dangerous places we didn't even have to say it—great stand-up.

"You film my hands while I point to the clothes and the shoe, and then you go wide while I pull the watch out of the earth, and I'll say it's the same time and date as the massacre."

Dubi interrupted. "What if it's a booby trap?"

"Well, yes, that could be a bit of a problem," I said, and we all pondered. If anything in the area was booby-trapped, this was likely to be it. Nobody would want to touch human hair or a jawbone, and the cash and ring were just lying on top of the earth. But who wouldn't pull the watch out of the earth? It's human instinct. The strap was half buried. What was on the other end? Nothing? Or a bomb?

"Great stand-up," I repeated, and everyone agreed. "So are we going to do it?" I asked. Hamdi, who did not work in television and was not a journalist, said, "No way!" Everybody else said, "Of course!" We knew we had only one go at this because, assuming the watch didn't blow our heads off, if I got the words wrong, I couldn't very well stick the watch back in the ground and do it again.

It didn't help our nerves that we couldn't protect ourselves with our flak jackets and helmets. We'd left them behind in the car and were too lazy to go get them. So we steeled ourselves, Dubi with the microphone close by to get the plop and, we hoped, not the bang, of the watch sucking free from the earth, Jeff close by with the camera on the tripod following the action, and I, trying to memorize what I wanted to say. Nobody really thought it was a booby trap, but it could well have been. We just didn't know, but we did know that we needed this shot for the story. So I counted down: "Three, two, one," and began to talk to the camera, explaining what I was finding and ending with the watch, which I then pulled out of the earth. There was a slight resistance and I flinched a tiny bit, but then the watch slipped out and lay harmlessly in my hand. I finished what I had to say, and we all burst into relieved laughter. It must have looked strange, three ghouls laughing on top of a mass grave. When I look back on my long career, I believe this must have been the most foolish, irresponsible thing I ever did, and I have done many. But it was a great stand-up.

During the winter of '99, half a year after NATO imposed peace and five months after Hamdi returned home, we went back to Kosovo to report on the 350,000 refugees still without a roof. As the daytime temperature sank below zero, tens of thousands were still living in tents, despite promises by the UN that every family would have four walls, a roof, and a heater by the end of autumn.

The population of the Kosovar capital of Pristina had tripled as refugees from the devastated villages sought to escape the bitter cold by moving in with relatives in the city. The UN fed half the population, most of whom had no work. But as I reported on the failed promises of the aid community and the homeless refugees, I was most interested in one thing: I wanted to find out what had happened to Yehona. I knew she came from a village called Ferizaj, but I had no idea where it was and had not yet had time to check it out.

Kosovo was not very large—around 6,800 square miles, a little smaller than Connecticut—but it still took many hours to drive its poor, damaged roads. One rare day, when the sun shone and the sky was blue and the temperature stood around fifty, my crew and I got lost about ten miles outside Pristina. We entered a small town of crumbling buildings with roads full of potholes and rain-filled craters. We stopped at a café to ask the way. "Where are we?" we asked. "Ferizaj," came the reply. That sounded familiar, so I flipped through my notebook. Sure enough, I found it: "Ferizaj, 20 mins Pristina, dad behind fighting, family lost Blace, Yehona, cute, dreams of mum, no cry."

"Do you know the Aliu family?" we asked the old lady serving us coffee.

"Which one?"

"Little girl called Yehona?"

"Up there, second on the right, one of the houses on the left on the edge of the field."

It was as simple as that. We downed the coffee, followed the instructions, and there was Yehona, swinging on the gate. Her little ears still stuck out, and she still looked like a pixie. "How are you?" I asked. She pushed herself off on the gate, and as she swung, she started singing over and over the same English words that she had probably learned from Captain Soper: "Good morning, I'm fiiine, thaaank yooouuu."

Yehona's mother, Sadie, a cautious woman with a sad smile, whom I was meeting for the first time, made tea and sat us down in her living room while Yehona played with her two brothers and two sisters. It was a warm room with a big, thick rug and a nice sofa with cushions. A little gray puppy bit at everyone's shoes. Yehona was laughing and giggling and fighting with her elder brother, and she kissed the baby, who had been only two weeks old when Yehona had gotten lost. Sadie told us, "For months I used to cry for Yehona. I saw her in dreams every night, and Yehona would tell me in my dreams, 'Don't cry, Mummy, I'm okay.'" She said that now Yehona was cold all the time, a legacy of her freezing, wet escape through the mountains.

Then, before I could ask what had happened to Sherif, Yehona's father, who had stayed behind to fight the Serbs, he walked into the room. He was a short, powerfully built man with graying hair and an unshaven face. He did not stop smiling and hugged everyone, especially Yehona. He gave her a doll to play with as she sat on his lap. It was the same big blond doll with chubby pink cheeks that Yehona had had in Stankovic 1 refugee camp near Skopje. She had kept that doll through her entire ordeal.

Sherif did not want to talk about himself, beyond saying that his time in hiding had been very hard. He'd watched from the hills as the Serbs burned his town, but miraculously his own house had emerged unscathed. Now he was focused only on providing for his family. He had a car, and he earned small amounts of money ferrying people around and delivering goods. They had no running water or power in the house, and when dinnertime came, all Yehona had to eat was a thin soup and white bread to dip in it. But as she ate, Yehona hummed happily to herself. Sadie had tears in her eyes as she filled her bowl again and said, "The only thing that counts is that Yehona is back with the family."

Watching Yehona eat and play, it was inevitable that my thoughts would pass to the refugees in my own family. We didn't have any lucky ones. There were no happy reunions. In London, my mother, Edith, a penniless young refugee, received rare, sad letters from her parents for two years, describing their increasingly forlorn attempts to flee Nazi oppression in Austria. They knew that, if they stayed, they were doomed, along with the rest of their families. Then, from late 1941, silence. Yehona lost her parents for two months. It took my mother five more years to discover her mother's fate.

Annelise, my mother's older sister, who had had the good sense to marry an American scientist and leave Austria in 1937, had apparently

been working hard to find their parents. She received this letter, dated
May 8, 1946, which I translate from the German:

Dear Mrs. Lisa,

*Although it is very hard for me to write about it, I am ready to tell
you what I know about your dear mother. I met your mother in January 1942 on a transport from Vienna to Riga and we became so
friendly that we ended up sharing a room for two years. Although I
am twenty-five years younger than your mother, sisters could not
have gotten on better. Even if I don't know you personally, dear Mrs.
Lisa, and your sister, Edith, still I know everything about you from
your earliest childhood. For there was nothing your mother liked better than to talk about her children and no day went by without us
talking about our lovely past years. But unfortunately fate wanted it
differently. In August 1944 we were dragged from Riga to a Polish
concentration camp, which was much worse than death. I don't want
to make it any harder for your heart. The whole world knows what
these brown beasts did with us. Nobody, dear Mrs. Lisa, can have as
much understanding as I for at the same time I lost my own mother
in a concentration camp. Your dear mother died of typhoid, as did my
own mother. Maybe it is a comfort for you to know that she did not
have to go through all the things that I did. One can hardly describe
in words all the horrors we had to put up with. It is a miracle that I
am still alive and it was only thanks to a deadly bomb attack that I
and four other women were able to escape. As sad as fate can be, we
can only console ourselves with the thought that there was nothing we
could have changed. I also, dear Mrs. Lisa, will never forget your dear
mother and will always remember her fondly. There is no relief for
such great pain.*

I don't know if the truth made life more bearable for my mother or
harder, because she wouldn't talk about it. As for her stepfather, Onkel

Max, it turned out he'd died in a hospital—the Nazis shot all the patients. Her real father, Otto Feibelmann, who was last seen by his other daughter, Annelise, at the train station in Kaiserslautern, Germany, simply disappeared in the concentration camps. She took a heartbreaking photograph of him gazing after her as she left for America, never to see him again. That photo now sits on a side table in Prescott, Arizona, in the home of Betsy, the granddaughter he never knew.

Three months before my mother read that letter, my father got as close as he ever did to finding out what had happened to his parents, Julius and Therese Fleischer. In a letter from his friend Walter, who wrote from Prague, he read the following: "There is, alas, no hope dear Georg, that your dear parents could be still alive. I received information that all Viennese Jews in summer 1942 were 'ausgesiedelt' from Lodz [Litzmannstadt], that means transport to Oswiecin [Auschwitz], from where there was no return for elder people at all."

My father lit memorial candles at every opportunity, but he could never talk about the end of his parents, and sisters, aunts, uncles, and cousins, without tearing up and breaking off the conversation. I think that, like those of many Holocaust survivors, my parents' experiences, even though they escaped the camps, were still too traumatic to express in words, so they retreated into silence. Because they could not express their pain, they could never emerge from their trauma, which, it has been written, is the encounter with the unspeakable. For my parents, there was no catharsis, no moment of healing. During sixty years of living in England, they had no English friends. Everyone they knew was a refugee and a Holocaust survivor, from Central Europe and the Balkans. They remained traumatized and passed some of that on to their children.

In Kosovo, for the first time in my journalistic career, I found myself completely sympathetic to one side in a conflict. The water was muddied somewhat by the fact that during the Second World War the Serbs were among the few Europeans who had actually helped the Jews. Now the good guys had become the bad guys, and the Muslims, who hated the Jews, were the good guys. Moreover, evil as it was, there was nothing the Serbs were doing to the Muslims that the Muslims hadn't done to the Serbs, ten times over and much worse, during the five-hundred-year reign of the Ottoman Turks in these same lands. It was the Ottomans, after all, who had stuck poles through the anuses of the Serbs until they poked through their chests or mouths, then hung the bodies on bridges, along with their severed heads, to terrify the townspeople. Now the Serbs were getting their revenge, and judging by the history books, it was still pretty mild stuff.

But Yehona did not know any of that. She was just an innocent child refugee, sweet as honey, and a tough little kid to boot. In all those weeks with the soldiers and then with foster families and aid workers, nobody ever saw her cry. When other lost children cried, Yehona would say, "Don't cry, I'm lost, too, and I'm not crying." Of course, that made all the adults cry. When a bigger boy gave her a ball to play with, she threw it straight onto his nose and laughed. And in quieter moments, Yehona would sit in a corner of the tent, take out the colored crayons and paper she had been given, and draw for hours, over and over again, the same stick pictures of her mother and father.

In my TV reports I've always tried to avoid that old chestnut, used about survivors of one kind or another: "These [ominous pause] are the lucky ones." But now, as I sat in her family's warm living room, watching Yehona slurp her soup on the thick rug, her mother and father smiling proudly, I thought, It fits.

Nine

Living with Terror

I magine this: **Murderers are trying** to kill your kids, yet every day at work it's your job to interview the murderers. That's the excruciating situation I confronted during the late 1990s and early 2000s. As residents of Israel, my children were on the front line, taking buses to school or to discos in Tel Aviv, all of which are favorite targets of the suicide bombers. I kissed my sons good-bye in the morning, then went to the West Bank and listened to al-Aksa fighters tell me how many Jews they wanted to kill. One day I interviewed Jewish victims of suicide bombers; the next day I interviewed bombers and the men who sent them.

My assignment challenged every journalistic tenet. How could I remain objective and nod politely as a killer explained why the Jews, my people, were dogs and pigs? You ignorant racists, I would think, as masked men wielding M16s and hand grenades browbeat me.

The first Palestinian suicide bombing campaign against Israel in the mid-nineties, and then the second in the early years of the new century, tore me up inside. While I shared the fear of the bombing victims, I also understood why Palestinians had been driven to such a ferocious and desperate tactic. What choice did they have? Nothing else had worked, and they weren't going to submit to Israeli power. Even Palestinians who condemned random killing defended the suicide bombers by pointing out that Israeli shells and planes killed more people than their martyr bombers. The Palestinians proudly called the suicide bombers "our F-16s." Palestinian children collected sets of cards depicting the martyrs much the way children elsewhere collect baseball cards. Kids wore lockets around their necks with photos of their favorite bombers. They adorned their bedroom walls with posters of dead men with bandannas and guns, dreaming of one day being brave like them.

The suicide bombing campaigns and the second Intifada grew directly out of the 1993 Oslo peace agreement. As soon as I read the Oslo text, arrived at secretly by Israeli and Palestinian negotiators, I understood that this agreement would lead inevitably to war. The document provided for the return of Yasir Arafat and the PLO to the West Bank and Gaza,* along with thousands of armed police, and the gradual establishment of a Palestinian state on land that Israel would cede. Most of the key issues, like Palestinian refugees' right to return to their homes, the future of Jerusalem, even the two states' future borders, were to be settled at a later date. It was obvious, however, that Israel would never grant Arafat everything he wanted. And at that point, from a position of greater strength, Arafat would launch a war to gain the rest. Arafat knew he didn't have to win the war; he just had to start it and hope that the world would force Israel to compromise further in order to restore the peace. And this was exactly what transpired.

Except for the last bit. The world didn't force Israel to compromise. The suicide tactic had already been introduced, in a comparatively limited way, in the mid-nineties, partly to influence Israeli elections, partly to force Israel to compromise on disputes emerging from the Oslo agreement, and partly as a result of Palestinian infighting.

Israeli intelligence judged that the campaign wouldn't last long. Profiles of the bombers themselves, analysts argued, suggested that only a

---

*The PLO's leadership had been living in exile in Tunis.

very limited pool of potential bombers existed—about a dozen. The supply of unemployable, single, mentally slow young men susceptible to terrorist brainwashing would soon dry up. Unfortunately for Israel, the analysts were dead wrong. Ten years later, terror groups were turning away volunteers. Fathers of large families, jilted females, angry young men, university students, schoolboys, men and women seeking a spot in Paradise for themselves and their families as promised by Jihad—all yearned for a chance to blow themselves up among the Jewish enemy. For every bomber who succeeded, a dozen more were stopped by Israel's secret service.

From 2001 to 2005, there were more than 120 suicide bombings, and I must have been on the scene of at least half of them. We stood in pools of blood as we filmed, stepped over torn-off hands and body parts as victims screamed and terrified parents searched the carnage for their children. We passed neatly severed heads sitting properly on the street* and saw limbs lying in bushes and on shop awnings. Once, I saw a bloodied man holding his foot and waving it at a medic. Religious Jews scraped flesh and tendons off the walls for proper burial. One bus was blown up next to the Megiddo jail in northern Israel, and the wailing of the Jews mingled with the delighted jeering of the Palestinian prisoners. On another occasion, we raced from Tel Aviv to the scene of a suicide bombing in Jerusalem, only to rush back because there had been an even bigger bomb in Tel Aviv.

All this was hard on the soul. The Israeli police spokesman, Gil Kleiman, a tough-looking guy with a strong jaw, cropped dark hair, and a Brooklyn accent, was always on hand to give the facts. In February 2005, somebody else took his place, but I didn't think anything of it until I read an interview with Gil in *The Jerusalem Post*. Describing the impact of witnessing his forty-seventh suicide bombing, he said,

---

*These would be the bombers; the blasts from their backpacks or belts around their chests often decapitated them.

I just started crying in my office. I picked up the phone to call the police psychologist but I could not speak in a coherent sentence. It was then I realized that I needed help. I could no longer deal with any kind of suffering—even down to a young child crying in the street. I could not deal with my emotions. The army and police give their officers flak jackets, but their souls are ripped apart with no protection whatsoever. It's not normal standing over a dead body and chit-chatting with a friend I haven't seen in ages, asking him why he hasn't been in touch. I don't want to slip on someone's jawbone again.

I wasn't feeling so great either. I was constantly torn in my emotions, appalled by the violence, sympathetic to the victims, and understanding of the terrorists, who themselves were victims, trapped in a vicious rut since birth. Most difficult of all was the sense of hopelessness. Only a genuine peace process that offered real hope to both sides had a chance of ending the daily violence, but with doubts persisting about the true motives of Palestinian and Israeli leaders, extremists succeeded in tripping up every step toward agreement. Day after day, as I trudged to another gut-wrenching scene, I wondered: How long will this tragedy go on? How in the world will it ever end?

It was another lovely late summer day when a family friend, Gilli Kucik, a sweet fourteen-year-old girl with beautiful big eyes and a smile to die for, strolled down Ben Yehuda Street in downtown Jerusalem with some school friends. She was licking an ice cream as she called home to tell her mother, Nirit, that she was going to a friend's place, she would be home later, and not to worry. It was 3:00 P.M.

This is what happened next, in Gilli's words. She spoke quietly and deliberately, still in the moment, describing a horror nobody can imagine:

"If I hadn't bought an ice cream I may have escaped. There we were on Ben Yehuda Street, and my ice cream stick broke, I had sticky fingers. I just remember a boom, I thought it was a sonic boom, then I don't remember much, I ducked, all was very quiet, then a huge blast, I felt a wave of heat, a huge ball of fire. I thought, I don't believe this is happening to me, seeing bodies is bad enough but . . . all my trousers were covered with burned skin from other people, blood, I got up and looked for my friend, she was a meter away, the bomb was four meters away by Atara Café, I was sheltered by tables and chairs, all was gray, my friend's hair was burned, not mine, she was bleeding in many places, my ears were singing, I caught her, I held her in my arms, there was blood, silence, then she screamed in horror, then people started to shout, freaky, a soldier came and took control of us and pushed us into a shop, everybody was hiding, we ducked again, there was another bomb and then another bomb. My friend Michal was badly burned from that one, and nails from the bomb entered her body. Me, I had only very light wounds. It only hurt later when I limped.

"I have a still photo in my mind of Smadar and Sivan and a dark unknown shape that I think was the terrorist. My bag fell on the ground and I lost it and I was frightened my parents would see it on TV and think that I was killed. As we walked away I looked only on the ground, I didn't want to look around me and see more bodies and people covered in blood and crying."

It was one of the most shocking suicide bomb attacks ever. Three Palestinian men blew themselves up. First one suicide bomber exploded his device. As Israelis died or fled, another bomber blew himself up in the crowd, and then, thirty seconds later, as survivors gathered, a third. The killers left a trail of carnage and hysteria. Five dead, a hundred and fifty wounded. Two of Gilli's girlfriends were blown up next to her. It seems that one of them, running from the first blast, ran right into the second bomber and died in his embrace as he detonated his bomb. Gilli has an image of the two shapes merging before the blast.

A year later, Gilli's huge dark eyes were ringed and had a haunted look as she told me she no longer knew how to walk down a street. Should she walk in the middle of the street to be far from the glass shopwindows, or should she walk next to the shops so that she could take shelter inside? Every person became a potential terrorist. She said she became like a radar machine, checking out people's distance from her, scanning everything, suspicious of everyone.

But hers was just the beginning of the suffering. In all the bombings, there was a ripple effect of pain. Entire families and circles of friends were traumatized by the death or injuries of each victim. I, too, was deeply upset by Gilli's experience. I've known Gilli all her life. Her mother, Nirit, is one of my wife's oldest and dearest friends. It struck me that when Nirit and Hagar were Gilli's age, they may have walked together down the same pedestrian street Gilli did with her friends. It was impossible to escape the stomach-knotting feeling that sooner or later it could happen to myself or my loved ones.

The suicide bombings also took a terrible toll on daily life. Living with the constant threat of bombs on Israeli buses or in cafés, and the possibility that the man next to you with the backpack was carrying explosives, meant that everyone, like Gilli, went around nervously seeking clues. On the bus, what's that guy carrying in that bag? On the street, why's he wearing a coat on a hot day? Is he hiding something? At the entrance to the mall, why is that man sweaty and nervous? Is he an Arab or a Jew? One woman in Jerusalem was alarmed to see an ultra-Orthodox Jew with a backpack of a kind that ultra-Orthodox men didn't usually carry. She called the police. Sure enough, he was a Palestinian suicide bomber disguised as a Jew, hiding a bomb in the bag.

Infants in kindergarten were educated not to pick anything up in the street. A bomb could be stuffed inside a loaf of bread. Don't touch anything: Call the police. Traffic jams were commonplace as little black robots wheeled up to abandoned shopping bags and shot them as a precautionary measure. Every café and restaurant had an armed guard at the entrance. Fifty cents was added to the bill for security. After every bomb attack, cell-phone systems were overloaded as people checked on the safety of loved ones. Sometimes two or three times a day.

I asked Gilli what it was like for her, now, a year later. Would she ever get over it? I wanted to understand. It was a question, I thought, that could easily be relevant for my own children.

"Crowds of people are still hard for me," she answered. "Before it happened I knew of the danger, I was careful of buses, but when the bomb went off, it was the last thing I ever thought of. Life goes on, you think it's happening to somebody else. Since the bombing, people have said to me, 'Wow, how lucky you are nothing happened to you.' No—I'm completely unlucky that I was there. Everything was unlucky. I was there. The timing was terrible. Bodies were smooched onto me, nothing like this should happen to anybody.

"Today I don't go to some places in Jerusalem, in fact most places. I don't take buses anymore, only taxis from school, no walking in the pedestrian street. I went once with Dad; it's contaminated for me, I saw my hands and shoes and hair covered with 'people stuff.' I couldn't go back to that street. I felt it was a betrayal if I went there and Smadar can't, because she died next to me that day."

As I spoke to victims and perpetrators, trying to reflect fairly the views of both sides, trying to stay above the pain of so many, I had difficulty making sense of what was going on. Each side was causing immeasurable pain to the other and gaining little. I had seen too many severed heads, smashed limbs, and crushed lives, Jews and Muslims, to take seriously any claims that this carnage was rational or in any way motivated by a "good cause," that the end justified the means. After a while, though, covering the hatred and the killing of the suicide bombing campaign brought me to a pivotal understanding, one that I had first begun to grasp in the first Intifada: The divide was not really between Israeli and Arab, Jew and Muslim, or even right and wrong. The divide was between those who put peace above all else and those who didn't.

I learned this simple truth from an unlikely teacher—the mother of the young girl who died next to Gilli. Smadar's mother, Nurit Peled-Elhanan, is quite a lady. After she lost her daughter in the Ben Yehuda bombing and received condolences from Arab friends, an Israeli reporter asked her how she could accept words of grief from the other side. She answered straightaway that she hadn't. Nurit explained that for her the other side, the enemy, is not the Palestinian people; the struggle is not between Palestinians and Israelis but between those who seek peace and those who seek war. Her people, she said, are not defined as Jews or Israelis but as those who seek peace. Her sisters, she said, are bereaved mothers, whether Jews or Arabs in Israel or Muslims and Christians in the West Bank and Gaza.

It was a remarkable testimony of faith by a mother who had just lost her only daughter. As for vengeance, Nurit asked, what is the point? And she quoted the Jewish poet Bialik: "Satan has not yet devised a vengeance for the death of a young child."

It turned out that Nurit had a friendship that lasts to this day with, of all people, Benjamin Netanyahu. They became friends at age fourteen. But when Prime Minister Netanyahu phoned to offer his condolences, she refused to speak to him. "He thinks like a terrorist," Nurit told me in her cozy, book-lined living room. "It's either you get me or I get you. That's the way he always thought, and when someone like that gets power, it's very dangerous."

"Do you blame him for the death of your daughter?" I asked.

"Well, indirectly, of course. The murderers are murderers, but I blame him for letting them and even inspiring them to do what they did."

"Why inspiring them?"

"Because by the way that he acts, it is the best inspiration for such monsters to do what they do. . . . They have this glory of being freedom fighters and martyrs and all this, I think we inspire this. . . . This is the glory of the guerrilla, the way they act is the only way for them to react."

Later, Nurit wrote in an article: "Each attack is a link in a chain of horrific bloody events that extends back thirty-four years and has but one cause: A brutal occupation."

Nurit's logic didn't go down well at a time when hardly a day passed without a bombing, a knifing, or a drive-by shooting, as Palestinians stepped up their war of terror against Israeli civilians. But her voice of reason and wisdom in the face of such suffering made a strong impact on me, partly because of the prime emotion she felt at her daughter's death: guilt.

When it was a matter not of whether but of when and where a terrorist would strike, every parent nursed the same fear: Will my child return home safely? I faced it with my own children regularly. When I had heard through NBC that there was a high police alert in a certain area, I would ask my children not to go there, and they always agreed. I remembered the story of one schoolgirl who told me how angry she was with her father when he forbade her to go to Tel Aviv on an outing with her three best friends. Her father said he had a feeling that something bad would happen. "Just a feeling, that's all it was, he wouldn't let me go and have fun just because of a feeling. I hated him!"

She told me this the next day, as her whole school filed silently past a wall of memorial candles and photographs in the main hall, and each child was offered psychological counseling to deal with the trauma. Her three friends, who went without her, were blown up by a suicide bomber outside the Dizengoff Mall in central Tel Aviv.

Everyone had those moments, when living with terror meant a possibly fatal choice between listening to your gut and giving in to the terrorists, or listening to your brain and carrying on with normal life. Smadar's mother, Nurit, wished she had gone with her gut that day. "I had this feeling, I always had this feeling," Nurit said. "But that morning Smadar said, 'It's so good that you let me go about,' and I said, 'Listen, I would like to keep you at home, but I can't really do that.'"

"That's what Smadar said the day she died?" I asked.

"Yes. Another friend's mother wouldn't let her go, and Smadar said, 'I'm so happy you let me go, because if you hadn't let me go, I would have gone anyway.' It was like an everyday talk, nothing special. Her friend didn't go because she was more frightened of her mother than of the terrorist. But she is alive, you see. I let Smadar go there, I gave my permission to go there; this is terrible, it's like you send your child to die."

Every word Nurit said resonated with me. In this war against the civilians, I was no longer a foreign correspondent, detached and somehow above the fray, but just another worried parent. I wasn't part of the battle, but I was certainly as much a target as anyone else. Being a journalist was no protection. One prominent Israeli reporter was rushing to a suicide bombing when he was stopped by a phone call and told to return to his office. The newspaper's photographer had already gotten to the scene and recognized the dead body of the reporter's son. Another foreign correspondent, Elias Zaldivar of Telemundo, who broadcasts out of our NBC office, was writing his report on a bombing in a Tel Aviv nightclub when he learned that his own son, a drummer, was among the severely wounded. In a suicide bombing campaign, all you could do was trust in luck. Which runs out.

"Smadar was in the first bombing," Nurit continued, "and she ran into the second one. She could have run into one of the stores, but instead she went down the street, and he caught the two of them."

"The terrorist held on to them?"

"Yes, she ran into his arms. She did the wrong thing, and she could have been saved if she did the right thing. There was one girl who ran the opposite way. But she was in a state of shock so she ran right into the smoke and into a shop, and she was saved."

That was Gilli, who lived. Smadar died. Suicide bomb victims were totally random. What wasn't random was the choice of target. A pedestrian road in the heart of Jerusalem, crowded with young people and shoppers on a Thursday afternoon. Police said one of the bombers was disguised as an old man and another as a woman.

My heart bled for the Jewish victims of terror, yet I came to sympathize with the people who sent the bombers. Not with their actions—I wasn't that much of a bleeding-heart liberal—but with their motives. Palestinians lived for a generation under brutal and pitiless occupation. Most young people knew nothing else; the only Israelis they saw wore army uniforms, carried guns, and made their lives a living hell. Of course the Palestinians would fight back. Even Israel's former prime minister Ehud Barak memorably admitted that, if he had been born a Palestinian, he would have joined the resistance.

My reporting brought me continually into contact with Palestinian gunmen from Hamas, Islamic Jihad, and the al-Aksa Martyrs' Brigades all over the West Bank and Gaza. Some of these militants were the people who recruited, trained, and dispatched the suicide bombers, although nobody ever admitted that to me. It was somebody else, they always said. But as my team and I roamed the cities of the Palestinian territories, we became familiar with some of them. We returned again and again to Nablus, the West Bank's largest Arab town, and often looked up the same group of gunmen from the al-Aksa Martyrs' Brigades, the militia responsible for many of the suicide bombs.

And that's how I got invited to the al-Aksa "wedding" in Nablus in the autumn of 2006 with which I opened this book. A gunman called our office and used the code word *wedding* to invite us to a murder of Palestinian collaborators that was about to take place. After some soul-searching, I did not accept the telephone invitation. I didn't want to witness a murder, even if it was going to happen anyway. I couldn't have prevented the killing of the two collaborators by calling the police in Nablus and informing on al-Aksa—half of al-Aksa were linked to the police. I understood why they thought they had to kill the man and woman who had caused the death of their friends—next time it could be them. On the other hand, collaborators were Israel's main tool in the fight against terror, and stopping suicide bombers from attacking Israeli targets was as much in my interest as in anyone's.

A few days after the killing of the collaborators, my NBC team and I drove to Nablus to meet up with the gunmen who had invited us. It was getting more dangerous; undercover Israeli special units hunted the gunmen by day, regular army patrols by night. Curfews were imposed on Palestinians for weeks at a time.

Colonel Noam, an Israeli army officer leading the fight against the Nablus militias, said 80 percent of all terrorism in Israel originated in Nablus, home to two hundred thousand Palestinians. It was the center of all the terror networks—Hamas, Islamic Jihad, al-Aksa. The biggest bomb laboratories operated here, and it provided many of the suicide bombers. Noam, a Harvard-educated Israeli, was clear about his task: "We make them live in shit," he said. "They should learn that they'll get nothing from terror, they will only suffer more. It works. People turn in their children so they won't become suicide bombers."

There was only one place more hostile to Israel than the ancient casbah in the heart of Nablus, with its narrow alleys, old rock tunnels and caves, and tightly packed population, and that was the Balata refugee camp on the edge of town. The camp housed about thirty thousand people in another warren of alleys and crumbling buildings packed densely along dirt paths, with rooftops that linked over an area of several square miles, like a raised ground level. Three or four al-Aksa groups operated in the camp, as well as Hamas and Islamic Jihad. They manufactured bombs, trained suicide bombers, fought street battles at night with Israeli soldiers, and were the only heroes to thousands of hopeless children. The militias were all financed and backed by different Palestinian institutions. Al-Aksa members were paid salaries indirectly by the Palestinian Authority—they were effectively Yasir Arafat's deniable hit teams.

That's where we were headed: Balata, the heart of Palestinian resistance to Israel. To Israelis, Alaa Sanakreh, leader of one of the camp's al-Aksa groups, was a terrorist killer, high on the most-wanted list. To Palestinians, he was a hero. Following my Smola Smola theory of news coverage, I preferred to get to know his group intimately rather than wander across the West Bank and Gaza getting superficial coverage of many groups. Alaa Sanakreh, his younger brother Ahmed, his sidekick Nasser Abu Aziz, and half a dozen more become my guides to the second Palestinian Intifada. It was much more violent than the first. No more sticks and stones—this one was fought with bombs, grenades, rifles, and suicide bombers.

The gunmen were still no match for Israel's army, but this wasn't a war that would be won or lost by uniformed men. However many were killed on either side, they would always be replaced. It was a war against civilians. Israel pressured Palestinian civilians with roadblocks and border closures, and by generally making life miserable, while the Palestinians terrorized Israeli civilians with bombs and roadside attacks. Each side hoped to deprive the other of popular support. But nobody caved in. Neither side understood the sheer obduracy and staying power of the enemy. In the absence of peace negotiations, both sides faced the same zero-sum choice—victory or defeat.

My old mate Jeff Riggins, who had shared so many adventures with me and whose apparent indestructibility had made me feel safe in Somalia, Rwanda, Kosovo, and now here at home, drove our bulletproof Jeep Cherokee up the coast road, leaving behind Herzliya's leafy suburbs. We turned right at Netanya and headed toward the West Bank, a mere eleven miles from the coast. On our right was the mess of razor wire and high white walls of the Beit Lid prison. We passed the nearby monument to twenty-one Israeli soldiers killed at an assembly point here in January 1995 by two Islamic Jihad suicide bombers. The industrial parks, villages, and citrus groves dropped away as we entered the narrow roads and pretty hills of the occupied West Bank, where Arab villages and Jewish settlements jostle for space and hilltop dominance. Then we cut across to the army roadblock at the Tapuach junction and drove down the winding hills into Nablus.

Each time we crossed into the West Bank, I marveled at the complete contrast of lifestyles. We left behind relaxed Israelis at the beach and trendy cafés, and within forty minutes were surrounded by army roadblocks, dejected, unemployed Palestinians, and fear. On the edge of the Balata camp, we pulled off to the side of the road. We waited with Kevin Monahan, our producer, while our street-smart Arab field producer, Lawahez Jaabari, walked into one of the alleys, cell phone pressed to her ear, to make contact with the al-Aksa member who would guide us to one of their safe houses.

We kept our meetings as brief as possible. These men were targets and at any moment could be attacked by an Israeli undercover unit or a smart bomb launched from a distant helicopter. During the first Intifada, the Palestinians were convinced that a CBS crew had been followed into Nablus by the Israeli secret service, which killed several people CBS had just interviewed. Early in the second Intifada, men posing as an ABC News crew drove into a Palestinian village, began to interview some wanted men, then pulled out their guns and arrested them. Now in our Jeep, wearing sunglasses, baseball caps, and hooded sweaters, we could easily have been mistaken for an Israeli undercover unit. Once, when we innocently pulled up alongside a car at the camp's entrance, three men leapt out of the car and ran away. We were often surrounded by suspicious gunmen. Anything could happen at any moment. But thanks to Lawahez and our repeated visits, we gained the trust of these hunted men.

Now we sat in a small, bare room with half a dozen Martyrs' Brigades members, including Alaa Sanakreh and Nasser Abu Aziz. I sat by Alaa on a narrow bed. His jet-black hair was shiny and combed back, emphasizing his high cheekbones and alarmingly sunken brown eyes. He was slightly built, wiry, and confident.

At first, the al-Aksa leader wouldn't show me his "wedding" movie. "It would make us look like animals," Alaa said. His men had killed the collaborator who betrayed two of their friends to the Israelis. But they didn't kill his lover, a married woman. "Her brothers killed her, outside the hospital," Alaa said, "to save their family honor."

With Lawahez translating, I began to persuade Alaa to show us his video of the killing. When he asked me, "Why should we show it to you?" I understood he just needed a good excuse. I began my spiel, explaining that we needed to see all sides of the story, that it was about being honest and having nothing to hide, believing in what you did, et cetera, et cetera. Before I had finished, Alaa stuck out his hand and hit the play button on his cell phone. After all, he was proud of this demonstration of his power. A smile creased his narrow, gaunt face as the men crowded around.

The small Nokia screen lit up and showed four masked men hauling the collaborator into the camp's center, by the butcher's shop. The collaborator had dark skin, a gap between his teeth, and greased-back hair like the rest of them. He wore a T-shirt with the logo "Special Forces." His expression was blank. He didn't resist but was dragged, like a heavy sack. They shot him twenty times, from close range. As he curled up on the ground, they pumped bullets into his head. The pops and cracks were shockingly loud and clear on the little cell phone. The collaborator's head jerked back again and again. Blood poured from his neck and body and spread on the street. Palestinians crowded around and began to cheer.

This was the "wedding" I had missed. The collaborator's name was Jefal Ayesh; he was a twenty-five-year-old father who fell in love with the wrong woman and was blackmailed by Israel. When Alaa's video ended, two other men in the room played their cell-phone videos: the same killing from different angles. They were all smiling and proud.

Alaa wouldn't show me the video of the killing of Jefal's lover, Wedad Mustafa, a twenty-seven-year-old mother of four who had betrayed her own husband. "She's the wife of a martyr, and we owe him that," Alaa explained, "even if she is a *sharmouta* [whore]!"

Alaa was twenty-six years old when we met. All his men were the same age or younger, apart from Nasser Abu Aziz, the father figure at thirty-five. He was a stocky, swarthy man with a shaved head, neatly trimmed black beard, and sad eyes. I never saw him without a small black beret and a big black M16 automatic rifle. He was first arrested by the Israelis at age thirteen for throwing stones at soldiers, despite his father's attempts to stop him. Nasser Abu Aziz looked fierce, but unless aroused he spoke softly and eloquently. He was the spokesman of the group, despite his limited horizon. In all his thirty-five years, he had never left the Nablus area, except to spend ten years in an Israeli prison.

Nasser remembered proudly the triple suicide bomb attack in a crowded pedestrian street in Jerusalem on September 4, 1997, when Gilli was hurt and her friends were killed. He knew well one of the planners, Muhanad Taher. Taher headed the rival Hamas military wing in Nablus and was number one on Israel's most-wanted list. I never met Taher, who was killed by Israel in 2002, but Nasser described him as a nice, honest guy who could be trusted. They worked together when it suited them. Taher specialized in explosives. Palestinians called him Engineer Number Four, and Israeli security sources believe he provided at least one of the Ben Yehuda bombs.

As Nasser described Taher and his bombs, I thought of Gilli, her wide eyes and her soft hair. It was painful to connect the dots between Nasser

Abu Aziz, Muhanad Taher, Gilli Kucik, and her dead friends. It was hard being close to the suffering of both sides, having your friends and family on the firing line, yet hardening your heart and staying on the fence, as my job demanded. Once, when I was with the al-Aksa fighters in Nablus, news came of a bombing that killed a dozen Israelis. The militants jumped up and celebrated, laughing and slapping one another's backs, saying, "Allah Akbar—God is great." It made me sick.

As Alaa defended the bombers, or Nasser described their night battles with the Israelis, or Ahmed related how he had almost been killed yet again, I couldn't put aside the thoughts of their Jewish victims. And yet, as I came to know the al-Aksa fighters, who talked of fathers jailed, brothers killed, of the almost complete lack of jobs and hope; as they spoke lovingly of their families and their land, all the while knowing with certainty that every day could be their last, I could understand them, too. They had been living underground for years, switching beds every night, rarely visiting their families, seeing one friend after another shot, wounded, or killed in their doomed struggle against the Israeli occupation.

Alaa and his friends told me that by now, after having fought since their early teens, they wanted more than anything to stop fighting, get real jobs, and live without fear of assassination. But that was no longer an option. They had blood on their hands, and the Israelis were hunting them. During the summer of 2006, even as we covered the Katyusha rockets raining down on Israeli cities near the Lebanese border, the struggle in Gaza and the West Bank continued. After an absence of about six weeks, Alaa asked Lewahez, "Why hasn't Martin come to see us lately? Do you think that when I am killed Martin will come to visit my family?" It was then I understood that this strange relationship had placed a heavy load on my shoulders.

Alaa Sanakreh was never far from death. At his army base on the outskirts of Nablus, an Israeli colonel showed me a video taken by a drone camera of one near miss. The video showed little dark figures on a rooftop shooting at other dark objects in a courtyard below, then crawling to another corner of the roof and shooting again. It was a nighttime gun battle between Israeli soldiers and Alaa and his men in the refugee camp. "Sanakreh got away this time," said the colonel, "but we'll get him."

"Yes, but he broke his leg when he jumped over the wall," I said.

"He did?"

Immediately I regretted what I had said. It wasn't my job to give information to the Israeli army, just as I wouldn't tell Alaa that he was being filmed by a drone at night. But I understood how right Alaa was when he said he could be killed at any moment. "Every morning I thank God that I am alive," he said. An Israeli secret service agent who called himself Captain Mor regularly called Alaa on his cell phone to hassle and intimidate him. "We know where you are. Take a rest today," Mor would say. "Don't make trouble."

In yet another visit at yet another safe house, we sat with Alaa and his guards, sipping coffee, for once taking our time. The house belonged to a family that had lost two sons in the fighting. The sons' posters—the usual heroic poses with big guns, bandannas, fixed stares, the images superimposed on pictures of a sun-sparkled, golden Dome of the Rock in Jerusalem—hung on the wall. Next to the two posters was a red plaque with the Arabic inscription "When you die, rise to the sky, leave the earth for the cowards." But on this day, after another night in the streets evading or challenging Israeli army patrols, Alaa was tired. This was an earlier meeting than usual. Normally the gunmen slept from about 8:00 A.M. till noon. The reason Alaa was up already surprised me.

"Today is the first day of university," he said. "I got up to be there on time. But now I can't go!"

He looked exhausted and bitter. He was slumped over in his chair, massaging his own shoulders, his forehead deeply creased. He bit his nails and fanned his face with his hands, fidgeting constantly. He was wearing his usual black shoes, a tight black T-shirt tucked into his jeans, and had a pistol stuck in the waistband. Nasser's M16 leaned against him, and as Alaa talked he stroked the muzzle and rhythmically inserted his finger. He said that he wanted to get married, lead a normal life.

I was amazed to learn that while he was on the run, Alaa had managed to study hard enough to achieve a seventy-two average on the high school matriculation exam. He smiled proudly, and Nasser beamed across the little room like an approving father. But there was a problem. That morning, just before setting off with his books for his first day at university, Alaa had received two phone calls. The first was from the disembodied Captain Mor, who warned him before abruptly hanging up: "Do not go to the university. We will kill you there."

That was followed by a nervous call from the university director, who begged Alaa not to come. "We don't want any trouble," he said. "Everyone would know that a wanted man is studying here." That was a bit rich, I thought, from an institution that had provided at least a dozen suicide bombers. One failed suicide bomber, whom I interviewed in an Israeli jail, told me that he had received his instructions by way of paper notes left under the mat at the entrance to the university library.

Then Nasser chimed in, making Alaa slump further in his chair. "How can he study? He slept two hours today, all night in the street. When will he study? When he was studying for high school exams, all the fighters surrounded him, protected him while he read the books and wrote the essays. We followed him, kept him safe while he studied." Damn, that would have been a good shot, I thought, the terrorist studying geography. "At university we can't follow him from class to class with our guns. How will he be safe?"

Alaa wanted to study political science and enter politics. He wanted to be a minister. "Of what?" I asked.

Silence. Alaa, lost in his own grim thoughts, suddenly said: "I worked in Israel for a year. Strauss ice cream. I was a distributor to shops in Petah Tikva. Bad ice cream."

Then Alaa's younger brother Ahmed entered the room with three of his bodyguards. They all looked the same: black shoes, black T-shirts tucked inside their tight jeans, short black hair shaved at the sides. Their remaining hair was shiny and stood up in little gelled spikes. They all carried pistols tucked into their pants. The small, hot room became oppressive as they crowded along the wall. I had asked on earlier visits why

Ahmed, a baby-faced young man who hardly shaved, needed bodyguards all the time, but nobody answered. I would soon find out why.

Alaa leaned over and stroked a new scar on Ahmed's forehead. Ahmed's hand was bandaged. Two weeks earlier, an Israeli bullet had shot off two of his fingers and left a third paralyzed. I had once asked if any of them had been shot. Every man in the room, half a dozen of them, lifted his shirt or rolled up his trousers, revealing an array of bullet holes, deep dents, long scars along their backs or chests and red weals from recent wounds. I asked Alaa what his mother thought about her two sons on the run. "Every morning she wakes up with tears in her eyes, crying. She begs us to stop. But how can we? It is too late. There are only two ways this will end. Either they kill me or arrest me. But there will always be someone to take my place." As Alaa talked, Ahmed drifted away, idly stroking the head of our tripod like a child.

"I don't care if they kill me," Alaa said, "but if they kill Ahmed, I'll go mad."

He had a reason to say this. Only a week earlier the Israelis had left Ahmed for dead. He had been hiding with eighteen of his militant friends in the old *muqata*, the destroyed headquarters of the Palestinian Authority in the center of Nablus. Israeli troops surrounded the ruined building, shelled it, and attacked it with bulldozers. One Palestinian was killed, three critically wounded. The rest surrendered. Ahmed was trapped beneath crushed concrete after two floors pancaked down on top of him. Two gas canisters supported the concrete, and he survived in a tiny crawl space. His mother and Alaa called him on his cell phone, begging him to surrender, but he refused. "I never felt so bad," Alaa said. "My brother was dying, and there was nothing I could do. I hid in a room, then later went onto the rooftops and into the alleys to see the compound, but I was helpless."

After three days the Israelis pulled out, and Alaa and Nasser and their friends dug Ahmed out of the debris. He was barely breathing. But it wasn't over yet. While Ahmed was recovering in the hospital, Alaa heard the Israelis were about to break into the ward to arrest his brother. The militants got there first and spirited him away.

I asked Alaa why the Israelis were so keen to get hold of Ahmed. Ahmed looked away with a grin, but for once Alaa gave a direct answer. "Remember the Israeli officer who was killed in a jeep at the entrance to Balata four months ago? Ahmed did it. Ahmed makes the bombs, too."

So that's it, I thought. Ahmed is the new bomb maker. That would put him right on top of Israel's hit list. Without the man who makes the bombs, a hundred suicide bomb volunteers are less dangerous than a boy with a peashooter. Since the age of fifteen, Ahmed had been trained to be another Muhanad Taher, whose bomb may have killed Smadar and nearly killed Gilli. I studied Ahmed with new interest. Could he still make bombs with those missing and paralyzed fingers? Certainly he could teach others. He seemed to have as many scars on his body as zits on his chin. He was a youngish nineteen, with pouting, fat lips, as if his mother had just scolded him. He stood against the wall, looking almost shy, his good hand still stroking the head of the tripod. Our eyes met, and he smiled. I thought, I hope they kill you before you kill anyone else.

Or did I? I didn't know what I hoped. I had become very familiar with these killers of Jews, if not close to them. Several times, on taking leave from Alaa and his men, I had almost asked if there was anything I could bring them from Israel when I came back, as if I was a friend passing through duty-free. Cigarettes, chocolates, something you can't get in Nablus? Aftershave? But I always stopped myself in time. What was this, a variation on the Stockholm syndrome? These gunmen were not my friends; they were just professional sources. However much I might understand their plight, I kept reminding myself, these men wanted to kill my children and their friends.

Midway through the second suicide bombing campaign, Shahar Bar-on, then a producer for NBC's *Dateline*, was visiting friends in Jerusalem. We were working on a magazine report: "Living with Terror." Four weeks after 9/11, and following anthrax attacks on Americans through the mail, *Dateline* wanted to show America how Israel had adapted to the daily threat. But Shahar couldn't think of an original way to tell the story, and I wasn't much help. After months of working around the clock, all I wanted was a day off. His deadline was approaching, and Shahar was getting desperate, kicking around a few second-rate ideas in his friend Joseph's living room after Saturday lunch. Then Joseph's mother, Tsippi Cedar, walked in, grinning smugly.

"Well, that's it," Tsippi said, "finished the e-mail."

"What e-mail?" her son asked.

"To my brother Jake in Philadelphia. He's terrified, poor man. Worried about bombs. Doesn't know what to do. He wanted advice—how to live with these terror threats."

Shahar's head jerked up. "Do you want to be on TV?" he asked.

And that's how Tsippi Cedar, a pretty, sixtyish grandmother with a quick, knowing smile, achieved her fifteen minutes of fame, even ending up on *The Oprah Winfrey Show,* dispensing sensible, hard-earned advice to Americans on how to live with terror.

Our ten-minute magazine report consisted of Tsippi reading her e-mail to her brother Jake, covered by relevant news footage. She was a huge hit. If the hope of Alaa Sanakreh and his al-Aksa Martyrs' Brigades, as well as Hamas, Islamic Jihad, and terrorist groups the world over, was to terrify ordinary citizens into submission, through their bombs packed with nails, ball bearings, and sometimes rat poison, then they didn't reckon on this tough little gray-haired lady, an art therapy teacher, mother of six, and grandmother of three. The unstoppable force had met the immovable object. Mohammed reached the mountain.

"Dear Jake," Tsippi read in a clear, strong voice in her Jerusalem living room. "You asked for it so here goes: a couple of pointers on how to survive the constant threat of terror. But before you read on, first . . . CALM DOWN!"

Tsippi knew what she was talking about. Only two months earlier, one of her students was eating a pizza in the Sbarro pizzeria in Jerusalem's center, about three hundred yards from where Gilli's friends were killed, when a suicide bomber carrying a guitar case full of explosives blew himself up among the lunchtime crowd. The ten-kilo bomb was packed with nails, screws, and bolts, and it killed fifteen people. "That girl's funeral was the hardest hour of my life," Tsippi said. But she didn't pause.

"Lesson One: As you go about your daily business, always be on the lookout. Extend your peripheral vision whenever you walk anywhere, i.e., be alert.

"Lesson Two: Teach your children to avoid touching any object found on the streets or sidewalks.

"Lesson Three: Keep up with the news," Tsippi continued.

I interrupted: "What's the first thing you think of when you hear that there's a terrorist attack?"

Tsippi reacted as if there had been a bomb. Her body language showed how close she lived to the edge.

"Who's there? Who's there! Who's there!" she replied with increasing intensity, slapping her cheek and pursing her mouth. She seemed transported. Her emotions were skin-deep, exposed. "We're always waiting for the next incident," she went on. "Always waiting. And when something happens, there's even a sense of relief. It usually doesn't happen two in a row, although sometimes it does . . . but when it happens, then you know: Okay, that's it for today."

Tsippi's Lesson Four: Search for patterns of terrorist behavior. Go to the bank or go shopping at times unpopular with terrorists. That morning Tsippi's husband, a scientist, had gone shopping in the market at 7:00. "Terrorists don't go to the market at seven o'clock in the morning," she said. "It takes them time to get there, and there's nobody there, it's not worth it for them. They're going to blow up the oranges and the nectarines."

Grimm's fairy tales had nothing on this granny's scary stuff. Tsippi continued with practical comments on how to drive, where to park, and how to be ready for searches. She ended with her most important advice to her worried brother: "Still pursue life the way you did before. Don't let the anger change your personality. Americans are happy people. Don't let that destroy your happiness."

Tsippi Cedar's survival notes drew upon years of living with terror, when ordinary people had become the targets. At least she's still talking about happiness, I thought as we said farewell and wished each other good luck. On the Palestinian side, all they aim for is survival.

One day in November 2006, I was at home reading some translations from the Hebrew press when I found a story on the Ma'ariv-NRG online news site. It began innocuously, like just any other poorly edited government report: "There was activity in all the sectors last night." But then I read the following: "Paratroopers from the Central Command operating in the Nablus area spotted two suspects involved in preparing a car bomb. The troops hurried to respond, and the two suspects were killed. Later on, they turned out to be the commander of El-Aksa Martyrs brigades in the city and his brother. The car was intended for use in a mass terror attack."

Holy shit, I thought, that's Alaa and Ahmed! I was stunned. Alaa had asked Lawahez if I would visit his family if he was killed, and now he was dead. I was glad the Israelis had stopped a car bomb, the new big weapon of terror, but still, I'd grown to know Alaa. I understood why he was fighting, and I also knew how desperately he wanted to stop, to study, to go into politics. He had never told me what his political goal was, whether ultimately he believed peace was possible with Israel, and now I'd never know. Would I go see his family, as he'd asked? Sure, I thought, it'll be important to them, why not? His mother worried about her son, just like any other mother. And only five months earlier in Jordan I'd visited the family of Abu Musab al-Zarkawi, the al-Qaeda leader killed in Iraq with a price of $25 million on his head. If I could shake hands with his family, surely I could visit Alaa's mom.

I read on: "The troops that operated in the Balata refugee camp spotted the two high-ranking wanted men near a suspicious-looking vehicle. The soldiers fired at the first terrorist and succeeded in killing him. Later on, it turned out that he was Ahmed Sanakra, the leader of El-Aksa Martyrs brigades in Nablus."

That's wrong, I thought, he's the younger brother; the Israelis always get the details wrong, and they always promote the dead man. Every terrorist killed is reported by the Israeli press as being the leader, a senior wanted man, a commander, never just some rank-and-file Joe Blow. Still, knocking off the bomb maker is a big success. They're hard to train. Alaa would have been on the warpath, though, I thought. He always said, "If they harm Ahmed, then they will pay." But now he's dead, too.

The report continued: "A short while later, his brother, Ibrahim Sanakra, arrived in the area, and the soldiers succeeded in killing him as well. A preliminary examination shows that the car contained an enormous amount of explosive material."

Who's Ibrahim? I thought. Never heard of him. Another brother? That's news to me. Alaa had told me his other brothers and sisters were not involved in the struggle. So if Ibrahim, whoever he was, was dead, did that mean Alaa was alive? Or did they get the names wrong?

I read on: "It appears that the car was intended to attack soldiers, exploding during an operation in the area and killing many of them. However, it is also possible that the car was supposed to arrive inside Israeli territory and perpetrate a terror attack on the home front. Sappers who arrived at the scene blew up the car, and said that it was a very large explosion that indicates the type and quantity of the explosives that the wanted men used."

So who's dead? I wondered. Ahmed, the bomb maker? Alaa, the leader? Ibrahim, the unknown brother? Some other people altogether? What about Nasser? Was he there? I had an uncomfortable mix of feelings. I wanted them to be alive, partly for selfish professional reasons, and also because they had become friends of a sort, but I also definitely wanted them to be stopped from their murderous intentions. And only death could do that. Or peace.

I called Lawahez and told her what I had read. "Ohmygod!" she said. "Are you sure?"

"No, I'm not, all I know is what I just read. Can you call Alaa's phone and see what happens?"

Lawahez phoned him immediately and then reported back. "He answered right away," she said. "He was speaking calmly, as if he was expecting this. He spoke as if he was talking about someone else. He had another phone going, too, a lot is going on. But he is alive, and so is his brother Ahmed. But Ahmed was wounded." Again? Was this kid bionic? How many lives did he have? Lawahez continued, "The person killed was another brother, fifteen years old."

"Anybody else killed?"

"He says no."

Israeli army reports often appear to be the product of wishful thinking, deliberate distortion, or just bad intelligence. The last seems hard to imagine, given how many collaborators the Israelis had operating among the Palestinians. In this case, though, the Israelis were wrong again. Alaa and Ahmed lived. I would not be visiting their family. Their war would continue. And I would keep reporting on it. Until their luck ran out—or mine did.

In Israel during the second Intifada, luck was the bottom line. For Gilli at the triple suicide bombing on Ben Yehuda Street; for Alaa and Ahmed and the rest in Balata still fighting the Israelis every night; for Tsippi and her family, despite all her wise precautions; and for me and my colleagues, too, despite our flak jackets and bulletproof cars, it was just a matter of luck.

It would be nice to think that after thirty years of covering wars I knew what I was doing. But when I look back, the old saw "I'd rather be lucky than good" rings truer than ever. During Israel's war with Hizbullah in the summer of 2006, a Katyusha rocket came as near as possible to wiping out Kevin Monahan, Amikam Cohen, and me. It exploded in the road right in front of our car, the blast of flame and shrapnel just far enough away to miss us. For many people, that might have been a life-altering experience; for us, it was just another day at the office. I recalled my mother's response when I told her once not to worry about me, because whenever I went to work in a war zone, I wore a flak jacket and a helmet. "Martin," she said, "if you have to wear a flak jacket and a helmet to work, you should get a new job."

But I can't. For me, this is more than a job. It's a way of life: traveling the world, overcoming obstacles, meeting people, telling their stories. Storytelling is not the world's oldest profession, but it might be the world's oldest art. Cavemen drew pictures on rock walls whereas we edit pictures on computers. If the means have changed, the result is the same. As for the danger, war correspondents accept the risks, because war is where the best stories—and also, I believe, the most important stories—are. I'd sooner give it all up than cover the Paris fashion show or the British royal family. I'd rather get a real job, or worse, go into management. Psychologists finance yachts analyzing people like me, but there still is no good explanation for why war correspondents so routinely put themselves in harm's way. Most people run from the blazing fire if they can. Others are drawn to it.

Not that it's been easy. Whether it was the moral compromises required to cover the news in South Africa and Somalia, or the beating the media took in Rwanda, or the hard confrontation with my own family's past in the Balkans, or the confusion of sitting on the fence in Israel, or the violent deaths of so many good friends in pursuit of our calling, or simply the accumulation of mental fatigue from witnessing the pain of so many people in so many places, I have sometimes considered my mother's advice to jack it all in. Even today, having witnessed every possible form of suffering inflicted by man and by nature, and at the urgent behest of my wife, I face seriously the question: Why do I still do this job? The question's subtext is: Give it up already!

After due consideration and some painful introspection, I still can't summon up a cogent answer. I can understand why a soldier may risk his life for his country; or why a fireman would enter a burning building to save a life. But it doesn't seem reasonable to risk your life with such frequency just to tell a story. It might sound like a cop-out, but I can only hope that some sort of answer has emerged from this book. The answer must lie somewhere near the convergence of a spirit of adventure, a certain recklessness, a competitive drive, and a need to do something worthwhile and important. In a world obsessed with celebrities, wealth, and success, I have focused on those left behind, on those who paid the price. I have tried to answer the question: Why should we care? I now believe my work also became something of a journey of discovery, in which I have sought to understand the suffering of my own family through witnessing and understanding the suffering of others.

In closing this book, I can only fall back on the crutch of every half-educated Englishman, offered up by our know-it-all bard William Shakespeare: "This above all: to thine own self be true."* And I can only hope that Shakespeare wasn't referring to storytellers like me when he wrote: "Life's but a walking shadow . . . it is a tale told by an idiot, full of sound and fury, signifying nothing."†

---

*Hamlet, 1.3.78.
†Macbeth, 5.5.23, 25–27.

Index

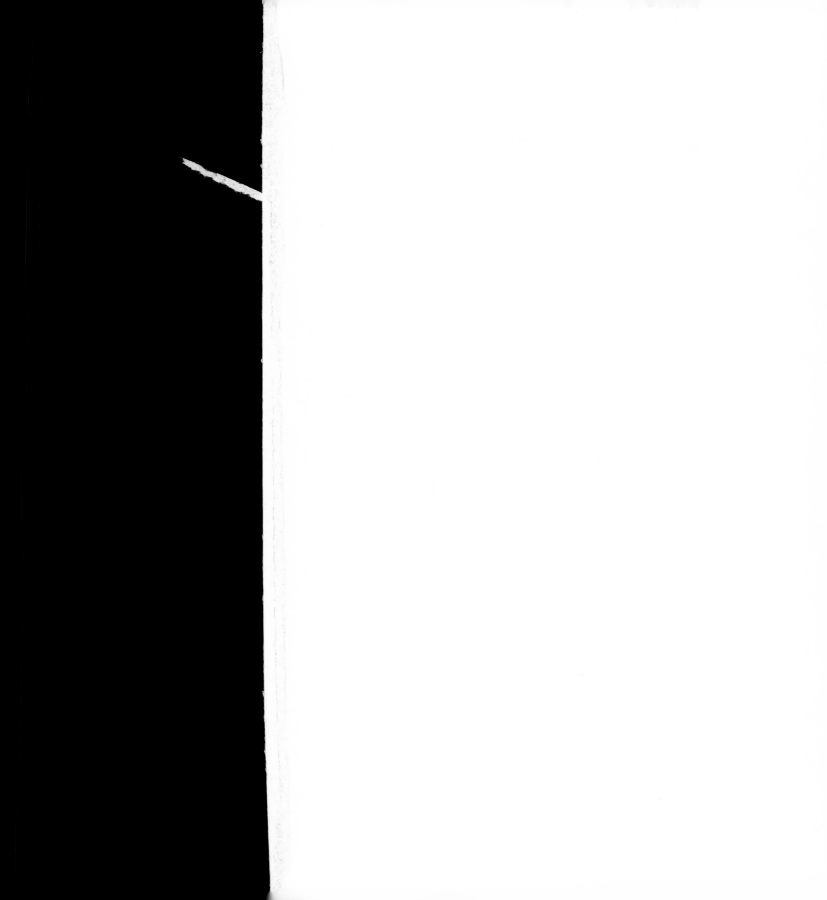